ENVIRONMENTAL BIOGEOCHEMISTRY AND GEOMICROBIOLOGY

Volume 3: Methods, Metals and Assessment

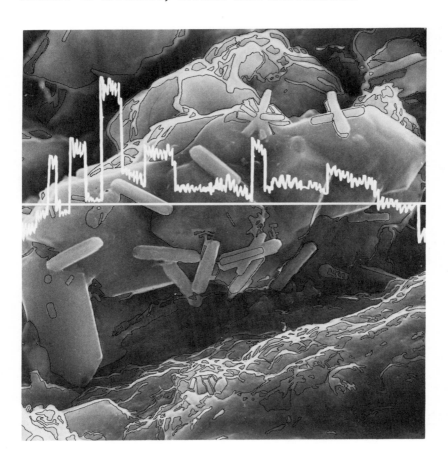

ENVIRONMENTAL BIOGEOCHEMISTRY AND GEOMICROBIOLOGY

Volume 3: Methods, Metals and Assessment

edited by
WOLFGANG E. KRUMBEIN
University of Oldenburg
Environmental Laboratory
Oldenburg, Germany

Proceedings of the Third International Symposium on Environmental Biogeo-chemistry organized by W. E. Krumbein, University of Oldenburg, and spon-sored by the Minister of Science and Arts of Niedersachsen, Deutsche Forschungsgemeinschaft, and the International Association of Geochemistry and Cosmochemistry. The symposium was supported ideally and scientific-ally by Deutsche Gesellschaft für Hygiene und Mikrobiologie, Gesellschaft für Ökologie, Deutsche Bodenkundliche Gesellschaft, German Local Branch of the American Society for Microbiology. The meeting was held at the Herzog August Bibliothek, Wolfenbüttel.

ANN ARBOR SCIENCE
PUBLISHERS INC
P.O. BOX 1425 • ANN ARBOR, MICH. 48106

Life on earth has produced earth's present atmosphere,
the uppermost parts of the lithosphere, soil structure, water
quality and man—to adore it, study it and possibly destroy it.
Life has managed to survive long periods of dangerous fluctuations of equilibrium and, according to the "Gäa hypothesis,"
life may survive even man. Energy and entropy may be more
important to our present-day situation but without a doubt,
life and its far-reaching consequences are the most prominent
factors to be considered in studying the environment and environmental cycles.

Certainly life and its processes may be regarded as mere
chemical reactions under certain physical conditions. But
though the driving forces are primary and secondary energy
sources and flows, and though chemical balances and budgets
are possibly more basic, and though the cycle of substances
in space and time can always be expressed in chemical terms
and reactions, it must be stressed that as long as this earth
can sustain life, man will look at it and its development in
terms of a living entity. Therefore, biogeochemistry, geomicrobiology, ecology and exogenic dynamics are always regarded as events controlled and modified, speeded up or slowed
down, by life and life processes.

The production cycle for reduced carbon compounds, their
growing degree of organization, their pathway through the food
or energy chain in nature, the apparent death and final anni-
hilation by mineralization and oxidation to simple compounds—
all this can take place in a small lake or in soil within a
single day. In other circumstances, it may require billions
of years to complete a cycle. Many examples may be given for
the hypothesis that any atom that has reached or established
itself in the outer few kilometers of the earth's crust will
have passed a living organism at least once since life emerged
or, at least, will have been influenced or modified in its
energy level, spatial position, or physical-chemical condition
by organisms. It therefore seems that biogeochemistry, though
relatively far from man—at least farther than medicine, soci-
ology or music—will increasingly attract the attention of
society. Geomicrobiology and biogeochemistry will probably

increase in importance with man's growing influence on the exogenic cycle, with man's accelerating sections of the huge "mill wheel" of masses passing up and down in the earth's crust and along the energy levels.

Regarding our consternation about the carbon dioxide cycle, the importance of nitrogen compounds in the atmosphere, enormous amounts of stored energy, and reduced carbon compounds, we see the need to increase our biogeochemical activities. If we consider the acceleration of metal cycles, if we look at the enormous number of organic chemical compounds, if we take note of the changes and manipulations man produces on genetic matrices and the stress we exert on the entire ecosystem, we see that the established parameters have been drastically altered in an incredibly short time.

The aim of biogeochemistry and geomicrobiology is to find scales and balances before we so totally change our environment that no traces of the entirely "natural" remain to study, analyze and compare.

The time of holistic approaches, which science lost only 100 years ago, has returned. One major aim of this symposium series on environmental biogeochemistry is to bring together students of the various disciplines concerned with dynamic processes on the earth's surface. The main concerns are not only understanding the importance of the major mineral cycles and their budgeting and balancing, but also analyzing systems and making prognoses on these cycles that control and are controlled by life. Additional factors and study areas will include the biogeochemistry of manmade compounds and their alteration products, and the need to build up new geochemical cycles, since the natural materials used through the centuries are no longer sufficient for humanity's still-growing needs. This means that man will need to study ways to accelerate natural mineral cycles by biological or technical methods.

Isotope fractionation, mobilization and immobilization, oxidation and reduction, mineralization and storage in biological material, transfer, volatilization, catalysis and equilibration of systems—all these are ruled mainly by biological processes in the microscale and most frequently by microorganisms. Therefore, microbiologists, isotope chemists, geochemists and ecologists, and a few botanists, zoologists and physicists were asked and responded to the call for papers for this meeting.

These volumes are based primarily on the papers given at the Third International Symposium on Environmental Biogeochemistry. It was our original intent to emphasize a more specific area, but the problems and the wealth of information were so broad it became necessary to expand the scope of the conference. Hence, one part of the proceedings is dedicated to defined environments, such as shallow water photosynthetic environments with dominance of blue-green algae, deep sea environments with dominance of manganese nodules, specific soil environments, or the microenvironment of one soil or rock particle, while other major segments of the proceedings are dedicated to the general cycles of elements and compounds and their alteration by man.

The study of biogeochemistry and geomicrobiology is only beginning. We wish to keep the field open and look forward to a time of organization, synthesis and perfection. The growing interdisciplinary field between biology, physical and chemical science, and geoscience cannot reasonably limit itself before the subject is more fully understood.

W. E. Krumbein

ACKNOWLEDGMENTS

The Third International Symposium on Environmental Biogeochemistry was sponsored by Deutsche Forschungsgemeinschaft, Ministry for Science and Arts of Niedersachsen, IAGC, Balzers, Cambridge Instruments, Jürgens und Co., E. Merck, Arbeitsgemeinschaft für meerestechnisch gewinnbare Rohstoffe, Ortec, Carl Zeiss. Their help is gratefully acknowledged.

The following persons were extremely helpful in planning and encouraging the development of the meeting: E. T. Degens, K. H. Domsch, W. Flaig, P. Hirsch, M. Kürsten, G. Müller, W. Schwartz, K. Wagener and D. H. Welte of the national committee; M. Alexander, G. Eglinton, H. Ehrlich, P. H. Given, R. O. Hallberg, G. W. Hodgson, I. R. Kaplan, K. A. Kvenvolden, A. D. McLaren, P. A. Meyers, J. O. Nriagu, E. A. Paul, M. Schnitzer, J. Skujinš and G. Stotzky of the international committee, and namely J. Skujinš, chairman of the IC, K. Kvenvolden and E. Ingerson of IAGC, J. W. M. la Rivière of SCOPE, and A. Meyl of DFG.

It is my pleasure to acknowledge the support of P. Raabe of the Herzog August Bibliothek, Wolfenbüttel, and his staff. Without their aid and acceptance, and especially the calm and efficient stability of D. E. Petersen, the meeting would not have been possible. I also wish to extend my thanks to W. Schwartz who was so kind to cooperate and coordinate the "Roundtable Conference on Leaching" with this symposium.

Christine Lange, Peter Rongen, Elisabeth Holtkamp, Joachim Leibacher, Cornelia Wilcken, Monika Michaelsen, Ulrike Kant and G. Koch have made a major contribution to the success of the practical arrangements and to the well-being of the participants.

Finally I wish to express my gratitude to all participants for attending and submitting their contributions on schedule.

W. E. Krumbein, Associate Professor at West Germany's University of Oldenburg, is the chairman and coordinator of the Third International Symposium on Environmental Biogeochemistry. An expert on microbiological rock weathering, his work has concentrated on geomicrobiology, environmental biogeochemistry, productivity and element cycles in natural environments.

Dr. Krumbein received his Vordiplom (BSc) in geoscience from the University of München, and his MSc and PhD (both magna cum laude) from the University of Würzburg. He studied soil microbiology and microbial ecology at the Institut Pasteur and the Sorbonne in Paris and the Landgebouwhoogeschool Wageningen in the Netherlands, and was the recipient of a research grant for postgraduate study at Jerusalem's Hebrew University. He then spent six years as a research scientist at the Biologische Anstalt Helgoland, a government laboratory for marine research.

The editor has taught on the faculties of the Universities of Würzburg, Freiburg and Hamburg. He was a guest scientist at the Scripps Oceanographic Institute in La Jolla, California, and was recently a Visiting Professor at Hebrew University.

Dr. Krumbein has been a speaker at many international scientific conferences, was active as Convener of the International Congresses of Sedimentology and Ecology, and has completed three lecture tours in the U.S. For his active promotion of the fields of geomicrobiology and biogeochemistry, Dr. Krumbein has received awards from the Deutsche Geol. Ges. (German Geological Society) and the Institut Pasteur. He is a member of the Advisory Board of the MBL, Elat, ISEB's International Committee, the National Building Research Council and ICES/ECOMOS. He is also Associate Editor of *Geomicrobiology Journal.*

At present, Dr. Krumbein and his colleagues are planning to establish an institute for salt water biology in Germany. In recent papers he has dealt with hypersaline environments and calcification in prokaryotic organisms as well as with nitrogen and phosphorus budgets of intertidal cyanobacterial communities of the Gulf of Aqaba and the North Sea coast.

TABLE OF CONTENTS

VOLUME 1

SECTION I
MICROBIOLOGY, CHEMISTRY, AND GLOBAL CYCLES
IN THE AQUATIC ENVIRONMENT

SECTION II
ELEMENT CYCLES, BUDGETS AND TRANSFER RATES IN LAKES AND
RIVERS AND THEIR ALTERATION BY MAN

SECTION IV
DIAGENESIS

VOLUME 2

SECTION I
GEOMICROBIOLOGY, BIOGEOCHEMISTRY AND ENERGY FLOW

SECTION II
PADDY SOILS, PEAT AND COAL

SECTION III
NITROGEN IN SOIL AND ITS IMPACT ON THE ATMOSPHERE

SECTION IV
INTERFACES AND SORPTION

SECTION V
DESTRUCTION, MINERALYSIS, WEATHERING

VOLUME 3

SECTION I
METHODS TO ASSESS BIOGEOCHEMISTRY AND GEOMICROBIOLOGY OF THE ENVIRONMENT

SECTION II
THE CYCLE OF CARBON AND OXYGEN AS DETERMINED BY
ISOTOPIC AND CONVENTIONAL METHODS

SECTION III
BIOGEOCHEMISTRY AND GEOMICROBIOLOGY OF METALS WITH
SPECIAL REFERENCE TO MANGANESE NODULE ENVIRONMENTS

SECTION IV
BIOGEOCHEMISTRY OF MAN'S FINGERPRINTS IN NATURE
(METAL-ORGANIC RELATIONS)

SECTION I

METHODS TO ASSESS BIOGEOCHEMISTRY
AND GEOMICROBIOLOGY OF THE ENVIRONMENT

CHAPTER 57

THE POISONED CONTROL IN BIOGEOCHEMICAL INVESTIGATIONS

THOMAS D. BROCK

Department of Bacteriology
University of Wisconsin
Madison, Wisconsin 53706 USA

INTRODUCTION

The problem to be considered is the separation of biological reactions from nonbiological reactions in the geochemical processes. Incubations of water, soil or sediment can be made and chemical changes or radioisotope uptake measured, but unless a suitable poison is available, it is not possible to distinguish biological from nonbiological agencies. The selection of a suitable poison is not a simple matter. The poison must be effective but must not itself enter into the reaction or interfere with the chemical assay being used. For many situations, formaldehyde (4%) or mercuric bichloride (100 µg/ml) can be used, but neither of these poisons can be used when studying sulfur or iron transformations. Probably the best general means of inhibiting biological activity is by the use of agents which reduce the water potential of the system, such as highly soluble solutes. Glycerol, sucrose and NaCl have been used effectively in some systems. One of the most certain ways of showing that a process is biological is to show that it has a distinct temperature optimum. As temperature increases, the rates of purely chemical reactions continue to increase, but the rates of biological reactions increase only until an optimum is reached, after which they fall to zero. With the appropriate agent, it should be possible to determine the extent to which a given reaction is mediated by biological as opposed to nonbiological means.

One of the major tasks of the biogeochemist is to sort biological from nonbiological transformations in natural environments. Biological transformations, carried out primarily by microorganisms, may in many cases be similar to nonbiological ones, differing primarily by rate or by nature of the end products. Organisms cannot change thermodynamic relationships, so that reactions will not take place biologically which cannot also go nonbiologically. The main role of the microorganism, at least from the viewpoint of the biogeochemist, is to catalyze and hence to greatly speed up the rate of the reaction. This increase in rate may be only minimal, or it can be of many orders of magnitude. As an example of the latter, the rate of oxidation of ferrous iron at acidic pH can be increased as much as 10^6 times by iron-oxidizing bacteria (Singer and Stumm, 1970). In addition to such dramatic increases in rate, microorganisms also have the ability to affect the nature of the products formed from the breakdown of a given substrate. For instance, the breakdown of glucose chemically proceeds under a given set of environmental conditions always in the same way, whereas microbial breakdown of glucose can result in the formation of differing products, depending on the particular microorganism which happens to be present.

Because of these obvious influences of microorganisms on biogeochemical reactions, it becomes important in studying chemical transformations in nature to sort out biological from nonbiological effects. This can to some extent be inferred from analyses of the products being formed (using knowledge from more defined systems to help in interpretation), or from measurement of fractionation of stable isotopes (making the assumption that since fractionation is primarily a low-temperature process, it is likely that it will only have occurred at a significant rate in nature if it has been catalyzed by microorganisms).

However, the most direct way of studying biogeochemical reactions is by an incubation method, in which a sample of water or sediment is incubated for a period of time under conditions as close to natural as possible and successive analyses made to determine changes in a constituent of interest. Given a sufficiently sensitive assay method, a chemical analysis can be used, but in many cases it is necessary to add a radioactively labeled compound and measure its transformation to products. Incubation methods permit not only a direct study of biogeochemical reactions, but make it possible to deduce rates, so that the geochemical significance can be assessed. But since chemical transformations in incubated materials may be due to nonbiological processes, it is essential to have poisoned controls, in which biological but not nonbiological reactions are inhibited, so that the relative importance of the two kinds of processes can be assessed. Despite the central importance of the poisoned control in biogeochemistry, there has been little consideration of its necessity or of appropriate kinds of poisons to be used.

The selection of a suitable poison for a biogeochemical investigation is not a simple problem. The poison must not only be active against microorganisms in the system under study, but it must have no effect on chemical reactions, and if a chemical rather than a radioisotope assay is being used, the poison must not interfere with the chemical assay. In a number of investigations, agents such as formaldehyde or anti- biotics have been used uncritically without assessing whether they are really being effective. Because many poisons are adsorbed or neutralized by materials present in the system, they may be ineffective, leading to the conclusion that a transformation being studied is nonbiological when in fact it is actually being carried out by microorganisms. For the past ten years, my laboratory has been studying biogeochemical reactions in geothermal environments. Because in such extreme environments, the importance of microorganisms can be seriously questioned, it was of especial importance to employ suitable and effective poisoned controls. We have also extended our studies in recent years to more normal environments, and have employed similar poisons successfully. In this paper, I would like to review some of the poisons we have used, and to sug- gest how they can be used in other systems.

In this paper, I am using the word "poison" quite broadly to mean any agent or treatment that will inhibit bio- logical reactions without at the same time inhibiting chemical reactions. In actuality, one of the most important agents we have used is high temperature, which, as will be seen, more clearly than any other agent reveals the biological nature of geochemical reactions.

SELECTION OF THE POISON

When defined laboratory systems are being studied, it is quite simple to test various poisons for effectiveness, but in natural systems such as water and sediment, the evaluation of an effective poison is difficult. The only procedure which is really effective is to test a series of poisons and see if they inhibit. If inhibition does not occur, it does not necessarily mean that the process being studied is nonbiologi- cal; the proper inhibitor may not have been used. Thus, we are faced with the situation that if the inhibitor works, firm conclusions can be drawn, but if the inhibitor does not work, nothing certain can be decided. In the latter case, the only thing that can be done is to continue testing more inhibitors, with the hope that an effective one will be found. Two examples of situations in which a variety of inhibitors were effective are shown in Table I. In these two cases, uptake of labeled compounds into bacterial populations at high temp- eratures was measured and it was essential to show that the uptake was indeed due to organisms, and not to nonspecific binding. Because all of the inhibitors used were effective, to one degree or antother, the conclusion was clear-cut.

Table I
Effect of Inhibitors on Uptake of Radioactive Compounds
by Bacteria from High-Temperature Systems

Inhibitor	Boulder Spring % Control	Octopus Spring (Pool A) % Control
None	100	100
Formaldehyde (4%)	2	8
Mercuric bichloride (100 μg/ml)	–	7
Mercuric bichloride (10 μg/ml)	2.5	–
Streptomycin sulfate (1000 μg/ml)	9	9
Sodium azide (1000 μg/ml)	48	3
Novobiocin (100 μg/ml)	–	2
Hydrochloric acid (0.1 N)	6	–
Incubation temperature	87C	86C

Control values: Boulder Spring, ^{14}C-acetate, 10,128 cpm;
Octopus Spring, ^{14}C-leucine, 4,622 cpm.

Boulder Spring data: Brock *et al.*, 1971; Octopus Spring,
Brock and Brock, 1971.

STABILITY OF THE POISON

It is essential that the poison be stable in the
system used, that it not be bound or otherwise neutralized.
The fact that the inhibitors listed in Table I were all effective suggests that they are stable at high temperatures,
at least for the duration of the experiments (one hour). However, these same inhibitors may not be stable at low pH, or
may be bound to soil or sediment particles, or may precipitate
in a system. It is important to find these matters out before
using the inhibitor for any critical experiments. Almost
certainly, mercuric ions are chemically stable at high temperature and low pH, but may not necessarily be stable in a
sulfide-rich environment, where mercuric sulfide could form.
Formaldehyde is a relatively stable inhibitor, and for this
reason has been widely used, but it is not completely unre-
active with natural systems, and may be inactivated or removed
from the system (as will be shown later).

In this regard, the kinetics of the process under
study may be considered. If short incubation times can be

used (possible with radioactive labels but not necessarily with chemical assays), then inactivation may be less of a problem, but another problem may crop up: the agent may not act instantaneously, but require time for binding or reaction with the cells. Thus, it is essential that the poison be added well before the reaction has been started, but the lead time necessary cannot be deduced directly. It is essential to do preliminary experiments, studying the effect of the inhibitor on the process, to see whether the rate changes during the incubation period. An ideal way to proceed, if it can be done, is to follow the time course of the reaction in uninhibited material, and then add the inhibitor during the course of the reaction. If the inhibitor is effective, the reaction rate should drop abruptly, preferably to near zero.

IMPROPER POISONS

Reactivity of the poison may preclude its use in the system. For instance, we have been trying to study the oxidation of the sulfide in lake waters, and to partition this process between biological and nonbiological components. Formaldehyde cannot be used as the poison, because it catalyzes and accelerates chemical oxidation of sulfide (Chen and Morris, 1971). (For this reason, all of the radioisotope studies on sulfide oxidation carried out by Ivanov (1968) are fallacious, since he used formaldehyde as his poison.) Mercury ions can obviously not be used, because they precipitate sulfide. Antibiotics probably would not be useful, because they inhibit growth processes, but not necessarily the activity of pre-existing organisms. In one system that we studied (low-pH geothermal waters), we were able to separate the organisms from the system by centrifugation, kill them by formaldehyde treatment, wash them thoroughly to remove the formaldehyde, and then replace them in the system. At low pH, where H_2S is relatively stable in the presence of O_2 (if Fe^{3+} is absent), it could be shown using this technique that sulfide oxidation was a bacterial process (Zinder and Brock, 1977). However, in most systems it would not be possible to use this approach.

TEMPERATURE AS A POISON

One of the best ways to show that a process is biological is to show that it has a temperature optimum. As temperature increases, the rates of purely chemical reactions increase proportionately, without showing any fall-off, whereas biological reactions show sharp temperature optima (Figure 1) and fall-off dramatically when the temperature is further increased (Arrhenius, 1915). In many of our studies, we have been able to easily show that a process has a definite temperature optimum. This has been true even of those processes

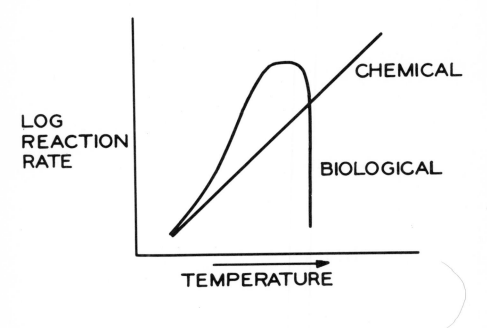

Figure 1.   Idealized graphs showing the effect of temperature
            on biological and chemical reactions.

occurring in geothermal systems, where the temperature optima
are quite high.   Thus, as seen in Figure 2, the temperature
optima for uptake of radioactive compounds by bacteria from
Boulder Spring and Octopus Spring are around 90°C, the temperature optimum for elemental sulfur oxidation by Moose Pool.
bacteria is 80°C, and the temperature optimum for ferrous
iron oxidation by Locomotive Spring bacteria is 80–85°C.   No
better evidence for a biological process can be obtained than
data showing a sharp temperature optimum.

WATER POTENTIAL AS A POISON

        Availability of water has a marked effect on biological
reactions.   Water availability can be expressed in terms of
water potential (Griffin 1969, 1972; Brock, 1975), and can be
most readily reduced by addition of solutes to the system.
Solutes commonly used include sucrose, glycerol and sodium
chloride.   At water potentials below about –300 bars   (equiv-
alent to about 30% w/v NaCl), very few microorganisms are able
to grow or carry out biochemical functions.   Most microorganisms
of frewshwater environments are inhibited at water potentials
around –50 bars, and marine organisms at around –100 bars.

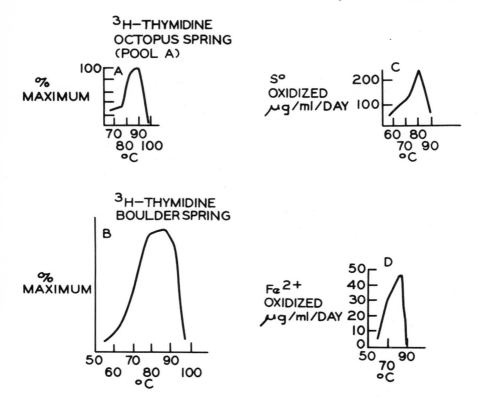

Figure 2. Typical data on the effect of temperature on biogeochemical processes in geothermal habitats. A. Incorporation of ³H-thymidine into heterotrophic bacteria from Octopus
Spring (Pool A) (Brock and Brock, 1971). B. Effect of temperature on ³H-thymidine incorporation into sulfur bacteria
at Boulder Spring (Brock *et al.*, 1971). C. Effect of temperature on rate of oxidation of elemental sulfur in Moose
Pool (Mosser *et al.*, 1973). D. Effect of temperature on
rate of oxidation of ferrous iron in Moose Pool (Brock *et
al.*, 1976).

Thus, water potential is an excellent way of stopping microbial
activity. Although it is probable that the addition of solutes
to reaction mixtures will have some effect on purely chemical
reactions, the effect is likely to be minor, since chemical
reactions do not involve movement of substances across semipermeable membranes.

     In our study of the biogeochemistry of ferrous iron
oxidation in geothermal habitats (Brock *et al.*, 1976), we
used reduced water potential for the poisoned controls. The
solute NaCl was used, at a concentration of 10% w/v. We had
already shown in cultural experiments that this concentration

completely inhibited growth of *Sulfolobus acidocaldarius*, the
organism responsible for the oxidation process. Further,
NaCl had no effect on the ferrous iron assay, whereas two
other common poisons, formaldehyde and mercuric bichloride,
strongly interfered with the assay. Thus, incubations were
set up in which samples of water containing ferrous iron
were incubated with and without added 10% NaCl. The results
were quite clear-cut: at the pH values involved (pH 1.8-2.0),
chemical oxidation was virtually nil, whereas the biological
process occurred at a rapid rate. As a further indication
of the biological nature of the process, the temperature
optimum was also determined.

Water potential, as controlled by addition of solute,
is probably the simplest and most general means of eliminating
biological activity without influencing spontaneous chemical
reactions. A wide variety of solutes are available which can
be used, including very soluble salts such as NaCl, alcohols,
sugars, urea, etc. It is of course always essential to be
sure that the solute used does not interfere with the assay
procedure used for the process, and does not itself increase
or decrease the chemical reaction. This latter possibility
can be easily tested by setting up model reactions in the
laboratory. To calculate the solute concentration necessary
to obtain a given water potential, concentrative properties
of solutes can be obtained from tables given in most handbooks
of chemistry. The most useful formula relates freezing-
point depression to water potential: water potential (bars) =
(13.32) x (freezing-point depression). One bar equals 100
joules/kg.

SEPARATING THE BIOLOGICAL AND NONBIOLOGICAL COMPONENTS OF A REACTION

Given the proper inhibitor, it is relatively simple
to separate the biological from the nonbiological components
in a biogeochemical reaction. All one need do is carry out
incubations on several replicates, some of which are poisoned
and some of which are not. Data from the poisoned experiment
will give the nonbiological rate, and data from the non-
poisoned experiment will give the combined rate. All one need
do to get the biological rate is deduct one from the other.
It is necessary to assume two things: (1) that the poison
has no effect on the nonbiological reaction; and (2) that the
biological reaction has no effect on the nonbiological reaction.
Assumption 1 can be tested in model systems in the laboratory,
but assumption 2 cannot be tested. In many cases, the biological rate is so much faster than the nonbiological rate
that interpretation of the results presents no difficulties.

REFERENCES

Arrhenius, S. *Quantitative Laws in Biological Chemistry* (London: G. Bell and Sons, 1915).

Brock, T.D. "Effect of Water Potential on Growth and Iron Oxidation by *Thiobacillus ferrooxidans*," *Applied Microbiol.* 29:495-501 (1975).

Brock, T.D., and M.L. Brock. "Temperature Optimum of Non-Sulfur Bacteria from a Spring at 90°C," *Nature* 233:494-495 (1971).

Brock, T.D., M.L. Brock, T.L. Bott and M.R. Edwards. "Microbial Life at 90°C: the Sulfur Bacteria of Boulder Spring," *J. Bacteriol.* 107:303-314 (1971).

Brock, T.D., S. Cook, S. Petersen and J.L. Mosser. "Biogeochemistry and Bacteriology of Ferrous Iron Oxidation in Geothermal Habitats," *Geochim. Cosmochim. Acta* 40:493-500 (1976).

Chen, K.Y., and J.C. Morris. "Oxidation of Aqueous Sulfide by O_2: 1. General Characteristics and Catalytic Influences," *5th International Water Pollution Research Conference,* July-August 1970, III, 32/1-32/17.

Griffin, D.M. "Soil Water in the Ecology of Fungi," *Annual Rev. Phytopathology* 7:289-310 (1969).

Griffin, D.M. *Ecology of Soil Fungi* (London: Chapman and Hall, 1972).

Ivanov, M.V. *Microbiological Processes in the Formation of Sulfur Deposits* (Jerusalem: Israel Program for Scientific Translations, Ltd., 1968).

Mosser, J.L., A.G. Mosser and T.D. Brock. "Bacterial Origin of Sulfuric Acid in Geothermal Habitats," *Science* 179:1323-1324 (1973).

Singer, P.C., and W. Stumm. "Acidic Mine Drainage: The Rate-Determining Step," *Science* 167:1121-1123 (1970).

Zinder, S., and T.D. Brock. "Sulfur Dioxide in Geothermal Waters and Gases," *Geochim. Cosmochim. Acta* (in press).

CHAPTER 58

SEASONAL MATRIX ANALYSIS OF RHIZOSPHERE AND
RHIZOPLANE MICROBIAL RESPONSES, CARBON DIOXIDE
EVOLUTION, AND OXYGEN UTILIZATION PROCESSES
IN SOILS ASSOCIATED WITH GRASSLAND PLANTS

J.P. NAKAS
D.A. KLEIN
A.L. GELLER

Department of Microbiology
Colorado State University
Fort Collins, Colorado 80523 USA

INTRODUCTION

The analysis of microbial responses in terrestrial
microenvironments is made difficult by the lack of access
without site disturbance. This problem becomes especially
pronounced in studying decomposer responses in the rhizosphere-
rhizoplane zone. To evaluate seasonal microbial responses in
these zones, a matrix analysis approach was used to relate
changes in a series of decomposition process parameters, including respiration indices and dehydrogenase activity in the
presence of five broad substrate classes. Earlier studies
from this laboratory (Klein, 1977) utilized a similar approach,
without having involved analyses in the rhizosphere and rhizoplane. This study was completed to determine if this type of
approach could be used to gain a better understanding of microbial responses and functions in rhizosphere and rhizoplane
microenvironments of a semiarid grassland.

MATERIALS AND METHODS

Sampling was carried out at the Pawnee National Grass-
lands, Colorado. Soil cores, 16.5 cm in diameter by 10 cm in
length, were taken at two-week intervals from March 11, 1976,
to December 20, 1976. Soil organic matter and root organic
contents were determined by ashing procedures, using whole
soil or the separated roots which were trapped using a 32-mesh

screen. The degree of mycorrhizal infection of roots was
carried out as described by Klein and Molise (1975). Preparations were observed using the 20X objective, and only hyphae
were counted that could be seen projecting away from the root
edges. Five contiguous fields were examined, with the root
tip area constituting the first field.

The quantity of fungal hyphae was determined by a
modification of the agar film method developed by Jones and
Mollison (1948). The microscope slide was prepared using
cover slips (0.7-mm thickness) as spacers positioned 8 mm
apart by use of tape, and after addition of the molten soil-
agar suspension, a clean cover slip was gently pressed down
until it contacted the taped cover slips. The slide was im-
mersed in cold deionized H_2O to solidify the agar and gently
wiped dry before examination. This procedure eliminated the
need to stain or to transfer the agar layer to a second slide,
as carried out in the original procedure.

For respiration rate and routine microbial analyses,
soil cores were prepared by removing all plant growth down to
the root crowns and slicing the core from the bottom to achieve
a gross weight of 250 ± 5 grams (length 5.5-6.0 cm) prior to
addition to respirometers, as carried out in previous studies
(Klein, 1977). The separation of whole free rhizosphere and
rhizoplane microbial populations was carried out using the
procedure of Louw and Webley (1959).

The dehydrogenase activity of the test soils was
evaluated by using a modification of the simplified procedure
developed by Klein, Loh and Goulding (1971). Two tubes from
each set received 0.2 ml of 1, 2, 3, 4 or 5% (w/v) triphenyl
tetrazolium chloride solution (TTC), followed by incubation
at 20°C for 24 hr. After incubation, 10 ml of methanol was
added, shaken for 30 sec and allowed to stand in the dark for
6 hr at room temperature. The methanol supernatant was removed
from each tube and absorbances were read at 485 nm.

Phosphatase activities were determined by the procedure
of Tabatabai and Bremner (1969) using buffers at 5.5 and 8.2,
and soil inorganic phosphorus levels were measured using
routine procedures after bicarbonate extraction.

RESULTS

The overall matrix analysis for decomposer parameters
of soils from the Pawnee site (samplings 1-19, 1976) is given
in Figure 1. Several interactions of interest can be noted:
(1) the interaction of CO_2 evolution and moisture is strong
(<0.01); (2) the percent organic matter in root materials was
correlated at the 5% level with changes in the rhizoplane
fungal population, as determined by plate counting procedures;
and (3) the microscopic fungal biomass was related to bacteria
and actinomycete levels, as determined by plating procedures,
but not to viable fungal counts.

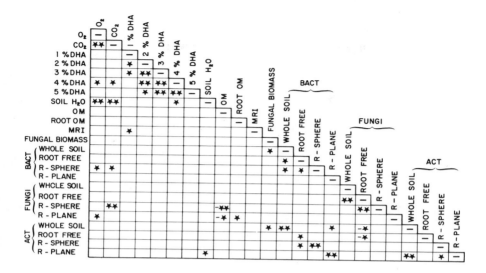

Figure 1. Matrix analysis of decomposer responses in rhizosphere and rhizoplane zones for the entire 1976 season.

In addition, several other points were of interest:
(1) no significant interactions occurred between viable count
populations of bacteria and fungi; (2) mycorrhizal hyphal
measurements were correlated with oxygen consumption; (3)
bacteria and actinomycete changes in the whole soil, free soil,
rhizosphere and rhizoplane were closely correlated, with three
of these four interactions being at the 1% level; and (4)
TTC gave the best correlations when using a 4% concentration
in the test system.

For the entire year, fungi in the rhizosphere and
rhizoplane showed significant (1 and 5 percent, respectively)
inverse relationships with soil organic matter changes. A
direct relationship of rhizosphere fungal changes with the
organic matter content of root materials also was observed.

The seasonal analyses provided additional information
on the functioning of this system. The strongest positive
respiration and dehydrogenase correlations were found in
summer when the single major precipitation event occurred.
In addition, the spring and fall periods tended to have a
greater number of significant inverse correlations, as noted
in Table I for all nutrient treatment experiments.

The interactions of interest for the spring period
included the following (Figure 2): (1) strong correlations
were observed between bacteria and actinomycetes; (2) fungal
and actinomycete relationship changes (based on viable counts)
were inverse; (3) the mycorrhizal hyphal infection changes
were inversely related to changes in the whole soil bacterial
population; (4) inverse relationships between fungal populations
in the rhizoplane and the soil water content and organic matter

Table I
Seasonal Variations in Total and Inverse
Significant Matrix Relationships

	Total Interactions	Inverse	% Inverse
Spring	73	35	48%
Summer	127	4	3%
Fall	78	27	35%

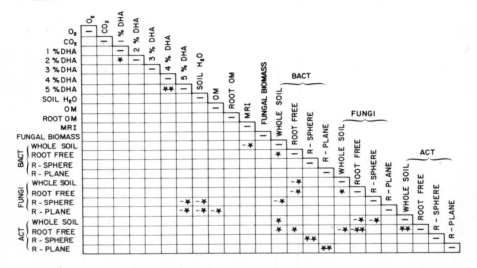

Figure 2.   Matrix analysis of decomposer responses in rhizosphere and rhizoplane zones for the spring 1976 season.

content were observed; and (5) the relationship between fungi
(rhizosphere and rhizoplane) with the 5% dehydrogenase assay
also was inverse.

During summer, in comparison with spring, many respira-
tion-related significant positive interactions were observed
(Figure 3). Both bacteria and fungi, especially in the rhizosphere area, showed significant positive correlations with O_2
use, soil water content and CO_2 evolution. Of interest was
the inverse relationship (P = <0.01) between changes in mycorrhizal fungi and the viable counts of fungi in the rhizoplane.
As observed previously, no interactions were observed between
viable counts for bacteria and fungi. The changes in soil
organic matter did show an interaction with the microscopic
assays for fungi and with viable counts for actinomycetes in
the rhizosphere. With 4% TTC, correlations with carbon dioxide
evolution occurred.

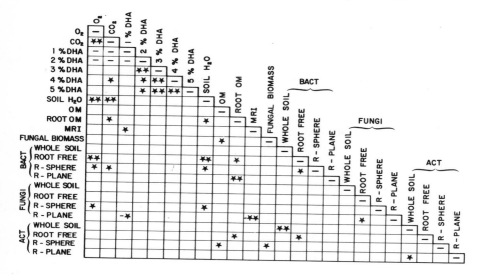

Figure 3. Matrix analysis of decomposer responses in the rhizosphere and rhizoplane zones for the summer 1976 season.

During the fall (Figure 4), as observed for spring, a
greater percentage of the significant interactions were negative, suggesting the absence of continuing primary productivity
or optimal water content conditions which would allow continued
decomposer activity. During this season, the respiration
correlations are predominantly with O_2 use, and interactions
between viable counts for fungi and bacteria were observed

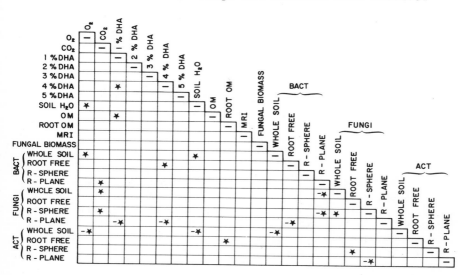

Figure 4. Matrix analysis of decomposer responses in rhizosphere and rhizoplane zones for the fall 1976 season.

(all inverse). During this time no interactions between
changes in soil organic matter, or microscopic fungi with other
other parameters were observed. Mycorrhizal hyphal development,
microscopic fungal biomass, and [1]acid and [2]alkaline phosphatase
parameters showed significant changes in September and October,
following this rainfall event (Figure 5). A decrease in
mycorrhizal development occurred, and at the same time increased
alkaline phosphatase activity was observed, usually considered
to be of fungal or bacterial origin. During the same period,
the acid phosphatase activity (considered to be predominantly
plant-derived) and the microscopic fungal biomass parameters
showed decreases (data not shown).

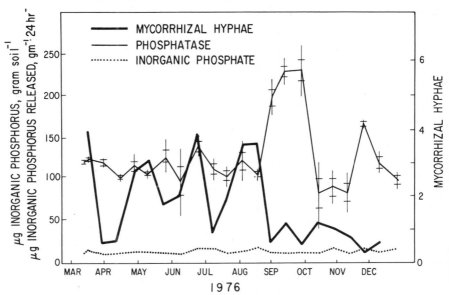

Figure 5. Mycorrhizal infection, bicarbonate-extractable
   inorganic phosphate and alkaline phosphatase activity
   relationships at the Pawnee Grassland site - 1976.

DISCUSSION

        In comparison with results obtained for 1972 (Klein,
1977) where the dominant primary production events occurred
in spring, during 1976 the primary production event occurred
in August. In response to this change in the time of the major
nutrient inputs to the decomposer compartment, the major
positive relationships also were observed in summer. The
respiratory parameters responded as might be expected, and a
point of special interest was the increased **correlation** obtained when using 4 or 5% TTC.

The microscopic procedures used for soil fungi and mycorrhizal hyphal measurements did show general responses which are of interest. The fungal biomass assay showed surprisingly good correlations with the viable counts of bacteria and actinomycetes, but not with fungi as determined by viable count procedures. On the other hand, the viable fungal count procedure gave best responses in the rhizosphere and rhizoplane in relation to changes in respiration parameters. This may be due to the ability of conidia or chlamydospores to germinate more easily in the root zone, either due to a relief of fungistatis, or an increased availability of nutrients (Brown, 1975; Richards, 1974). In any event, it suggests that the fungi, at least as measured by viable counts, may be a sensitive indicator of periods when substrates are increasingly available in the rhizosphere.

The decreases in mycorrhizal infection, free fungal biomass and acid phosphatase activity which occurred following the late summer rainfall event, together with the increase in alkaline phosphatase activities, suggest that bacterial and nonmycorrhizal fungal phosphatases may have been releasing phosphorous for plant use in the late fall period. This would make it possible for the grassland community to function with a lower level of mycorrhizal fungal development.

The ability of matrix analysis procedures to provide information on seasonal changes in relationships between decomposer parameters, especially in the rhizosphere and rhizoplane zones, suggests that this experimental method may be useful in analysis of other environments. These data also suggest that in the study of microbial functions and responses in the rhizosphere zone, that the fungal components of such systems should not be neglected, in spite of the greater experimental difficulties which might result from the use of these organisms. Studies are in progress to determine the seasonal contributions of fungi versus bacteria in mineralization processes in the rhizosphere and rhizoplane, utilizing procedures of Harrison, Wright and Morita (1970) in combination with antibiotic combinations recommended by Anderson and Domsch (1973). It is hoped that in this way it will be possible to more fully assess seasonal changes in the contributions of fungi to nutrient cycling processes in the plant root zone of a grassland community.

ACKNOWLEDGMENTS

This research was supported under project DEB 7518765 "Ecosystem Analysis of Seasonal Carbon Flow and Decomposer Compartment Control Relationships," carried out with support from the Office of Ecosystem Studies, National Science Foundation. Laboratory assistance and general technician support has been provided by Gayle Greenslade, Greta Klein, Nicholas Nagle, Sharon Pauli, Terry Praznik and Gayle Robison.

REFERENCES

Anderson, J.P.E., and K.H. Domsch. "Quantification of Bacterial and Fungal Contributions to Soil Respiration," *Arch. Mikrobiol.* 93:113-127 (1973).

Brown, M.E. "Rhizosphere Microorganisms--Opportunists, Bandits or Benefactors," in *Soil Microbiology*, N. Walker, Ed. (New York: Halstead Press, John Wiley and Sons, 1975), pp. 21-38.

Harrison, M.J., R.T. Wright and R.Y. Morita. "Method for Measuring Mineralization in Lake Sediments," *Appl. Microbiol.* 31:714-717 (1970).

Jones, P.C.T., and J.E. Mollison. "A Technique for the Quantitative Estimation of Soil Microorganisms," *J. Gen. Microbiol.* 2:54-69 (1948).

Klein, D.A. "Seasonal Carbon Flow and Decomposer Parameter Relationships in a Semiarid Grassland Soil," *Ecology* (January 1977).

Klein, D.A., T.C. Loh and R.L. Goulding. "A Rapid Procedure to Evaluate the Dehydrogenase Activity of Soils Low in Organic Matter," *Soil Biol. Biochem.* 3:385-387 (1971).

Klein, D.A., and E.M. Molise. "Ecological Ramifications of Silver Iodide Nucleating Agent Accumulation in a Semiarid Grassland Environment," *J. Appl. Meterol.* 14:673-680 (1975).

Louw, J.A., and D.M. Webley. "The Bacteriology of the Root Region of the Oak Plant Grown Under Controlled Pot Culture Conditions," *J. Appl. Bact.* 22:216-226 (1959).

Richards, B.N. *Introduction to the Soil Ecosystem*   (London: Longman, Ltd., 1974), p. 163.

Tabatabai, M.A., and J.M. Bremner. "Use of *p*-nitrophenyl Phosphate for Assay of Soil Phosphatase Activity," *Soil Biol. Biochem.* 1:301-307 (1969).

CHAPTER 59

A METHOD OF DETERMINATION OF VARIOUS SULFUR COMPOUNDS IN SEA SEDIMENTS AND ROCKS

N.N. ZHABINA
I.I. VOLKOV

P.P. Shirshov Institute of Oceanology
of the USSR Academy of Sciences
Moscow, USSR

The process of bacterial reduction of sulfates taking place in bottom sediments of modern reservoirs is one of the most important processes of the early stages of diagenesis. This process affects transformations both of silt (pore) waters impregnating the sediments and of the solid phase. For this reason, studies of the regularities of sulfur compound formation and transformation in bottom sediments are of great importance and interest. This explains the need for a reliable method for determining the composition of sulfur compounds in bottom sediments. The method we presently use involves investigating the solid phase of sediments and silt waters.

In the studies of reduced sediments with the developed process of sulfate reduction, free H_2S and sulfur contained in sulfates (SO_4^{2-}), sulfites (SO_3^{2-}), and thiosulfates ($S_2O_3^{2-}$) are identified and quantitatively determined in silt waters (Volkov, 1959). Free H_2S is determined by displacement from a suspension of the natural sediment (a separately weighed sample with added water free of oxygen) with inert gas (N_2 or Ar) without heating. H_2S is absorbed with cadmium acetate or zinc acetate solution and determined iodometrically or photometrically, respectively. Sulfate sulfur in silt water samples (3-5 ml) is determined by sulfate reduction to H_2S with a Sn (II)/strong H_3PO_4 reagent followed by iodometric or photometric analysis, depending on the amount of sulfate sulfur in the sample. The determination of sulfur contained in thiosulfates and sulfites is carried out in accordance with the method of A. Kurtenacker (1938) specially modified for silt waters of sediments (Volkov and Ostroumov, 1957). In this case a sample

of silt water (50-100 ml) is analyzed iodometrically. Often
the sensitivity of iodometry is insufficient for the determination of sulfites,and therefore only thiosulfates are
determined.

The present communication is devoted to the description
of various sulfur forms determination, the forms appearing in
the sediment solid phase as a result of the bacterial process
of sulfate reduction to hydrogen sulfide. Hydrogen sulfide
or its transformation products interact with mineral or organic
constituents of sediments. As first demonstrated by E.A.
Ostroumov (1953) for Black Sea sediments, and confirmed later
for the sediments of other basins, the reduction of sulfates
and the process of hydrogen sulfide metabolism in bottom sediments give rise to the following sulfur forms: sulfide, elemental, pyrite, and organic sulfur; a certain amount of sulfate always remains in the sediments.

Sulfide sulfur is bound in colloidal iron sulfide,
i.e., hydrotroilite. Mackinovite and greygite are its crystal-
lized varieties in sediments. The decomposition of greygite
with acids always gives rise to elemental sulfur. Apart from
iron sulfides, sulfides of other metals may also be present
in the sediments of hydrotherms (*e.g.*, sphalerite in the sediments of the Red Sea depressions).

In most cases, elemental sulfur is present in sediments
in a finely dispersed state. Only under certain conditions does
microscopic observation reveal "droplets" of elemental sulfur
in the bodies of sulfide-oxidizing bacteria. The aggregates
of elemental sulfur are also sparse and ephemeral on the surface of shallow water sediments where a rapid oxidation of
hydrogen sulfide, entering intensely from the mass of sediments,
with oxygen of overlying water occurs. Evidently, one should
distinguish between indigenous elemental sulfur and sulfur
precipitated in the course of analysis (as a result of acidification with HCl in the determination of sulfide sulfur).
The sources of elemental sulfur formation in the course of
treatment with HCl are as follows: (1) sulfide sulfur in the
case of greygite presence in the sample. (2) sulfide sulfur
from hydrotroilite or another monosulfide decomposed with
diluted HCl at heating (sphalerite) if trivalent iron is
present in the sediment sample, (3) sulfur of thiosulfate in
silt water in the case of acidification and heating of a sample,
and (4) sulfur from decomposed polysulfide possibly present in
silt water; the formation of polysulfide under the conditions
existing in sediments is presently admitted by some researchers.

Pyrite sulfur, a predominant form of reduced sulfur in
sediments, one of the final products of hydrogen sulfide transformation, is represented by pyrite finely dispersed in the
bulk of sediments. Large pyrite aggregates or concretions,
visible with the naked eye, are very rarely met in modern marine

sediments. On the contrary, in ancient (particularly shale and carbonaceous) rocks, pyrite concretions of different sizes are found frequently.

Organic sulfur or sulfur as a part of the organic matter of marine sediment is, as a rule, a second large form of reduced sulfur, after pyrite. The formation of organic derivatives of sulfur results from the interaction of elemental sulfur (or hydrogen sulfide) with the products of metamorphosed organic matter during the processes of its bituminization and humification in the diagenesis of sediments. The nature of sulfur organic compounds formed under anaerobic conditions of marine sediments has not been studied sufficiently, but this organic sulfur can by no means be regarded as identical with the sulfur existing in living organisms, *e.g.*, protein sulfur. The results of chemical and isotopic studies show that organic sulfur of sediments, as other reduced sulfur forms, has been formed from hydrogen sulfide, a product of bacterial sulfate reduction.

Sulfate sulfur determined in the course of analysis is mainly represented by silt water sulfates. However, a certain amount of sulfates (apart from possibly present $BaSO_4$) is present in the solid phase of sediments in acid-soluble form, partly as a constituent of carbonate skeletons of organisms, partly as a component of the argillaceous portion of sediments.

A scheme for the separate determination of the above-mentioned forms of sulfur compounds in marine sediments was first developed by E.A. Ostroumov (1953). According to this scheme, sulfide sulfur was determined iodometrically and element sulfur was determined photometrically, from the color of iron thiocyanide. The content of pyrite, organic and sulfate forms of sulfur was found from the weight of $BaSO_4$. Later, the method was slightly improved (Volkov, 1959), with volumetric analysis (iodometry) substituted for the final gravimetric determination due to the utilization of a bivalent tin/strong phosphoric acid reagent $(SN(II)/H_3PO_4)$ for the reduction of sulfates to H_2S (Kiba, 1955; Volkov and Ostroumov, 1958). However, even in this form the method of determination of sulfur in modern sediments was time-and labor-consuming. The separation and determination of pyrite sulfur conducted by oxidation was the longest stage.

In our opinion, the methods of direct transformation of various sulfur compounds into hydrogen sulfide are the most promising. They are rapid and make it possible, dependent on sulfur content, to finish the determination either iodometrically or photometrically. The utilization of photometry (methylene blue formation) is needed in the case of samples containing, together with pyrite in high concentrations, minute amounts (less than 0.001%) of sulfide and elemental sulfur which cannot be measured iodometrically because of the low sensitivity of this method.

Our recent works dealing with the application of metallic chromium and bivalent chromium salts in analytical chemistry of sulfur made it possible to simplify and accelerate the determination of elemental and, particularly, pyrite sulfur (Volkov and Zhabina, 1971, 1975, 1977a,b). These studies have demonstrated that in the presence of metallic chromium or $CrCl_2$ in a hydrogen chloride-containing solution, a quantitative reduction of elemental sulfur and a quantitative decomposition of pyrite with H_2S evolution occurs. It has also been ascertained that at a low acidity (less than 1.2 *N* HCl), $CrCl_2$ solution allows free and pyrite sulfur to be determined in the presence of large amounts of sulfates. Organic sulfur is not affected during the application of metallic chromium or $CrCl_2$ in solution.

These methods were included in the general scheme of determining various sulfur compounds in sediments and thus simplified and accelerated the analysis. The method as a whole has been verified and utilized in the studies of samples obtained during the expedition to the Pacific Ocean (Volkov *et al.*, 1972; 1976). During the cruise of the research ship *Academician Kurchatov* in the Indian Ocean and the Red Sea (March-June 1976), the analysis of sulfur compounds described below was used (without the last stage of organic sulfur determination) in the laboratory onboard the ship. Organic sulfur was analyzed for later in the laboratory onshore.

Below is given the scheme of analysis for various forms of sulfur compounds in marine sediments which we presently utilize; the analysis procedure and instruments are briefly described. All results are calculated in percent with respect to the dry matter of sediments. Moisture content is determined for a parallel weighed sample by drying at 105-110°C to constant weight (see Scheme).

The material is sampled immediately after arrival onboard and is stored, prior to analysis for sulfur forms, in glass tubes tightly closed with rubber plugs from both ends and refrigerated at 2-4°C.

SULFIDE SULFUR DETERMINATION

First a sediment sample of natural moisture content (1-2 g of dry matter) placed on a glass tray or piece of polyethylene film, is introduced into the decomposition flask of an assembly for the determination of sulfide sulfur (Figure 1). Before the determination, the assembly is washed with inert gas (CO_2, N_2 or Ar) for the displacement of air. Hydrochloric acid (80 ml 1.5 *N* solution) is added through the gas inlet tube and inert gas is again passed through the flask at the rate of 2 bubbles per second. When the decomposition of sulfides slows down, about 20-30 minutes later, the contents of the reaction flask are heated until they just begin to boil. Inert

Scheme of the Determination of Various Forms of Sulfur Compounds in the Marine Sediments

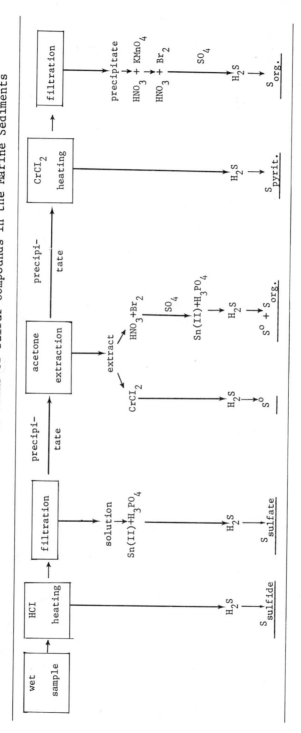

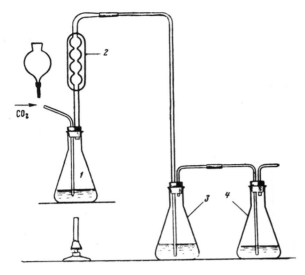

Figure 1. Scheme of an apparatus for sulfide sulfur determination.

gas is passed 20–25 minutes more. The flask is disconnected, the gas inlet tube and the cooler washed, and the contents of the flask are kept for further operations.

Emanating hydrogen sulfide is absorbed with cadmium acetate in flasks or with zinc acetate in the case of iodo-metric (Figure 1) or photometric determination. In the latter instance, a wide test tube is used as an absorbing vessel (see Figure 3, p. 742). After absorption, the vessels are discon-nected and the final stage of determination for sulfide sulfur is conducted either iodometrically or photometrically depending on the amount of sulfur.

SULFATE SULFUR DETERMINATION

The contents of the reaction flask are mixed with macerated paper pulp and filtered ("white ribbon" dense filter) into a beaker. Residue on the filter is washed with warm water until no chlorine is detected in eluate. The filtrate together with the eluate is evaporated and transferred into a 50-ml volumetric flask. An aliquot of the solution (10 ml) is placed in a quartz tube in the apparatus for the reduction of sulfates (Figure 2) and thoroughly dried.

A $Sn(II)/H_3PO_4$ reagent (8 ml) is added to the dry residue in the tube (the reagent's preparation was described by Volkov and Ostroumov, 1958), and the tube is hung on a wire hook in the reaction vessel of the apparatus for the reduction of sulfates. The apparatus is closed with a rubber plug having a gas inlet tube and a thermometer sheath. A thermometer is inserted, absorption vessels are connected, and inert gas is let through the apparatus for 2–3 min. The temperature is

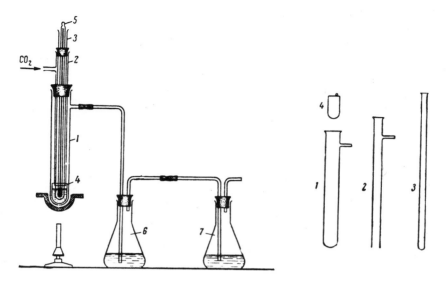

Figure 2. Scheme of an apparatus for the determination of sulfates by reduction to H_2S. a. Assembled apparatus; b. Transparent quartz parts of the apparatus.

1. Reaction vessel (length 225 mm, i.d. 27 mm);
2. Gas inlet tube (length 285 mm, i.d. 13 mm);
3. Thermometer sheath (length 340 mm, i.d. 13 mm);
4. Tube with an eye on top and a 8-ml volume mark on the wall (height 50 mm, o.d. 26 mm);
5. 360°C thermometer;
6 and 7. Absorber flasks (200-ml capacity).

raised to 300°C in 15-20 min by means of a gas burner or an electrical oven, the heating is continued 20-25 min more, with the temperature kept constant. The completion of reduction and the end of the process can be checked by disconnecting the absorbers and analyzing for hydrogen sulfide in the outgoing gas by smell or with the help of paper wetted with lead acetate solution. At the end of the process, absorbing vessels are disconnected and the final stage of determination is carried out iodometrically or photometrically, depending on the amount of sulfur.

ELEMENTAL SULFUR DETERMINATION

The residue on the filter after filtration of the solution containing sulfate sulfur is dried as completely as possible by pressing it at once between pieces of filter paper; the residue is dried together with the filter. After drying, the edges of the filter are turned up and the filter with the residue is placed into the tube of an extraction apparatus.

Acetone is introduced into the tube and the flask of the extractor and the extraction of elemental sulfur on a weakly boiling water bath is started. The duration of extraction is 16 hours. After extraction and the evaporation of most of the solvent from the flask, the extract is transferred into a volumetric flask and acetone is added to the 50-ml mark. The extract contains all the elemental sulfur and a portion of the organic sulfur from the bituminous component of the organic matter contained in sediments.

For the determination of elemental sulfur, an aliquot of acetone extract containing no more than 100 μg S is introduced into the reactor tube of an analysis assembly (Figure 3). The assembly consists of two identical tubes, *i.e.*, reactor and absorber, closed with glass ground-in stopper. HCl (10 ml, density 1.12), is added to the aliquot in the reactor tube. The reactor is closed with a stopper having a gas inlet tube, the absorber filled with zinc acetate solution is connected, and gas is passed through the absorber at a rate of 60 bubbles per minute. 1-2 minutes later, the gas flow is interrupted and $CrCl_2$ solution (10 ml) introduced through the gas inlet tube by means of a pear-shaped funnel; then gas is passed again. The time required for a complete reduction of sulfur

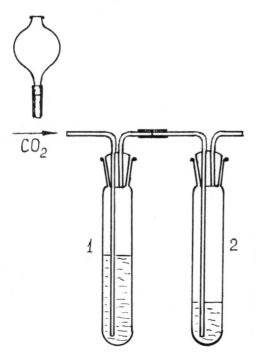

Figure 3. Apparatus for the determination of elemental sulfur by reduction to H_2S.
1. Reaction test tube.
2. Absorber: length 180 mm, diameter 30 mm.

CO_2

and the distilling of the H_2S formed is 15-20 min. The
absorber containing zinc sulfate is disconnected 20 minutes
later and dimethyl p-phenylene diamine solution (8 ml) is
added through the gas inlet tube by means of a pipette. The
contents of the absorber tube are vigorously mixed and 2 ml
of ammonium iron alum are immediately added. The stopper with
gas tubes is replaced by a rubber plug and the absorber is
shaken for 30 sec. After the formation of methylene blue, the
contents of the absorber tube are transferred into a 50- or
100-ml volumetric flask, depending on the intensity of coloring.
The determination is completed with the measurement of light
absorption on a spectrophotometer or a photoelectric colorim-
eter.

BITUMINOUS ORGANIC SULFUR DETERMINATION

Another aliquot of the above acetone extract, usually
25 or 50 ml, is introduced into a beaker; the acetone is
disposed of by evaporation on a water bath. Bromine solution
in CCl_4 (2:3 by volume; 3-5 ml) is added to the dry residue
in the beaker, the beaker is closed with a watch glass and
the system is kept at room temperature for about 10 min and
occasionally stirred. Concentrated HNO_3 is added (5-10 ml)
and the mixture is stirred for another 10-15 min. With the
glass remaining, the beaker is put into a closed weakly
boiling water bath and carefully heated until most of the
bromine evaporates. The glass is removed, the beaker is
inserted into the opening of the bath, and the contents are
dried by evaporation. For a complete removal of nitric acid,
the dry residue in the beaker is treated with 3-5 ml HCl
(density 1.19) and dried by evaporation once again. The
treatment with hydrochloric acid is repeated 2-3 times.
Afterwards, the contents of the beaker are transferred into
the tube of the apparatus for the reduction of sulfates (see
Figure 2) and dried by evaporation. The rest of the operations
are conducted as in the sulfate-sulfur determination procedure.
The figure obtained represents the sum of elemental and bituminous organic sulfur concentrations. The latter is found by
difference.

PYRITE SULFUR DETERMINATION

The insoluble residue, left after elemental sulfur
extraction, is removed from the extractor together with the
filter, is placed in a weighing cup, and dried until all
acetone is removed. The sample, together with the filter,
is placed in the reaction flask of the pyrite decomposition
apparatus (Figure 4) and the determination of pyrite sulfur
is started. Ethanol (10-12 ml) is added to the sample and

mixed.   The flask is connected with the apparatus and CO_2 (nitrogen, argon) is passed in order to displace air.   After 3–5 minutes, gas flow is cut off and $CrCl_2$ solution (50 ml) and HCl (20 ml; density 1.19) are introduced into the reaction flask by means of a dropping funnel.   A constant gas flow is established in the absorbers (80–100 bubbles per minute).   Depending on the intensity of H_2S evolution, the first 10–15 minutes of the process is carried out in the cold; subsequently, the contents of the flask are heated to boiling and slowly boiled for 30–40 minutes.   After the evolution of hydrogen sulfide has stopped, absorption flasks containing cadmium sulfide are disconnected.   The final stage of analysis is iodometric titration.

$CrCl_2$ solution is obtained by the reduction (with amalgamated zinc) of an analytical-grade $CrCl_3$ solution containing 40–50 mg Cr in 1 ml and acidified to 0.5 N concentration.

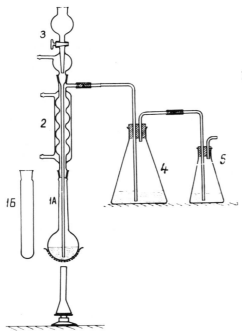

Figure 4.   Scheme of an apparatus for pyrite sulfur determination.   1. Reaction flask (capacity 150 ml, neck diameter 22 mm, height 230 mm). 2.   Ball reflux condenser. 3.   Dropping funnel with stopcock and gas inlet tube. 4 and 5.   Hydrogen sulfide absorbers.

ORGANIC SULFUR DETERMINATION

For the determination of the main amount of organic sulfur, the insoluble residue after the distillation of pyrite sulfur as H_2S is taken.   The reaction flask is disconnected from the apparatus and the gas inlet tube is washed with water.   The insoluble residue in the flask is filtered through

a "white ribbon" dense filter and repeatedly washed with distilled water acidified with several drops of HCl, the washing
removing chromium ions. The washed residue together with the
filter is placed in a 100-150 ml beaker, dried in a drier oven
and subjected to exhaustive oxidation, transforming organic sulfur into sulfate. To this end, the dry residue in the beaker
is treated with 20-30 ml of concentrated HNO_3; a few crystals
$KMnO_4$ on the end of a spatula are added, the beaker is covered
with a watch glass and placed on low heat on an electrical
stove. The contents of the beaker are boiled under the glass
to almost dry the residue. The glass is then removed, the
residue dried, and the operation repeated. The final dry
residue is treated with bromine and nitric acid in compliance
with the method of determination of bituminous organic sulfur
described previously; nitrates are removed by repeated evaporation with hydrochloric acid and the sample is transferred into
a 50-ml flask. An aliquot of the solution is introduced into
the tube of the apparatus for the determination of sulfates
(Figure 2); the further operations are carried out as before.
The final stage of determination is iodometric or photometric
analysis, depending on the amount of sulfur. The total content
of organic sulfur is found by adding the figure obtained to
the content of bituminous organic sulfur.

REFERENCES

Kiba, T., T. Takagi, Y. Yoshimura and I. Kishi. "Tin(II)--
Strong Phosphoric Acid. A New Reagent for the Determination
of Sulfate by Reduction to Hydrogen Sulfide," *Bull. Chem.
Soc. Jap.* 28:641-644 (1955).

Kurtenacker, A. *Analytische Chemie der Sauerstoffsäuren des
Schwefels* (Stuttgart: Enke, 1938).

Ostroumov, E.A. "Method of Determining the Form of Combined
Sulfur in the Sediments of the Black Sea," *Acad. Nauk SSSR
Insti. Okeanologii Trudy* 7:57-69 (1953).

Volkov, I.I. "Determination of Different Forms of Sulfur
Compounds in Marine Sediments," *Acad. Nauk SSSR Inst.
Okeanologii Trudy* 33:194-208 (1959).

Volkov, I.I., and E.A. Ostroumov. "Determination of Thiosulfates in Interstitial Water of the Black Sea," *Acad.
Nauk SSSR Doklady* 114:853-856 (1957).

Volkov, I.I., and E.A. Ostroumov. "Determination of Sulfates
by Reducing to Hydrogen Sulfide," *J. Analyt. Chem. Rus.*
13:686-690 (1958).

Volkov, I.I., A.G. Rozanov, N.N. Zhabina and T.A. Jagodinskaja. "Sulfur in the Pacific Sediments Toward the East from Japan," *Litol. Polez. Iskop.* 4:50-64 (1972).

Volkov, I.I., A.G. Rozanov, N.N. Zhabina and L.S. Fomina. "Sulfur Compounds in the Sediments of the California Gulf and Adjoining Region of the Pacific Ocean," in *Biogeochemistry of Diagenesis of Sediments of the Ocean,* I.I. Volkov, Ed. (Moscow: Nauka, 1976), pp. 136-170.

Volkov, I.I., and N.N. Zhabina. "Determination of Free Sulfur by the Reduction to Hydrogen Sulfide with Metallic Chromium," *J. Analyt. Chem. Rus.* 26:359-364 (1974).

Volkov, I.I., and N.N. Zhabina. "Determination of Elemental Sulfur by its Reduction to Hydrogen Sulfide with Chromium (II) Chloride," *J. Analyt. Chem. Rus.* 30:1572-1576 (1975).

Volkov, I.I., and N.N. Zhabina. "Determination of Pyritic Sulfur with Metallic Chromium and Chromium (II) Solution," in *Chemical Analysis of Marine Sediments,* E.A. Ostroumov, Ed. (Moscow: Nauka, 1977a), pp. 5-14.

Volkov, I.I., and N.N. Zhabina. "Photometric Method of the Determination of Element Sulfur in Marine Sediments, " in *Chemical-Oceanographic Investigation,* B.A. Skopintcev and V.N. Ivanenkov, Eds. (Moscow: Nauka, 1977), pp. 157-161.

CHAPTER 60

INFRARED SPECTROSCOPY OF TWO SOILS AND THEIR COMPONENTS

Z. FILIP

Department of Agricultural Microbiology
Justus Liebig University
6300 Lahn-Giessen
Federal Republic of Germany

INTRODUCTION

Identification or simple detection of microorganisms (biomass) in natural heterogeneous systems is an important part of microbiological investigation of the environment. Various physicochemical methods, *e.g.*, gas chromatography, radiometry and microcalorimetry, are recommended for this purpose (Johnston and Newsom, 1977). However, most of these methods are rather complicated for use in routine microbiology, and may destroy valuable samples during analysis. In order to overcome such disadvantages, an attempt was made to check the possibility of biomass and other organic substance identification in a heterogeneous soil system using IR-spectroscopy, which is both exact and relatively simple to use. In soil science, IR-spectroscopy has often been used either for identification of soil mineral parts (Beutelspacher *et al.*, 1972; van der Marel and Beutelspacher, 1976) or structural characterization of soil humic substances (Schnitzer and Khan, 1972; Flaig *et al.*, 1975). Few studies exist on IR-spectroscopy of whole soil samples (Fieldes *et al.*, 1972; Stepanov, 1974) and they do not consider soil biomass detection.

METHODS

Soil fraction less than 2 mm from arable soil (chernozem) and forest soil (podzol) were used in the experiments. Portions of those soils were extracted using a mixture of 0.1 N NaOH with 1.0 M $Na_2P_2O_7$. After acidification to pH 1.5, the precipitated humic acids were dialyzed and dried at 50°C.

Portions of extracted soils were additionally oxidized, using 30% H_2O_2 at room temperature and at 80°C until the reaction indicating the presence of organic matter did not occur. In this way, C_{ox}-content (originally 2.2% by chernozem and 2.7 % by forest soil, respectively) was totally excluded from respective soil samples. Furthermore, the biomass of soil microorganisms was enriched. For this purpose, a nutrient solution with glucose and peptone as the only C- and N-sources, containing soil extract, was inoculated with a diluted sus- pension of soil microorganisms (10^{-3}) and cultivated by permanent shaking at 25°C. The biomass yielded after five days was dialyzed and thoroughly dried at 50°C. For IR- spectroscopy, the KBr-pellets were uniformly prepared from the mixtures of 1-5 mg of dry samples with 300 mg KBr using precautions to eliminate moisture. These were examined in a Perkin-Elmer Model 283 IR-spectrophotometer over a wavelength of 2-30 μm.

RESULTS AND DISCUSSION

The possibility of the IR-spectroscopical detection of microorganisms in the soils could have been based on the IR- spectra of microbial biomass given in Figure 1. Both the biomass from chernozem (A) and forest soil (B) are distinguished by a very complicated IR-spectrum, containing a number of sharp adsorption bands at several wavelengths. Most of them

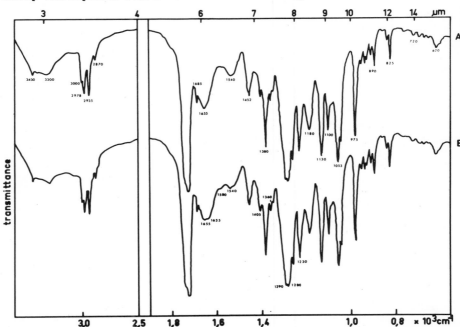

Figure 1. IR-spectra of microbial biomass from chernozem (A) and podzol (B).

can be associated to various cell constituents, such as proteins, glycoproteins, glycopeptides, polysaccharides, lipids and nucleic acids. They can be explained in agreement with data published by Bellamy (1975) and Parker (1971).

A weak absorption in the region of 3400-3300 cm^{-1} is due only to a low moisture content in the KBr pellets. As a free water band at 1613 cm^{-1} is not present at all, the absorption band at 3300 cm^{-1} can be partially attributed to NH$_2$ stretching vibrations in residues of purine and pyrimidine bases in the microbial biomass. A number of sharp peaks are laying in the typically C-H stretching region at 3000-2870 cm^{-1}. Cell wall and capsular polysaccharides may be responsible for this partially overlapping band. According to Fieldes *et al.* (1972), the absorption band at 2925 cm^{-1} is characteristic for soil organic matter (leaf litter) and peat.

Dry matter of bacteria and especially of fungi consists of 10-50% lipids, which contain both esterified and free fatty acids. Carboxyl groups of these compounds as well as ester carbonyl groups absorb very strongly at 1730 cm^{-1}. Additionally COOH-groups of un-ionized amino acids participate on absorption in that region. Furthermore, the terminal carbon atoms of microbial fatty acids are indicated by a doublet in the range 1380-1360 cm^{-1}, whereas P-O-C groups in phospholipids absorb at 975 cm^{-1}. Some other bands in the region of 970-910 cm^{-1} indicate P-O-P groups of pyrophosphate and polypyrophosphate which are present in fungal mycelium.

In the same spectrum, cell proteins are indicated by a number of amide absorption bands. These appear at 1660-1650 cm^{-1} (amide I), 1550-1540 cm^{-1} (amide II), 1300-1200 cm^{-1} (amide III), and 620 cm^{-1} (amide IV). A shoulder at 1685 cm^{-1} (amide I region) is due to C=O stretching vibration of cyclic amides. At 720-700 cm^{-1} N-H groups of amide V absorb, whereas a middle strong absorption band at 890 cm^{-1} is due to β-configuration of hexose molecules in cell polysaccharides. Carbonyl groups of cell wall glycopeptides absorb rather strongly at 1100 cm^{-1}. Compared with the soil biomass, rather simple and monotonous spectra in some extent were prepared from whole soil samples (Figure 2). Except C-H stretching bands in the 2960-2855 cm^{-1} region, no distinct absorption bands are present until 8 μm wavelength. However, the absorption bands of Si-O, O-Si-O and Si-O-Si atomic groups of soil minerals are sharply expressed in the spectra of both soils. They indicate the presence of quartz (1168 cm^{-1}), montmorillonite (1090-1030 cm^{-1}), and kaolinite (1032-1008 cm^{-1}) mixed with some other silicates. In the region of 1000-690 cm^{-1} absorption bands of Me (Al, Fe, Mg)-OH (-O) atomic groups of clays and other silicates and also -CO$_3$ and -HCO$_3$ groups of carbonates and bicarbonates appear.

In order to increase the intensity of "nonmineral" absorption bands, the soil concentration in KBr pellets was

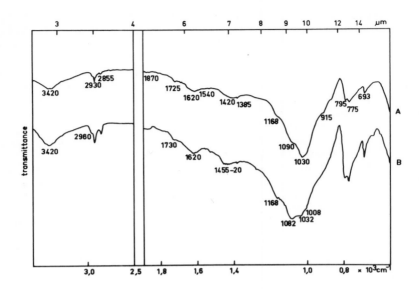

Figure 2.   IR-spectra of whole soil samples (1 mg in 300 mg
KBr) from chernozem (A) and podzol (B).

enhanced from 1 to 5 mg. In Figure 3, which shows the preparations of forest soil, one can see that it was not very helpful.
Only the C-H stretching vibrations absorbing at 2930-2855 cm⁻¹
resulted in more intensive bands, and NH-, NH₂- stretching
vibrations of some aromatic compounds occurred at 2330 cm⁻¹
(where also P-OH groups of organic compounds absorb). The
other weak absorption bands at 2350 cm⁻¹ can be attributed to
O-N=O group of nitrites. Carboxyl bands at 1730 cm⁻¹ of high
intensity in the pure biomass spectra can only be found in
the form of very low peaks.
          The preparation of humic acid extracted from the
forest soil shows strong stretching bands of C-H groups
(2930-2855 cm⁻¹), N-H groups in aromatics at 2330 cm⁻¹, C=C
stretching vibration of double bonds in both cyclic and
acyclic compounds at 1615 cm⁻¹ and aliphatic C-H deformation
at 1400 cm⁻¹. At the same time, the IR-absorption in the
respective regions was little diminished in spectra of extracted
forest soil. Total minimization of some absorption bands
occurred first after full oxidation of organic matter in soil
sample, however (Figure 3 D). This is especially true for
the absorption bands of C-H stretching vibrations at 2930-
2855 cm⁻¹, which disappear almost completely. An absorption
band of N-H stretching in aromatics at 2330 cm⁻¹ is present
only as a weak shoulder, whereas the carboxyl groups are no
more detectable at 1730 cm⁻¹.

Figure 3. IR-spectra of (A) whole soil sample (5 mg in 300 mg KBr); (B) humic acid from the same soil; (C) soil sample after h.a. extraction; (D) soil sample after oxidation with H_2O_2.

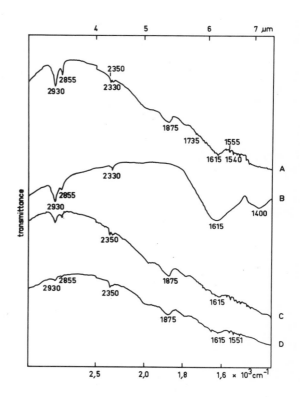

Counting of microorganisms by dilute plate methods resulted in 3×10^6 bacterial cells and 2×10^4 fungal cells and 6×10^2 actinomycete per gram of untreated forest soil. These counts were reduced to 3×10^1 for fungi and to zero for actinomycete by alkaline extraction of the soil, whereas bacteria were still present. The latter were excluded by oxidation in fact, when only some bacterial spores ($13 \times 10^1/1$ g) survived in the soil.

In conclusion, soil biomass possessing a number of well-expressed absorption bands in the wide wavelength region can only be detected by the presence of C-H stretching absorption bands at 2930-2855 cm^{-1} in soil, as all other bands in the IR-spectrum of whole soil samples are effectively masked by strong absorption peaks belonging to different mineral components of the soil. Experiments are in progress which should throw light on the quantitative aspects of biomass detection using IR-spectroscopy.

REFERENCES

Bellamy, L.J. *The Infrared Spectra of Complex Molecules* (London: Chapman and Hall, 1975).

Beutelspacher, H., H.W. van der Marel and E. Rietz.   "Boden-kunde," in *Handbuch der Infrarot-Spektroskopie*, H. Volkmann, Ed. (Weinheim/Bergstr.:   Verlag Chemie GmbH, 1972), pp. 297-327.

Fieldes, M., R.J. Furkert and N. Wells.   "Rapid Determination of Constituents of Whole Soils Using Infrared Absorption," *N.Z.J. Sci.* 15:615-627 (1972).

Flaig, W., H. Beutelspacher and E. Rietz.   "Chemical Composition and Physical Properties of Humic Substances," in *Soil Components*, Vol. 1, J.E. Gieseking, Ed. (New York: Springer-Verlag, 1975), pp. 109-118.

Johnston, H.H., and S.W.B. Newsom, Eds., *Rapid Methods and Automation in Microbiology*, 2nd Internat. Symposium, Cambridge, England (1977).

Parker, F.S. *Applications of Infrared Spectroscopy in Bio-chemistry, Biology and Medicine* (London: Adam Hilger, 1971).

Schnitzer, M., and S.U. Khan. *Humic Substances in the Environment* (New York: M. Dekker, Inc., 1972).

Stepanov, I.S.   "Interpretation of Soil Infrared Spectra," *Pochvovedeniye* 6:76-88 (1974) (in Russian).

van der Marel, H.W., and H. Beutelspacher. *Atlas of Infrared Spectroscopy of Clay Minerals and Their Admixtures* (Amsterdam-Oxford-New York: Elsevier, 1976).

CHAPTER 61

NITROGEN FIXATION RATES IN ANAEROBIC SEDIMENTS
DETERMINED BY ACETYLENE REDUCTION,
A NEW ^{15}N FIELD ASSAY, AND SIMULTANEOUS TOTAL N
^{15}N DETERMINATION

M. POTTS[*]
W.E. KRUMBEIN[*]
J. METZGER

Universitaet Oldenburg
Postfach 2503
D-2900 Oldenburg, Federal Republic of Germany

INTRODUCTION

The acetylene reduction assay technique has been used extensively for detecting the presence of nitrogenase activity in a variety of aquatic environments (Peterson and Burris, 1976). Advantages of the method include its sensitivity, the portable and inexpensive apparatus required, and the rapid analysis of samples using gas chromatography (Hardy *et al.*, 1973). This method is generally preferred to the use of ^{15}N-enriched N_2, even though a number of investigators have stressed the importance of carrying out experiments with acetylene and ^{15}N$_2$ simultaneously to obtain appropriate conversion factors (Burris, 1974; Peterson and Burris, 1976). However, it is now apparent that the validity of the acetylene reduction assay technique may be questionable when studying certain anaerobic environments, particularly those where bacterial communities using methane and lower hydrocarbons are present (Oremland and Taylor, 1975; de Bont, 1976a, 1976b; de Bont and Mulder, 1976).
After preliminary studies of several blue-green algae and photosynthetic bacteria communities along the northern coastline of West Germany, it was decided to develop methods for the simple and reliable measurement of nitrogen fixation rates in these semi-anaerobic and anaerobic populations.

[*]Present Address: H. Steinitz Marine Biological Laboratory, Hebrew University Jerusalem, P.O. Box 469, Elat, Israel.

The following account describes a simplified $^{15}N_2$ reduction assay technique and a new method of estimating $^{15}N_2$ uptake by the direct combination of a CHN-O analyzer, gas chromatograph and mass spectrophotometer. Data are presented on conversion factors obtained by simultaneous estimations of acetylene and $^{15}N_2$ reduction, in laboratory-grown axenic cultures of blue-green algae and, also, in field populations.

METHODS

Algae

The heterocystous blue-green alga *Nostoc carneum* Agardh was used for laboratory experiments (Oldenburg Collection No. 02).

Nutrient Media

The nutrient solution of Allen and Arnon (1955) was used in modified form; major elements were used at one-quarter concentration; trace elements (minus vanadium) in full concentration; Fe (as EDTA complex) at 4 mg 1^{-1}; K_2HPO_4 at 0.348 g 1^{-1}, autoclaved separately.

Laboratory Culture

Axenic cultures were obtained by repeated streaking of algal suspensions on solid media (1% agar), and then isolation and transfer of single hormogonia into liquid media.

Stock culture aliquots of 0.1 ml were inoculated into 250-ml Erlenmeyer flasks containing 100 ml of sterile liquid media. The flasks were then enclosed in a large clear polyethylene bag; the end was sealed around a rubber bung through which two glass tubes passed (inlet/outlet). The bag was flushed for five minutes with a gas mixture of 95% N_2/5% CO_2, sealed and placed in a light incubator such that the flasks received a light regime of 760 x 10^{17} Q m^{-2} sec^{-1} (Quanta Spectrometer, Techtum Instruments, Sweden), and a temperature of 32°C. The bag was flushed once daily (5 minutes) with the gas mixture.

After 7 days the contents of each flask was centrifuged at 3000 rpm (10 minutes), washed with sterile medium, re-centrifuged, resuspended in 100 ml sterile medium, and left at 32°C for 30 minutes. This procedure was repeated twice, and finally the centrifuged material from all flasks were combined in a single flask containing 100 ml of sterile medium. This flask was incubated under the above conditions for 24 hours.

Field Populations

    In situ experiments were carried out at an intertidal mud- and sandflat on the southern coast of Wangerooge Island, 8 km off the German North Sea coast. The blue-green alga *Microcoleus chthonoplastes* Thuret forms a "Farbstreifen-Sandwatt" community (Schulz, 1936), together with the photosynthetic bacteria *Thiopedia* sp. and *Chromatium* sp. A detailed description of this community, together with physicochemical data on the sediments will be presented elsewhere (Krumbein, Potts and Rongen, in preparation).

Generation of ^{15}N-enriched N_2

Theory

    The theoretical basis of the method is that relatively pure $^{15}N_2$ may be generated by the action of a concentrated solution of hypobromite (alkaline) with an ammonium salt containing ^{15}N.

$$2\ ^{15}NH_3 + 3\ NaBrO \rightarrow 3\ NaBr + ^{15}N_2^\uparrow + 3\ H_2O$$

$$(or\ LiBrO \rightarrow LiBr)$$

Although this reaction is well-known and has been implemented by a number of investigators (for references, see Burris, 1974), the apparatus used has often been complex, fragile and expensive (*e.g.*, Porter and O'Deen, 1977). In the present method, vacutainers are used as reaction chambers in which to generate $^{15}N_2$.

Practical Applications

    Two milliliters of a solution of $(^{15}NH_4)_2SO_4$ (27 g 1^{-1}; 97.7% ^{15}N, MN-524 (Merck, Sharp and Dohme, Montréal), was injected with a gastight syringe into a 5-ml draw vacutainer (Becton and Dickinson, cat. no. 3206 U). This was followed by the injection of 1 ml of a concentrated hypobromite solution consisting of 40-ml NaOH solution (480 g 1^{-1}), 50-ml KI solution (1.8 g 1^{-1}), 10 ml Br_2. The vacutainer was then immediately inverted and shaken vigorously to ensure complete mixing of the reactants. After the effervescence had subsided, 100 µl of the gas phase in the vacutainer was removed with a gastight syringe to check the purity of the $^{15}N_2$ (See p. 757). This reaction was carried out a number of times in separate vacutainers to provide sufficient $^{15}N_2$ for assays (see p. 756, $^{15}N_2$ Reduction Assay).

    To minimize any contamination with $^{14}N_2$ during the reaction, both the $(^{15}NH_4)_2SO_4$ and hypobromite solutions were

kept in 100-ml glass bottles, fitted with perforated screw
caps and serum liners, and flushed with 99.9% Ar. All gastight syringes were flushed with Ar prior to use. The use
of a concentrated alkaline solution ensured the absorption
of any nitrogen oxides formed during the reaction.

$^{15}N_2$ Reduction Assay

Laboratory Assay

An attempt was made to develop an assay method which
enabled a direct comparison with the acetylene reduction
assay technique (see page 758, Acetylene Reduction Assays).
Glass serum bottles (7 ml) with perforated serum caps were
used for all incubations, and gases were introduced or removed
through the rubber serum seal by gastight syringe.

Two-milliliter aliquots of the algal suspension from
the Laboratory Culture (see page 754) were pipetted into
the bottles and allowed to equilibriate for one hour. The
caps were then secured and each bottle flushed with 30 ml of
a gas mixture of 95% Ar/5% CO_2. Replicates were prepared
for light and dark incubations and, in addition, several
were used to check the purity of gases and temperature changes
during the experiment.

After flushing with the Ar mixture, the bottles were
allowed a further incubation period of 15 minutes. From
separate vacutainers (see page 755, Practical Applications),
1 ml of $^{15}N_2$ was then taken with a gastight syringe (Ar-
flushed), and injected into each bottle. One reaction
chamber vacutainer was used for a single incubation bottle.
The partial pressure of $^{15}N_2$ in each bottle was approximately
20%, the same as the pC_2H_2 used in the acetylene reduction
assays (see page 758, Acetylene Reduction Assays). The
bottles were then incubated for 2 hr at 32°C, under a light
intensity of 760×10^{17} Q m^{-2} sec $^{-1}$. At the end of the
incubation period, 100 µl of the gas phase in each bottle was
removed with a gastight syringe (Ar-flushed) and analyzed using
a mass spectrophotometer (see page 757, Laboratory Assay).
The caps were then removed and the contents of each bottle
immediately vacuum dried at 50°C. When completely dry, approximate 1-mg aliquots from each bottle (weighted to ± 0.1
µg, Sartorius Electronic balance) were analyzed as described
in the Field Assay section below.

Field Assay

The field assays were essentially the same as those
used in the laboratory. Circular cores 5-mm deep were taken
of the Farbstreifen-Sandwatt sediment and transferred carefully to the 7-ml serum bottles. Filtered sea water was then

added to bring the final volume of sediment plus sea water to about 2 ml. Assays were terminated by a 0.5-ml injection of concentrated formaldehyde. The bottles were then inverted to seal any puncture holes and returned to the laboratory for immediate analysis.

Purity of Gases

All gases and gas mixtures used above were of spectroscopy-grade quality (Messer. Griesheim GmbH). A number of experiments were carried out to check the purity of these gases and to also check sources of error in handling and transfer of gas phases.

Measurement of Total N and $^{15}N_2$ Uptake

Quality of $^{15}N_2$ and Percent Excess in Gas Mixtures

One-hundred-μl gas samples were removed from reaction chamber vacutainers as well as incubation bottles and analyzed using a Varian MAT 111 Gas Chromatograph/Mass Spectrophotometer (GC/MS) system with accessory Varian Mat Kompensograph and Oscillofil. Masses 28, 29 and 30 were measured.

Analysis of Algal and Sediment Samples

A new method was developed and tested not only for the generation of $^{15}N_2$ but also for measuring the total N and ^{15}N content of each sample simultaneously, using a direct combination of a Carlo-Erba CHN-O Elemental Analyzer 1104 and the Varian MAT 111. Each 1-mg sample was pyrolyzed at 1060°C under addition of oxygen. The gases (N_2, CO_2 and H_2O) were separated by GC (Poropak Q) and the chromatograms were integrated on an automatic integrator-calculator. The outlet of the GC channel of the CHN-analyzer was directly connected by means of stainless steel capillaries (1/16 in. outer diameter) and a simple swagelok adapter to the slit separator of the Varian MAT GC/MS system. The carreer gas flow was 30 ml min^{-1} helium. We measured the masses of 28, 29 and 30, respectively, at a scanning speed of 100 masses sec^{-1}. For a single sample, we recorded at least 10 mass spectra. The error was ± 0.02% at ^{15}N concentrations of 0.5%.

Thus for each mg dry weight of the sample, it was possible to measure directly and without further manipulation of the gases (a) total N and (b) the masses 28, 29 and 30. This system was easily disconnected so that the normal gas analyses could be carried out as described in Quality of $^{15}N_2$ and Percent Excess in Gas Mixtures. No Kjeldahl N-analyses and no gas vacuum line was thus needed.

Acetylene Reduction Assays

The method given by Potts and Whitton (1977) was used, modified to the incubation times and partial gas pressures as described previously. For field assays, controls were run with Ar-flushed sediments, as well as those not flushed. In addition to dark controls, replicates were incubated with DCMU (7 μM), and 0.5-ml additions of glucose solution (100 g 1^{-1}).

Ethylene and acetylene were measured in 1-ml samples using a Varian Series 3700 Gas Chromatograph-CDS 111 Data system. The chromatographic column was packed with carbon molecular sieve (CMS 60/80, Serva International) and maintained at 190°C. The FID detector was operated at 170°C. Nitrogen was used as carrier gas, at a flow rate of 40 ml min^{-1}.

Pigment Analyses

Samples of the Farbstreifen-Sandwatt community were collected for pigment analysis. Pigments were extracted in 95% methanol using the methods given in Potts (1977). Chlorophyll *a* and bacteriochlorophyll *a* were both estimated.

RESULTS

Table I shows the purity of the $^{15}N_2$ generated in vacutainers and, also, after transfer to a second or third vacutainer. Each value is the mean of five readings.

Table I
The Purity of Generated $^{15}N_2$ in Vacutainers

Reaction Vacutainer	Transfer to 2nd Vacutainer
84.5% ± 0.8%	75.5% ± 0.8%
82.0% ± 0.8%	75.5% ± 0.8%
82.6% ± 0.8%	76.0% ± 0.8%

The percentage purity of $^{15}N_2$ as measured on the mass spectrophotometer (MS) is shown in Table II, and compared when the gastight syringe was flushed with Ar prior to removing a gas sample or not flushed before sampling. A comparison of the Ar purity (contamination with air) from several different sources is shown in Table III.

Table II
Effects on the Purity of $^{15}N_2$ by Ar Flushing
of Gastight Syringes

$^{15}N_2$% in Initial Vacutainer	Transfer to MS Syringe Ar Flushed	Transfer to MS Not Ar Flushed
85.3% ± 0.8%	83.0% ± 0.8%	60.0% ± 0.8%

Table III
The Purity of Argon Used in Experiments

Direct From Cylinder	From Football Bladder	From Glass Bottle[a] (to over pressure)
99.9% ± 0.5%	84.5% ± 3.6%	95.5% ± 0.7%

[a]Used in field assays.

The results of all acetylene and $^{15}N_2$ reduction assay experiments with *Nostoc carneum* are given in Table IV, and a set of representative $^{15}N_2$ data in Table V. Total N is for samples analyzed on the CHN-O analyzer, rates have been expressed as n*M* N$_2$ fixed per mg N/hr.

Table VI shows the mean chlorophyll *a* and bacterio-chlorophyll *a* concentration in four different areas of surface sediment, in the region of *in situ* C$_2$ H$_2$ and $^{15}N_2$ reduction assay experiments. A summary of these rates is shown in Table VII. Simultaneous rates of C$_2$H$_2$ and $^{15}N_2$ reduction in the light for the *M. chthonoplastes, Thiopedia* sp.,*Chromatium* sp. community are compared in Table VIII.

DISCUSSION

Two electrons are required to reduce C_2H_2 to C_2H_4, and six for the reduction of N_2. This relationship has persuaded many authors to adopt the theoretical conversion factor of one-third N$_2$ reduced per acetylene reduced, when expressing nitrogen fixation rates in terms of acetylene reduced. However, experimentally determined factors appear to vary between different experimental systems; Hardy *et al.* (1973) summarized much of the literature and gave a range in factors between 2 and 25. Deviations from the theoretical value of 3 are explained in terms of the greater solubility

Table IV

Simultaneous Acetylene and $^{15}N_2$ Reduction Assays with *Nostoc carneum*

Assay	n	Total N in Aliquot (mg)	Average nM C_2H_4 (mg N^{-1} h^{-1})	Average nM N_2 (mg N^{-1} h^{-1})	Conversion Factor (C_2H_4/N_2)[a]
1	5	0.0194	301	83.77	3.64
2	5	0.0193	355	70.18	5.06
3	6	0.0270	220	69.72	3.16
4	5	0.0291	183	75.02	2.44
5	6	0.0211	448	73.14	6.13

[a]Mean conversion factor = 4.1   [n]number of N and ^{15}N-replicate measurements.

Representative Data from an Initial $^{15}N_2$ Reduction Assay Experiment with *Nostoc carneum*

Table V

Aliquot wt (mg)	Total N (mg)	%N	[a] atom % ^{15}N excess	Total N Fixed (μg)	nM N_2 Reduced (mg N^{-1} h^{-1})
0.8950	0.01771	1.97	0.0761	0.02657	53.6
0.6350	0.01198	1.89	0.0998	0.02276	67.9
0.5510	0.00899	1.63	0.0957	0.01708	67.9
0.8690	0.01696	1.95	0.0894	0.03053	64.2
0.6580	0.01174	1.78	0.0767	0.01761	53.8
0.5730	0.01081	1.79	0.1208	0.02594	85.7
0.6060	0.01015	1.67	0.0966	0.01929	67.8
0.9380	0.02036	2.17	0.0751	0.03054	53.5
0.6610	0.01216	1.84	0.0659	0.01582	46.4
0.8230	0.01645	1.99	0.0712	0.02302	50.0
1.3250	0.14178	10.7	0.0000 (atom % ^{15}N = 0.360)[b]		

[a]Corrected for enrichment of $^{15}N_2$ gas used, and naturally occurring ^{15}N in samples.

[b]Control sample from a culture grown in the presence of combined nitrogen.

Table VI

Concentrations of Chlorophyll *a* and Bacteriochlorophyll *a* from the
Surface Sediments of the Farbstreifen-Sandwatt Community of
M. chthonoplastes, *Thiopedia* sp. and *Chromatium* sp.

Area	n	x̄ µg chl *a* cm^{-2}	x̄ µg Bchl *a* cm^{-2}	Ratio
a	4	145	12.2	11.9:1
1b	4	184	12.4	14.8:1
c	4	245	18.3	13.4:1
d	4	123	18.3	6.7:1

[1] Experimental area.

Table VII

Simultaneous Acetylene and $^{15}N_2$ Reduction Assays in the Surface Sediment of the Farbstreifen-Sandwatt Community of *M. chthonoplastes*, *Thiopedia* sp. and *Chromatium* sp.

Assay	Average Total N (mg)	L nM C_2H_4 (mg N^{-1} h^{-1})	D nM C_2H_4 (mg N^{-1} h^{-1})	G nM C_2H_4 (mg N^{-1} h^{-1})	DCMU nM C_2H_4 (mg N^{-1} h^{-1})	L nM N_2 (mg N^{-1} h^{-1})
1	2.373	687	—	514	856	146
2	2.189	745	—	557	928	130
3	1.476	1104	442	826	1376	204
4	1.303	1250	—	936	1560	182
5	2.769	589	515	440	734	126
6	2.009	811	—	607	1011	168

L = light assay;   D = dark assay;   G = with glucose in light;   DCMU = with DCMU in light.

Table VIII

Conversion Factors Obtained from the Comparison of C_2H_2 and $^{15}N_2$ Reduction Rates in the Surface Sediment of the Farbstreifen-Sandwatt Community

nM C_2H_4 mg N^{-1} h^{-1}	nM N_2 mg N^{-1} h^{-1}	Conversion Factor (C_2H_4/N_2)[a]
637	146	4.71
745	130	5.73
1104	204	5.41
1250	182	6.87
589	126	4.67
811	168	4.83

[a]Mean rate = 5.37.

of acetylene in water, and the depression of H_2 production in the presence of acetylene (Hardy and Burns, 1971; Benemann and Weare, 1974). As a result, experimentally determined factors are closer to 4 (Burris, 1974). In a study of natural populations of lake phytoplankton (*Aphanizomenon* sp., *Anabaena* sp., *Gloeotrichia* sp.) Peterson and Burris (1976) found a conversion factor of 4.4 (4.2-4.8). This is close to the factor of 4.1 found in the present study with axenic laboratory-grown cultures of *Nostoc carneum*. The rates of acetylene reduction found for this species are similar to those found by Stewart (1967.1968), for *N. muscorum* and *Nostoc* sp., *i.e.*, 0.100 nM C_2H_4 mg dry wt^{-1} min^{-1}, 0.152 nM C_2H_4 mg dry wt^{-1} min^{-1} and 0.144 nM C_2H_4 mg dry wt^{-1} min^{-1}, respectively. The latter two rates have been calculated assuming a factor of 0.08 for N to dry weight, although as Table V shows, the percentage N in laboratory cultures of *N. carneum* was closer to 2%, suggesting the cultures to be nitrogen-starved before the commencement of assays.

Significant rates of C_2H_2 and $^{15}N_2$ reduction were detected in the *Microcoleus chthonoplastes*, *Thiopedia* sp., *Chromatium* sp. community, associated with anaerobic marine sediments. The rates of acetylene reduction are similar to those found by Potts and Whitton (1977) for a Farbstreifen-Sandwatt community dominated by the nonheterocystous blue-green alga *Hyella balani*, in the intertidal zone of the lagoon of Aldabra Atoll, Indian Ocean. The rates found by these authors for communities of *M. chthonoplastes* in similar habitats were somewhat lower than those of the present study; however, these authors carried out assays without first flushing with Ar. It is not possible to state with certainty which of the dominant species in the Farbstreifen-Sandwatt community is responsible for the observed rates of nitrogen fixation. The greater abundance of *M. chthonoplastes* as demonstrated by microscopic study and pigment analysis (Table VI), as well as depression of acetylene reduction rates in the dark and insignificant or no stimulation of rates in the presence of glucose, indicates that nitrogen fixation is mostly associated with this species. The somewhat higher rates observed in sediment samples incubated with DCMU, also suggest that nitrogen fixation was stimulated by lower oxygen levels, and in part possibly due to photosynthetic bacteria. However, Gallon *et al.* (1975) have shown in studies with a species of *Gloeocapsa* (nonheterocystous blue-green alga), that levels of DCMU which completely inhibited oxygen production had little effect on the ability to reduce acetylene, and reduction in the light in the presence of DCMU was approximately 30% greater than that in the dark. Recently, Cohen *et al.* (1975) demonstrated that the non-heterocystous filamentous blue-gree alga *Oscillatoria limnetica* Lemmerman could use H_2S as the sole electron donor in the photoassimilation of CO_2 with photosystem I, when photosystem II was inhibited with DCMU. At Wangerooge Island, E_h measurements from the Farbstreifen-Sandwatt community ranged from +295 mV at the surface, to -232 mV just below the layer of photosynthetic bacteria. In addition, the sediment had a strong smell of H_2S. It is therefore possible that the nonheterocystous *M. chthonoplastes* is able to use H_2S as an electron donor and to assimilate CO_2 and maintain rates of acetylene reduction when incubated in the presence of DCMU.

Another possible explanation of our field fixation data may be that in the interior of *Microcoleus* bundles, lower photosynthetic activity coupled with higher nitrogenase activity occurs comparable to the specialization between normal cells and heterocysts in heterocysteous blue-green algae. This on the other hand would imply material transfer between different trichomes. These assumptions remain speculative until further experiments have been carried out with this community. (See also Krumbein and Cohen, 1977). The conversion factor determined by simultaneous C_2H_2 and $^{15}N_2$ light reduction assays in the *M. chthonoplastes* community was 5.4, significantly higher than that found in laboratory experiments with *Nostoc carneum* using the same assay methods. This shows that a factor of 3, if applied to this system, would give a substantial error (80%) and overestimate rates of N_2 fixation.

There appear to be no reports of simultaneous C_2H_2 and $^{15}N_2$ reduction assays with anaerobic marine sediments, yet these are essential in view of the increasing interest in the study of these environments. Oremland and Taylor (1975) have shown that acetylene can inhibit methanogenesis in some marine sediments, yet they were unable to state if this would over- or underestimate nitrogen fixation rates. A number of recent papers also question the validity of the acetylene reduction technique when applied to these systems (*e.g.*, de Bont and Mulder, 1975).

The main facts we recollect from the study of literature and our own preliminary laboratory and field data concerning the question of estimating N fixation in the laboratory and in nature have already been summarized by Burris (1974) and Peterson and Burris (1976). Burris (1974) wrote: "Remarkably few have felt compelled to determine a proper conversion factor."

The present work was meant to clarify the situation that many data are presently based on field acetylene reduction assays, and converted into nitrogen fixation values per volume or surface unit by using arbitrary and theoretical conversion factors. Using the more rapid method of direct combination of N-determination with the mass determination of ^{15}N-compounds and the rapid and reliable field method of generating $^{15}N_2$ directly in the field, we were able to compare acetylene reduction rates with $^{15}N_2$ reduction and incorporation rates by measuring both the changes in the gas phase and the relative masses of N within the samples at the same time. The laboratory data and the field data we collected are reproducible and in agreement with the few reports on factors obtained in laboratory experiments using pure cultures and field samples. This suggests that within the limits of the method, our field data on anaerobic sediments are also reliable. The conversion factors of Burris and Peterson (1976) from an aerobic plankton community ranged from 2.7 to 6.5 (C_2H_2 reduced/N_2 reduced). Our field data on an anaerobic sediment with its complicated aspects of inhibition and/or enhancement of acetylene reduction and fluctuating environmental conditions range from 4.67 to 6.87 (C_2H_2 reduced/N_2 reduced). Besides naturally occurring influences on the rates, the greatest source of error in the simplified $^{15}N_2$-assay is contamination of the $^{15}N_2$ with $^{14}N_2$. However, provided a standard technique is followed in flushing syringes, incubation bottles and argon containers, this can be kept to a minimum. The new method of estimating total N and $^{15}N_2$ uptake simultaneously and of generating $^{15}N_2$ in the field is accurate, rapid (one sample every ten minutes in the CHN-O analyzer-MS combination) and much easier to use than the Kjeldahl method combined with MS.

The problem lies elsewhere. As has been discussed, several sources of error exist in the use of direct or theoretical conversion factors in transferring acetylene reduction data to N fixation. This inconvenience is further increased in anaerobic sediments (Oremland and Taylor, 1975; de Bont and Mulder, 1976). Though our conversion data obtained in the laboratory and field experiments, respectively, varied even less than in other reported comparisons of the two methods, we conclude that accurate conversion factors cannot be given so far even if linearity is observed in the two assay methods (Peterson and Burris, 1976). The conversion "factors" reported in literature vary from 2-25, while our conversion rates in laboratory and field experiments varied much less than that and were always higher than the theoretical value of 3. Therefore, it still seems better to calibrate the acetylene reduction assay in the laboratory and in the field with a few parallel assays using the ^{15}N method.

A conversion factor of 4.1 or 5.4, as in our study, is still more meaningful than the theoretical value which is almost never reached in the field. On the other hand, it is necessary to further refine the field assay described here as well as the new methods described for simultaneous N and ^{15}N determination. In environments in which it is essential to quantify the nitrogen cycle it may be advisable to use the new ^{15}N method exclusively instead of the environmentally influenced conversion rates.

SUMMARY AND CONCLUSIONS

Two new methods for the simultaneous measurement of acetylene reduction and ^{15}N reduction are presented here:

1. a new laboratory and field assay method for simultaneous C_2H_2 reduction and $^{15}N_2$ reduction by generating $^{15}N_2$ directly in the field with simple equipment; and

2. a new method for estimating total N simultaneously with $^{15}N_2$ uptake rates using a direct on-line combination of a CHN-O Elemental Analyzer with gas chromatography and mass spectrometry.

Simultaneous rates of acetylene reduction and $^{15}N_2$ reduction were measured by using these methods with laboratory-grown axenic culture of *Nostoc carneum* and an anaerobically growing field population of *Microcoleus chthonoplastes*. The conversion "factors" obtained were 4.1 and 5.4, respectively. Simultaneous estimations of the acetylene reduction and $^{15}N_2$ reduction are considered essential in the study of N_2 fixation in semi-anaerobic and anaerobic environments with populations

of photosynthetic prokaryotes associated with chemoheterotrophic anaerobic prokaryotes. In order to be able to
differentiate between the latter, it is also necessary to use
glucose to enhance heterotrophic activity, DCMU to block
oxygenic photosynthesis and to analyze for biomass and chloro-
phylls of the photosynthetic prokaryotes present in the
environment.

ACKNOWLEDGMENTS

This work was supported in part by grant Kr 333/12 of
the Deutsche Forschungsgemeinschaft. We thank P. Rongen for
field asssistance and excellent technical aid during this project. M. Shilo critically read the first version of the manu-
script and helped us improve the text. P. Köll was helpful in
approaching the MS methods. The experimental work was carried
out during a post-doctoral stay of M. Potts in the environmental
labratory of the University of Oldenburg.

REFERENCES

Allen, M.B., and D.I. Arnon. "Studies on Nitrogen-Fixing
    Blue-Green Algae. 1. Growth and Nitrogen Fixation by
    Anabaena cylindrica Lemm.," *Pl. Physiol.* 30:366-372 (1955).

Benemann, J.R., and N.M. Weare. "Hydrogen Evolution by
    Nitrogen-Fixing *Anabaena cylindrica* Cultures," *Science N. Y.*
    184:174-175 (1974).

Burris, R.H. "Methodology," in *The Biology of Nitrogen Fixa-
    tion,*" A. Quispel, Ed. (Amsterdam, Oxford: North Holland
    Publishing Co., 1974), pp. 1-769.

Cohen, Y., E. Padan and M. Shilo. "Facultative Anoxygenic
    Photosynthesis in the Cyanobacterium *Oscillatoria limnetica,*"
    J. Bacteriol., 123:855-861 (1975).

De Bont, J.A.M. "Oxidation of Ethylene by Soil Bacteria,"
    J. Microbiol. Serol. 42:59-71 (1976a).

De Bont, J.A.M. "Bacterial Degradation of Ethylene and the
    Acetylene Reduction Test," *Can. J. Microbiol.* 22:1060-
    1062 (1976b).

De Bont, J.A.M., and E.G. Mulder. "Invalidity of the
    Acetylene Reduction Assay in Alkane-Utilizing, Nitrogen-
    Fixing Bacteria," *Appl. Environ. Microbiol.* 31:640 (1976).

Gallon, J.R., W.G.W. Kurz and T.A. Larue. "The Physiology of
    Nitrogen Fixation by a *Gloeocapsa* sp.," in *Nitrogen Fixation
    by Free-Living Microorganisms,* W.D.P. Stewart, Ed. Inter-
    national Biological Programme 6. (Cambridge, New York,
    Melbourne: Cambridge University Press, 1975), pp. 1-471.

Hardy, R.W.F., R.C. Burns and G.W. Parshall. "The Biochemistry of Nitrogen Fixation," *Adv. Chem.* 100:219-247 (1971).

Hardy, R.W.F., R.C. Burns and R.D. Holsten. "Applications of the Acetylene-Ethylene Assay for Measurement of Nitrogen Fixation," *Soil Biol. Biochem.* 5:47-81 (1973).

Krumbein, W.E., and Y. Cohen. "Primary Production, Mat Formation and Lithification: Contribution of Oxygenic and Facultative Anoxygenic Cyanobacteria," in *Fossil Algae*, E. Flügel, Ed. (Berlin, Heidelberg, New York: Springer-Verlag, 1977), pp. 1-367.

Oremland, R.S. and B.F. Taylor. "Inhibition of Methanogenesis in Marine Sediments by Acetylene and Ethylene: Validity of the Acetylene Reduction Assay for Anaerobic Microcosms," *Appl. Microbiol.* 30:707-709 (1975).

Peterson, R.B. and R.H. Burris. "Conversion of Acetylene Reduction Rates to Nitrogen Fixation Rates in Natural Populations of Blue-Green Algae," *Anal. Biochem.* 73:404-410 (1976).

Porter, L.K., and W.A. O'Deen. "Apparatus for Preparing Nitrogen from Ammonium Chloride for Nitrogen-15 Determinations," *Anal. Biochem.* 49:514-516 (1977).

Potts, M. *Studies on Blue-Green Algae and Photosynthetic Bacteria in the Lagoon of Aldabra Atoll*. Ph.D. Thesis, Univeristy of Durham, England; p. 421 (1977).

Potts, M., and B.A. Whitton. "Nitrogen Fixation by Blue-Green Algal Communities in the Intertidal Zone of the Lagoon of Aldabra Atoll," *Oecologia* 27:275-283 (1977).

Schulz, E. "Das Farbstreifen-Sandwatt und seine Fauna, eine ökologisch-biozönotische Untersuchung an der Nordsee," *Kieler Meeresforschungen* 1:359-378.

Stewart, W.D.P., G.P. Fitzgerald and R.H. Burris. "*In situ* Studies on N_2 Fixation Using the Acetylene Reduction Technique," *Proc. Natl. Acad. Sci. U.S.* 58:2071-2078 (1967).

Stewart, W.D.P., G.P. Fitzgerald and R.H. Burris. "Acetylene Reduction by Nitrogen-Fixing Blue-Green Algae," *Arch. Mikrobiol.* 62:336-348 (1968).

SECTION II

THE CYCLE OF CARBON AND OXYGEN
AS DETERMINED BY
ISOTOPIC AND CONVENTIONAL METHODS

CHAPTER 62

THE INFLUENCE OF THE BIOSPHERE ON THE ATMOSPHERIC CO AND H_2 CYCLES

W. SEILER

Max Planck Institute
  for Chemistry
Department of Air Chemistry
65 Mainz, Federal Republic of Germany

INTRODUCTION

The main constituents of atmospheric air are nitrogen, oxygen and argon, which together comprise about 90% of the total mass of the atmosphere. The rest subdivides into a greater number of trace gases having volume mixing ratios in the range from several 10^{-6} (ppmv) down to 10^{-12} (pptv) and lower. With exception of the rare gases, these trace gases are not permanent atmospheric constituents. They occur in the atmosphere because each of them is injected into the atmosphere from certain sources and is removed by certain sinks. The mixing ratios observed in air are the result of a dynamic equilibrium, often called the cycle of the trace gas under consideration. Processes acting as sources or sinks are chemical reactions, biospheric processes, photodissociation, rain and wash-out, adsorption on aerosol particles, and anthropogenic activities.

Recent studies by several laboratories have shown that the biosphere contributes significantly to the cycles of several atmospheric trace gases and thus influences the composition of the atmosphere. For some gases such as CH_4, N_2O, H_2S and several hydrocarbons, the biosphere represents the dominant source. Furthermore, the biosphere was found to consume many gases produced anthropogenically, even those with high breakdown energies like DDT, so that the biosphere acts also as a regulative for the increasingly negative influence of anthropogenic emissions on our environment.

This paper summarizes the results of measurements from this laboratory concerning the production and destruction of carbon monoxide and hydrogen by different biological processes. The data also provide estimates for the production and destruction rates of individual biospheric sources and sinks of carbon monoxide and hydrogen.

METHOD

The program we carried out during recent years included three separate subprograms concerned with the biosphere, *i.e.*, the production and destruction of CO and H_2:

1. in surface waters of the oceans and fresh-water lakes,

2. in continental soils, and

3. by plants.

These programs required different methods which are briefly discussed in the following pages.

Methods for the Measurements of
Dissolved CO and H_2 in Water

Two sampling methods have been developed for the determination of dissolved CO and H_2 in water, a discontinuous method and a continuous one. The first method was used for the analysis of single water samples in conjunction with the determination of vertical concentration profiles in the oceans; the second method was used to assay dissolved CO and H_2 in the surface waters of the oceans in depths of 2-3 m.
In the discontinuous technique (M1), a 5-liter sample is sucked into an evacuated 10-liter glass flask. Because of the instantaneous dispersion of the fluid into small water droplets during this process and the low pressure in the glass flask, an equilibrium between the gaseous and liquid phases is rapidly established. Immediately thereafter the flask is filled to atmospheric pressure with CO- and H_2-free air. Subsequently, the entire air sample is fed into a CO and H_2 analyzer as described later. This discontinuous method permits the analysis of 1×10^{-6} cm^3 CO/liter H_2O and 5×10^{-6} cm^3 H_2/liter H_2O, respectively, with a relative error of about 10%.
Water samples were taken in different depths down to 3000 m by means of 10 1-liter Niskin water bottles. They were analyzed within 20-30 minutes after the Niskin bottles were brought to the ocean surface. During this time, the Niskin bottles were kept closed so that contamination by atmospheric CO and H_2 was avoided. It was found in samples that were analyzed later that the CO and H_2 concentrations increased with time, probably due to microbial activities. This increase, however, did not exceed 10% of the amount of CO and H_2 originally dissolved within a period of two hours,

as was observed in a number of tests. Thus, CO and H_2 production in water samples during storage will not have a significant effect on the results.

Due to the rolling of the ship, the data on the depths where water samples were taken are uncertain by approximately 80-150 cm, depending on the weather situation. This situation does not cause significant errors for depths greater than 20 m, but it prevents measurements of the vertical CO and H_2 concentration profile in the uppermost ocean layer; particularly between the surface and 2 m where most of the biological activities occur. The knowledge of the vertical distribution of the dissolved CO and H_2 in the upper layer, however, is very important when one wishes to calculate the fluxes of CO and H_2 through the ocean surface rising from air-sea interchange. Therefore, a second method (M2) for discontinuous CO and H_2 measurements in water was developed. This technique requires water samples of less than 25 cm^3. This method was employed onboard small rubber rafts at a distance of about 300 m from the main vessel. Then the vertical CO and H_2 profiles were not disturbed by the ship, *e.g.*, by action of the propellers. This second method used an evacuated glass flask (V = 50 cm^3) mounted on a plastic plate floating on the water surface. The glass flask was connected to a narrow-bore tubing whose length was varied from a few centimeters up to about two meters and through which samples were taken. After sampling about 25 cm^3 of water, the glass flask was filled with CO- and H_2-free air up to a pressure of 2 atm and was then brought on board the research vessel. Small air samples (V = 5-10 cm^3) were withdrawn from the flask by means of gastight syringes and injected into a CO- and H_2-free carrier gas flow which flushed the air sample into an improved version of our combined CO/H_2 analyzer. In this instrument CO and H_2 are separated by use of a column filled with molecular sieve (10 Å) and then analyzed in series.

For the continuous measurements of CO and H_2 dissolved in sea water, the water was sucked in by a pump near the bow of the vessel through a hose ending at depths of about 2-3 m. The sea water was then pumped at high flow rates into the laboratory where a part of the sea water flow was used for the continuous CO and H_2 analyzer. Comparisons between results obtained by the continuous registration and the discontinuous measurement technique carried out near the sea water inlet of the ship did not show any significant difference of the dissolved CO and H_2. Clearly, neither the sea water pump of the ship nor the conducting pipes influence the CO and H_2 concentration of the sea water.

A schematic of method M3 used for the continuous measurements of dissolved CO and H_2 in water is shown in Figure 1. This method employs an upright 1.5-m long glass cylinder with a volume of 7 liters into which a continuous

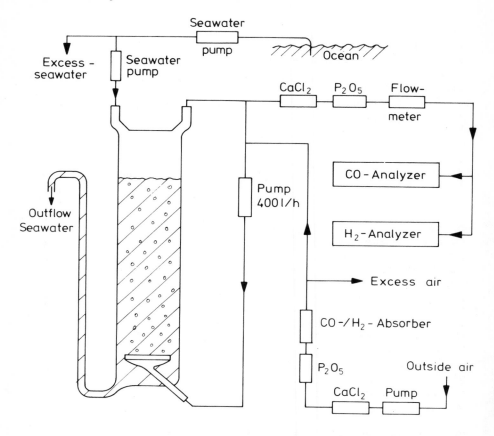

Figure 1.   Schematic of the continuous sampling method
for dissolved CO and H_2 in surface waters of
the ocean.

flow of sea water is directed downwards. The water column
is purged by air which is recycled with a flow rate of about
400 liter/hr. Careful tests have indicated that the duration
of the residence time of sea water in the glass cylinder is
sufficient to obtain an equilibrium between the CO and H_2
remaining in the liquid and that part entering the gas phase.
Due to their low solubilities, about 97% of the dissolved CO
and H_2 is transferred into the gas phase and only 3% is
lost by the outflow of the sea water. A constant flow of
60 liter/hr of the recycled air is fed into the continuous
CO and H_2 analyzers. The same amount of CO- and H_2-free air
is injected into the recycling system at the bottom of the
glass cylinder. From the registered rate at which sea water
flows through the system, that of air flowing through the CO
and H_2 analyzers, and the measured CO and H_2 mixing ratios,

the amount of CO and H_2 dissolved in sea water is calculated. Tests carried out periodically during the registration indicated that there occurred no production or destruction of CO and H_2 in the tubings and the glass cylinder. The latter was kept dark during the total time of measurements. The lower detection limit of the method M3 is 0.5×10^{-6} cm^3 CO/liter H_2O and 2.5×10^{-6} cm^3 H_2/liter H_2O, respectively, when a sea water flow of 60 liter/hr was employed. The relative error is about ± 10%.

Methods for the Determination of the Influence of Soil on CO and H_2

Measurements have been carried out in the laboratory as well as in the field, using several methods. For laboratory experiments, about 60 liters of natural soil were placed into a thermostated glass vessel having a volume of 123 liters. Experiments were started after an incubation time of more than five days during which the glass sphere was flushed with ambient air containing CO and H_2 mixing ratios of 0.5 ppm. The connecting lines to the glass vessel were then closed off and the temporal variation of the CO and H_2 mixing ratios was measured by withdrawing small air samples (V = 10 cm^3) from time to time which were analyzed with the CO and H_2 analyzers. During the time period between the experiments, the glass sphere was flushed continuously with ambient air so that the soil was kept under natural conditions with respect to the mixing ratios of the atmosphere constituents. When the temperature of the glass vessel was changed to a new setting, new runs were started 24 hours afterwards to let the system equilibrate. An entire series of runs usually lasted 3-4 weeks. As a check whether the soil underwent a change with respect to its ability to assimilate CO and H_2 during the experiments, a soil temperature of 20°C was re-established after a period of four days and the CO and H_2 uptake rates were compared with the results obtained initially.

In situ measurements were performed using two different methods. In the first method (M4), the natural soil surface was covered by a glass box (V = 30 liters) filled with a test atmosphere containing CO and H_2 mixing ratios of about 0.3 ppm and 0.5 ppm, respectively. The variation of the mixing ratios of these two gases with time was then determined in the same way as described above. Owing to the dependence of the CO and H_2 uptake rate on the soil temperature, this method could be used only for time periods during which the soil temperature remained constant. This situation occurred mainly on rainy days and at night.

Because of this restriction, a second method (M5) was employed which allowed the measurements of the CO and H_2 uptake rates independently of the weather situations. This method worked continuously and automatically so that measurements over long periods could be obtained. In this method, the glass box was flushed continuously with a constant flow of air at a rate of 200 liter/hr. Air containing a constant CO and H_2 mixing ratio of 0.2 ppmv and 0.6 ppmv, respectively, was used. The barometric pressure inside the glass box was kept equal to the outside pressure so that the exchange rate of air in and above the soil was not influenced by pressure changes (Seiler *et al.*, 1977a). Measurements of the CO and H_2 mixing ratios were carried out every ten minutes alternately at the inlet and outlet of the glass box. The uptake rates for both gases are calculated from the flow rate, which was registered continuously, and the difference of the CO and H_2 mixing ratios at the inlet and the outlet. The lowest uptake rates detectable by methods M4 and M5 are 4×10^{-14} g/cm^2 sec for CO and 1×10^{-14} g/cm^2 sec for H_2. These values correspond to a linear deposition velocity of 1×10^{-14} cm/sec for CO and 2×10^{-14} cm/sec for H_2 using CO and H_2 mixing ratios of 0.2 ppm and 0.6 ppm, respectively. Comparisons of uptake rates measured simultaneously by these two methods showed agreement within a difference of less than $\pm 15\%$.

The *in situ* measurements of the soil surface were supplemented by measurements of the CO and H_2 distributions in soil at depths from 5 cm down to 100 cm. For these experiments, several stainless steel capillaries of various lengths were driven into the soil. Double samples with a volume of 10 cm^3 each were taken from each depth with gastight syringes and analyzed directly afterwards.

Methods for Determination of the Influence
of Higher Plants on CO and H_2

Figure 2 shows schematically the setup used for the *in situ* measurements involving plants. A branch of the plant with a leaf area of approximately 15×10^2 cm^2 was enclosed with a glass sphere having a volume of 10 liters. The glass sphere was sealed at the bottom by a plastic plate and silicone rubber, both covered by a 1- to 2-cm-thick water layer. The glass sphere was flushed continuously with a carrier gas at a flow rate of approximately 100 liter/hr. The CO, H_2 and CO_2 mixing ratios of the carrier gas could be varied within a range of 0.1 to 0.5 ppm for CO and H_2 and 300-700 ppm for CO_2 by adding certain amounts of CO, H_2 and CO_2 to an airflow devoid of these compounds. Before entering the glass sphere, the carrier gas was bubbled through a thermostated container partially filled with water. In this way, a constant relative humidity of the carrier gas of about 70% was achieved.

The occurrence of drastic temperature variations inside the glass sphere due to changes of the sun's radiation

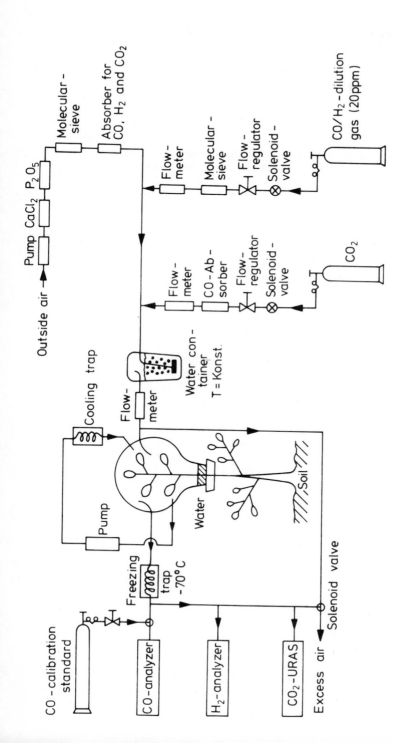

Figure 2. Schematic of the test setup used for the determination of the influence of higher plants on atmospheric CO and H_2.

flux had to be avoided. For this purpose, the air was recycled
with flow rates of F = 600 liter/hr through a cooling trap
whose temperature was set between 0°C and +15°C as the weather
situation required. The CO and H_2 mixing ratios were measured
periodically at the inlet and outlet of the glass sphere using
our continuous-registering CO and H_2 analyzer. The CO_2 mixing
ratios were determined with a URAS instrument. The radiation
flux of the sunlight was measured outside the glass sphere
with a Kipp and Zonen solarimeter-type CM5. Simultaneous
measurements of the radiation fluxes inside and outside the
glass sphere did not show any significant difference between
these two sets of data in that part of the radiation spectrum
important for photosynthesis.

The instruments were installed in a van placed next to
the plant under test so that connection pipes were kept as
short as possible. The total measuring system has been
improved with time and now works completely automatically so
that measurements on plants can be obtained over longer periods
and for different weather situations.

CO and H_2 Analyzers

The CO and H_2 analyzers used for the experiments
described above were developed in this laboratory. A short
description is given by Seiler and Junge (1970) and by Schmidt
and Seiler (1970). The instruments used here do not differ
in principle, but incorporate improved electronics. Both
analyzers are based on the reduction of HgO to mercury vapor
occurring upon the reaction of HgO with CO and H_2 at temperatures of 210-250°C. The mercury vapor is determined by flameless atomic absorption using the Hg 2537 Å line.

Both continuous measurements of CO and H_2 in air and
the analysis of air batch samples may be made. The lower
detection limit of the continuous registration and discontinuous
measurements of 5-liter air samples are 0.5 ppb for CO and
2 ppb for H_2. The relative error of both instruments is + 3%
at CO and H_2 mixing ratios of 0.1 ppm and 0.5 ppm, respectively.
For the analysis of air samples with volumes of 10 cm^3, the
lower detection limit increases to 2 ppb for CO and 8 ppb for
H_2. The calibration curves of the CO and H_2 analyzers are
checked and rechecked routinely by using calibration standards
available in our laboratory. The calibration generally remains
stable over periods of several days. Interferences by other
gases, *e.g.*, hydrocarbons, olefins, ozone and sulfur dioxide
which may also be influenced by plants was not observed
(Seiler *et al.*, 1977b).

RESULTS

Ocean

Dissolved CO and H_2 in ocean waters have been measured during several cruises covering various parts of the northern and southern Atlantic Ocean as well as the southern Pacific Ocean. Measurements were carried out in different seasons and at a variety of locations differing with respect to nutrient concentrations, water temperature and biological activities. Sufficient data are now available to give a representative distribution of dissolved CO and H_2 in ocean waters. Data obtained before 1973 were published by Seiler and Schmidt (1974) and therefore will only be mentioned briefly. Table I summarizes some data on the CO and H_2 concentration in surface waters. For completion, Table I also includes data obtained by researchers from the Naval Research Laboratory, Washington D.C.

From the CO and H_2 concentrations C in surface waters and the CO and H_2 solubilities α in sea water, the corresponding equilibrium values E in air are calculated by $E = C/\alpha$. When the equilibrium values are compared with the measured CO and H_2 mixing ratios in ambient air above the ocean surface, the so-called saturation factors are obtained. Saturation factors greater than unity indicate a supersaturation of the sea water with respect to the mixing ratio of the corresponding gas in air.

The data summarized in Table I show high variations of the dissolved CO. The highest values were found in nutrient-rich waters with the accompanying high biological activities. In these areas, the CO concentrations exceeded values of 21×10^{-5} ml CO/liter H_2O, corresponding to a saturation factor of more than 140. The lowest values were observed in tropical waters and during rough seas, when wind speeds exceeded 70 km/hr and correspondingly a rapid air-sea interchange occurred. Then, the CO values sometimes approached the equilibrium values. Small undersaturations were found only during short time periods (several hours), so we can assume that the surface waters of the oceans are generally supersaturated with respect to CO. Similar observations were made for dissolved H_2, although the H_2 concentrations were generally lower than the CO concentrations. The maximum observed supersaturation of the ocean surface water did not exceed a value of 5.

The data obtained so far for dissolved CO in surface waters at different locations, when averaged with respect to time, result in similar concentrations. The same is true for H_2. Hence, it can be assumed that similar values can also be encountered for the rest of the oceans. If this is the case, the average CO concentration would amount to approximately 6×10^{-5} ml/l, corresponding to a supersaturation

Table I

Dissolved CO and H_2 Concentrations in Ocean Surface Waters

Author	Location	Concentration (x 10^{-5} ml/l)	Equilibrium Value E (ppmv)	Surface-Air Mixing Ratio M (ppmv)	Saturation Factor F = E/M	Number of Samples
Swinnerton et al. (1969)	Tropical Western Atlantic	2-5	1-3	0.10-0.25	10-30	8
Swinnerton et al. (1970)	Western Atlantic	1-10	0.5-50	0.09-0.15	5-100	26
Seiler and Junge (1970)	Middle & Northern Atlantic	3-10	2-5	0.15-0.25	15-33	20
Lamontagne et al. (1971)	Western Atlantic &	6-19	3-10	0.10-0.18	20-100	11
	Northern Pacific } CO	2-14	1-7	0.08-0.16	10-60	52
Seiler and Schmidt (1974)	Norwegian Sea	1.5-18.5	0.8-9.0	0.13-0.30	3-56	cont.[a]
Seiler and Schmidt (1974)	Northern Atlantic	0.3-15.0	0.1-7.0	0.1-0.3	0.8-70.0	cont.
Seiler and Schmidt (1974)	Southern Atlantic & S. Pacific	0.2-21.0	0.1-10.0	0.05	1-140	cont.
Schmidt and Seiler (1974)	Northern Atlantic	0.8-5.0	0.48-3.03	0.55-0.60	0.8-5.4	cont.
Schmidt and Seiler (1974)	Southern Atlantic & S. Pacific } H_2	1.8-5.7	0.96-3.04	0.54-0.59	1.7-5.3	cont.

[a]cont. = continuous registration.

factor of 30. The average H_2 concentration is 2.2×10^{-5} ml/l. With an average H_2 mixing ratio in air of 0.56 ppm, this value corresponds to a supersaturation factor of 2.4.

In addition to regional variations, the concentration of dissolved CO showed high diurnal variations. Figure 3 shows as an example the concentration of dissolved CO as a function of time obtained with the continuous sampling technique at 3-m depth in the northern Atlantic Ocean (Gulf of Cadiz). Each data point represents the average over 20 minutes. These data indicate a direct correlation between the concentration of dissolved CO and the intensity of sunlight. The highest daily maximum values were observed on sunny days. When the skies were overcast, the CO concentration in sea water remained constant with values falling into the range of the equilibrium value. High variabilities of the CO concentrations observed on cloudy days were found to be caused by the variation of the radiation fluxes of the sun due to the changing cloud cover. In contrast to these observations, no systematic diurnal variations have been found for the H_2 concentrations in sea water.

Figure 4 shows a typical CO concentration profile from the surface down to the ocean bottom obtained in the northern Atlantic Ocean. The profiles are characterized by a rapid decrease of the CO concentration in layers a few meters above the sea bottom to values in the range of the equilibrium values. Apart from slight maxima often found in depths of 100-500 m, the CO concentrations remain constant in the total ocean column and increase again in the euphotic zone towards the surface. The highest values were generally observed in the early afternoon in the uppermost sample of the profile at about 2 m depth.

More detailed information on the CO distribution in the uppermost layer of the ocean is given in Figure 5 for different times of the day. Water samples in the layer between the surface and 2 m depth were obtained from a rubber raft 200 m away from the main ship. Samples from layers below 2 m were taken from the main ship using the Niskin water bottles. Figure 5 clearly indicates that the diurnal variations of the dissolved CO as shown in Figure 3 are not restricted to a shallow layer near the surface but occur simultaneously in the entire euphotic zone. The amplitudes of the diurnal variations are small in layers below 50 m depth. They increase in strength as one approaches the surface. Very high CO concentrations were sometimes observed in the uppermost 30-cm deep layer. In the vertical profile shown in Figure 5, the CO concentration reached values of 388×10^{-5} ml/l, corresponding to a supersaturation factor of about 1000. Due to the small number of measurements taken using method M2, we presently do not know whether these high values are representative for the entire oceans and further measurements are required.

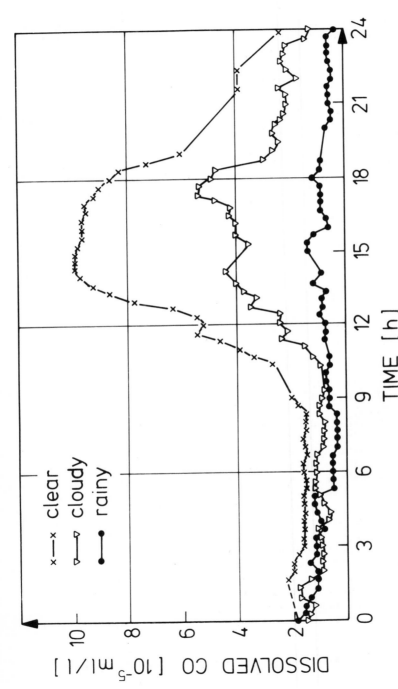

Figure 3.   Diurnal variations of dissolved CO in ocean surface waters over the northern Atlantic Ocean; data are obtained on three days with different weather situations.

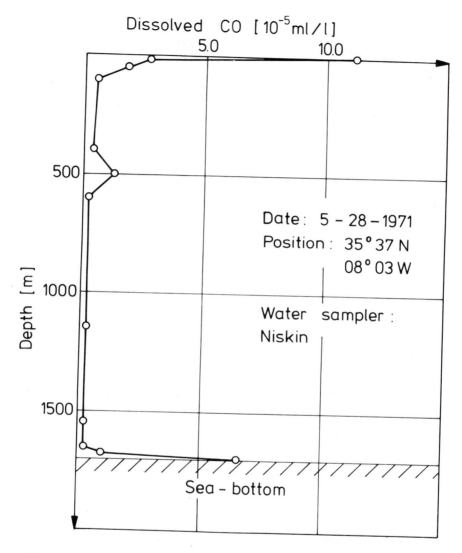

Figure 4. Vertical profile of dissolved CO obtained over the northern Atlantic Ocean.

Figure 6 shows the vertical profile of dissolved H_2 obtained at three different stations over the northern Atlantic Ocean. The individual profiles show little similarity; specifically they exhibit no recurrent maxima and minima in preferred layers as was found for the dissolved CO. At all depths, water was supersaturated by a factor of 1.4 to 3.5. Exceptions were found for concentration profiles measured in the Gulf of Cadiz in that zone affected by the outflow of

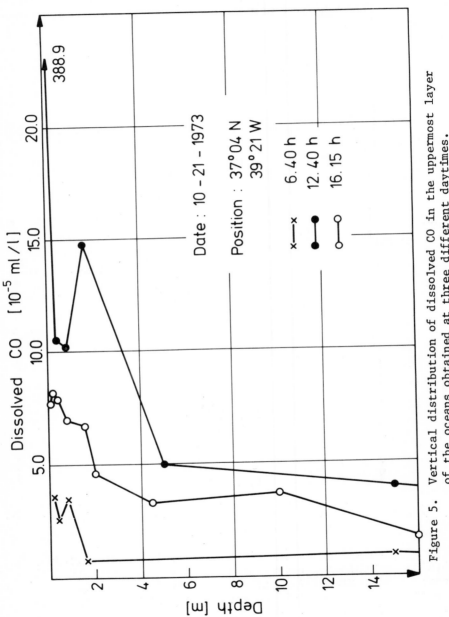

Figure 5.   Vertical distribution of dissolved CO in the uppermost layer of the oceans obtained at three different daytimes.

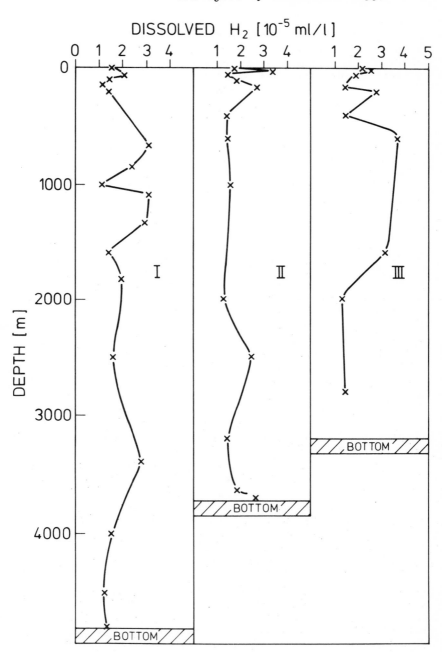

Figure 6.   Vertical profile of dissolved H_2 obtained at three different stations over the northern Atlantic Ocean.

Mediterranean waters into the Atlantic Ocean. At the upper
boundary of the layer of Mediterranean origin occurring at
about 500 m depth, a very pronounced maximum of H_2 was found
with saturation factors of 25. Similar values were often
found near the ocean bottom also (Seiler and Schmidt, 1974).

Soil

Laboratory experiments were carried out with three
different types of soil, *i.e.*, loess, loess loam and soil
from a greenhouse. Temperatures ranged from the freezing
point up to 45°C. A typical example of the influence of soil
on carbon monoxide is shown in Figure 7. The variation of
the CO mixing ratio in the glass vessel over loess loam was
measured as a function of time. At temperatures between 4
and 40°C, the CO mixing ratio decreases exponentially with
time, with a maximum rate at 25°C. It is interesting that the
CO mixing ratio never dropped to zero but reached a final
value. This value remained constant with time even over
periods of several days, indicating an equilibrium between
CO production and destruction. At temperatures below 40°C,
the equilibrium values varied between a few ppbv and 40 ppbv
with a minimum at 30°C and a maximum at 40°C. Above this
temperature, the equilibrium value increased abruptly with
increasing soil temperature and became 0.65 ppm at 41°C, a
value which was higher than the CO mixing ratio of the test
atmosphere.

Apparently the heating to temperatures higher than
40°C caused a change of the general behavior of the soil with
respect to the CO removal. Measurements made at a soil temperature of 20°C one day after the heating of the soil up to
45°C showed a considerably slower CO decrease with time and
higher CO equilibrium values than found initially. After a
regeneration time of approximately 14 days, the experiments
showed the same dependence of the CO decay and equilibrium
values on the soil temperature as measured before. A more
rapid decrease with time was found for the H_2 mixing ratios
(Liebl and Seiler, 1976). In contrast to CO, the H_2 mixing
ratio always decreased to values less than 10 ppb, close to
the detection limit of the H_2 instrument. An increase of
the H_2 mixing ratios as found for CO at temperatures higher
than 40°C was never observed. Furthermore, the periodic
measurements of the decrease of the H_2 mixing ratios at 20°C
before and after the heating of the soil up to 45°C did not
show any difference in the shape and gradient of the curves,
indicating that the soil, in contrast to CO, did not change its
behavior with respect to the H_2 removal.

In situ measurements were carried out over five different types of soil near Mainz: Eolian sand, Clay, Brown
soil, Loess loam and Tschernosem. A detailed description of

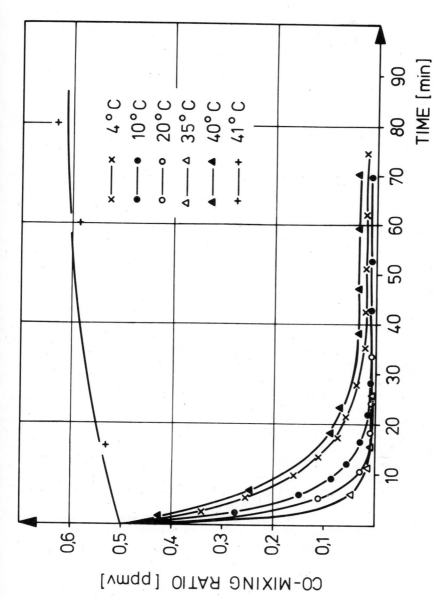

Figure 7. Variations of the CO mixing ratios within the glass vessel as a function of time and soil temperature.

the properties of the soil used for the experiments is given
by Seiler *et al*. (1977a). The results of the *in situ* measurements were similar to those obtained in the laboratory.
Figure 8 shows a variation of the H_2 mixing ratio within the
glass vessel as a function of time and the type of soil obtained in April 1975. The soil temperature varied between
15°C and 27°C during the experiments due to changes in the
weather situation. The H_2 removal rates were generally lower
compared to those obtained in the laboratory. Maximum removal
rates were found over Brown soil, minimum removal rates
occurred over loess loam. A similar dependence on the type
of soil was found for carbon monoxide.

  Surprisingly, the *in situ* measurements in April 1975
indicated no significant influence of the soil temperature on
the CO equilibrium values over the soil. Although temperatures up to 45°C were reached, the CO equilibrium values
remained nearly constant with values of 0.1 ppm (Liebl and
Seiler, 1976). This observation is in complete contrast to
measurements made during the summer season which showed high
variations of the CO equilibrium values depending on the soil
temperature. An illustration is given in Figure 9 which
shows the CO equilibrium values as a function of the time of
day measured on two following days in August 1969 over loess
loam. The CO equilibrium values exhibit marked diurnal
variations with maximum values of 0.6 ppm at noontime at
soil temperatures of approximately 50°C (measured at 1-cm
depth) and minimum values of less than 10 ppb when the temperature has decreased to about 17°C. Compared with the CO
mixing ratios measured simultaneously in atmospheric air
about 5-m aboveground, the soil acted as a netsink for CO at
nighttime and a source around noon. These observations were
confirmed by more recent measurements in 1976 over Eolian
sand. As the same method has been used for all our CO
measurements on soil, we assume that the difference in the
results obtained in April and during the summer season is due
to a seasonal effect, possibly the difference of temperature
gradients in the upper soil layers.

  The influence of the soil temperature on the CO mixing
ratio has been observed for the entire soil layer between the
surface and 1-m depth. Figure 10 shows the vertical distribution of CO in Eolian sand measured on three different days
in July 1976 and with different soil temperatures. Although
the temperature in 7-cm depth varied only between 32°C and
38°C, the CO mixing ratios showed marked variations. The
lowest CO values were found on July 9, when the soil temperature was lowest (32°C). For a soil temperature of 38°C,
the CO mixing ratios were generally higher in the entire
layer between the surface and 1-m depth. They often exceeded
values of 4 ppm and are considerably higher than the maximum

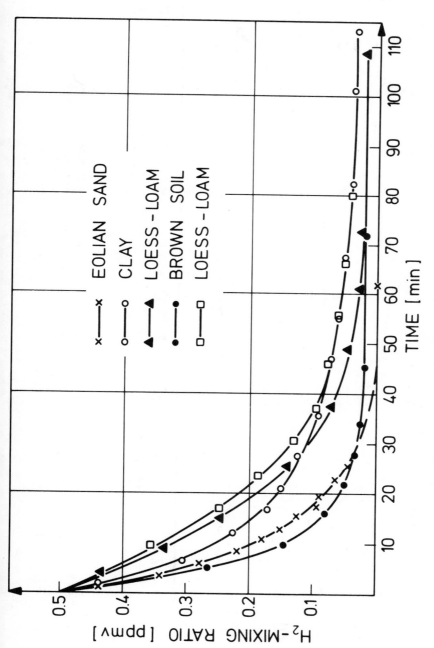

Figure 8. Variation of the H_2 mixing ratios within the glass vessel as a function of time and type of soil.

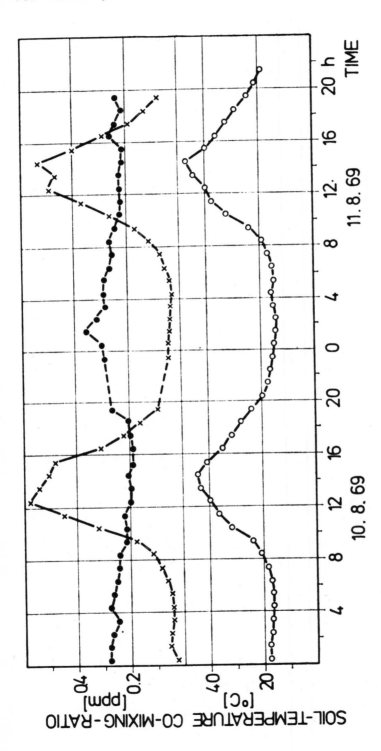

Figure 9.   CO equilibrium values (x-x) as a function of soil temperature (o-o) obtained over loess loam. The CO mixing ratio in atm air 4 m above-ground is indicated by filled dots.

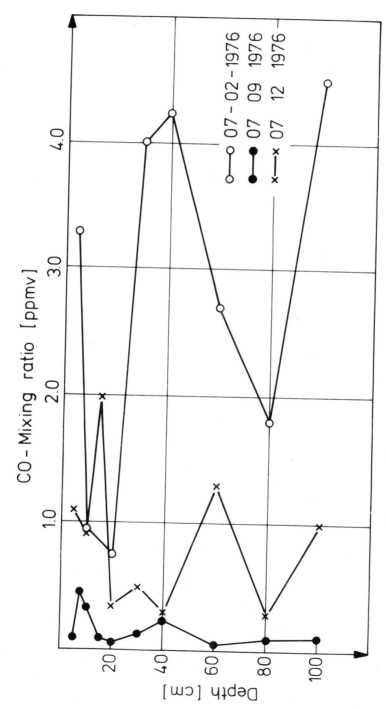

Figure 10. Vertical distribution of CO mixing ratios in soil (Eolian sand) obtained on three different days with different soil temperatures in 7-cm depth.   o–o = 32°C;   x–x = 35°C;   o–o = 38°C.

CO mixing ratios observed at the same time in the astmospheric
air above the ground. In spring and autumn, when the soil
temperature was less than 20°C, CO was not detectable in soil
layers lower than a few centimeters. Exceptions occurred in
layers above ground water in waterlogged soil. In this
case, CO mixing ratios of a few ppm have been observed
(Liebl and Seiler, 1976).

The H_2 mixing ratios in soil were generally found to
be lower than 0.1 ppm. Even on days with high soil temperatures (Figure 11), the H_2 mixing ratios did not exceed values
of 0.6 ppm. This value is identical with the H_2 mixing
ratios found in atmospheric air. These observations indicate
that the soil always acts as a sink for atmospheric H_2. Production of H_2 was found only in shallow layers above ground
water (Liebl and Seiler, 1976).

Plants

We have studied the influence of plants on atmospheric
CO and H_2 both in the laboratory--using the *Vicia faba* and
Platanus Acerifolia--and in the field--using *Fagus silvatica*
and *Pinus sylvestris*. The experiments indicated that these
plants had no significant effect on the H_2 mixing ratios of
the test atmospheres. On the other hand, the plants were found
to have a strong influence on the CO mixing ratios. Table II
summarizes some results obtained by the laboratory experiments. Two different radiation fluxes were used, *i.e.*,
2.5×10^4 erg/cm^2 sec and 4.5×10^4 erg/cm^2 sec. The table
lists the CO and CO_2 mixing ratios of the carrier gas used,
the flow rate of the carrier gas through the glass sphere
and, in the last column, the differences ΔCO of the CO mixing
ratios measured at the inlet and at the outlet of the glass
sphere. The given ΔCO values are normalized to a flow rate
of 200 liter/hr and a leaf area of the plant under test of
1.2×10^3 cm^2.

During darkness there was no difference between the
CO mixing at the inlet and at the outlet of the glass sphere.
During illuminations with artificial light, the CO mixing
ratio at the outlet increased with increasing light intensity.
Maximum ΔCO values were 6.8 ppb at 4.5×10^4 erg/cm^2 sec for
the maximum radiation flux available. Although the experi-
ments were carried out on different days with different CO
and CO_2 mixing ratios of the carrier gas, the ΔCO values
obtained for both plants are in good agreement.

A similar dependence of the ΔCO values on the light
intensity was found also in the *in situ* measurements. As
an example, Figure 12 shows the ΔCO values as a function of
daytime when using *Fagus silvatica*. The data were obtained
during a two-day period under different weather conditions,
i.e., a sunny day and a cloudy day. During the sunny day,

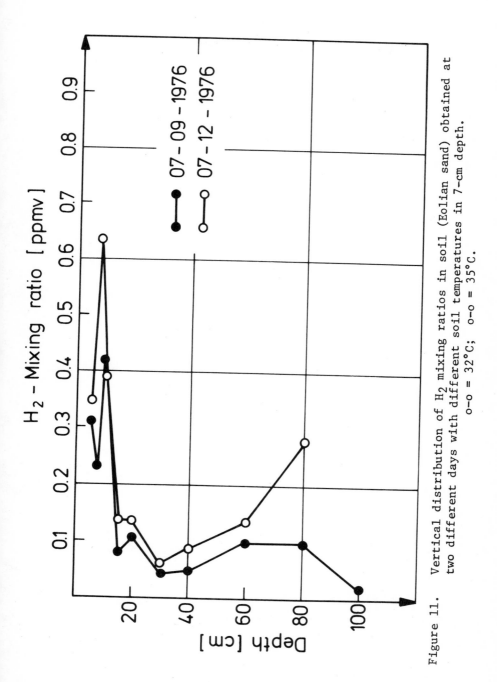

Figure 11. Vertical distribution of H$_2$ mixing ratios in soil (Eolian sand) obtained at two different days with different soil temperatures in 7-cm depth. o—o = 32°C; o—o = 35°C.

Table II

CO Production Rates Obtained by Laboratory Experiments Using the *Vicia faba* and *Platanus acerifolia*; ΔCO Values Normalized to a Flow Rate of 200 liter/hr and a leaf area of 1.2×10^3 cm^2

Light Intensity (10^4 erg cm^{-2} sec^{-1})	CO2 Mixing Ratio of the Carrier Gas (ppmv)	CO Mixing Ratio of the Carrier Gas (ppmv)	Flow Rate (1 hr^{-1})	ΔCO_{norm} (ppbv)	
0	369	< 0.2	181	0	\} *Vicia faba*
2.5				2.9	
4.5				5.1	
0	383	161	210	0	
2.5				–	
4.5				4.3	
0	383	276	215	0	
2.5				2.3	
4.5				5.3	
0	376	< 0.2	210	0	\} *Platanus acerifolia*
2.5				2.1	
4.5				6.8	
0	376	≈ 0.2	190	0.5	
2.5				2.5	
4.5				4.2	
0	377	269	200	0	
2.5				2.1	
4.5				4.2	

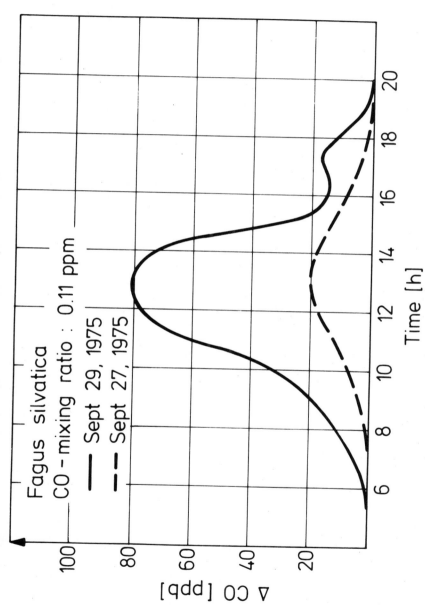

Figure 12. CO values as a function of daytime obtained during a sunny and cloudy day using the *Fagus silvatica*.

the ΔCO values show a marked diurnal variation with maximum values of 80 ppb at noon at a radiation flux of 40×10^4 erg/cm^2 sec. The slight minimum values observed in the after- noon are caused by clouds covering the sun for about two hours from 2 to 4 PM. On days with an overcast sky, the ΔCO values reached maximums of less than 20 ppb. On rainy days, the CO mixing ratio at the outlet of the glass sphere remained nearly constant. During the night, the CO mixing ratios at the inlet and outlet of the glass sphere did not differ by more than 0.2 ppb which is within the accuracy of the CO instrument.

DISCUSSION

The results of laboratory experiments and *in situ* measurements summarized in the preceding section show a sig- nificant influence of the biosphere on the CO and H_2 cycle in the atmosphere. The individual biospheric sources and sinks are discussed in the following sections.

Water

The high CO and H_2 supersaturation of the ocean surface waters indicate a chemical or biological production of CO and H_2 in sea water. Purely physical processes at the ocean's surface are not considered since they lead to super- saturation of only 10 to 20% at the most (Seiler and Schmidt, 1974).

Several chemical or biological CO and H_2 production processes are known. Laboratory experiments by Wilson *et al.* (1970) demonstrated the production of CO in sterilized water when enriched with organic material and subjected to UV- radiation. The CO production rate was found to be proportional to the amount of dissolved organic material. The production of CO by various types of algae has been reported by several authors (Langdon, 1916; Loewus and Delwiche, 1963; Chapman and Tocher, 1966). More recently, it has been found that several species of siphonophores also generate CO (Barham and Wilton, 1964). CO concentrations up to 20% were found in the floats of the *Physalia physalis* (Portuguese man-of-war) which can be explained only by the production of CO in the float cells (Wittenburg, 1960).

Our own investigations have demonstrated the production of CO by algae, *e.g.*, *cocolithinae*, isolated from sea water samples and by pure cultures of *Chlorella vulgaris*. The production rates were found to be dependent on the radiation fluxes with maximum values at high light intensities. Further- more, it was found that a variety of heterotrophic bacteria in aqueous solution can generate carbon monoxide and hydrogen (Junge *et al.*, 1971; Junge *et al.*, 1972; Radler *et al.*, 1974).

On the other hand, the rapid decrease of the dissolved CO in the ocean surface waters (Figure 3) from 10 to 2×10^{-5} ml/hr within a few hours during the afternoon, as well as the rapid fluctuations correlated to the cloud coverage indicate that CO must also be consumed in the water. Since the decrease of CO content occurs simultaneously throughout the entire euphotic layer, physical processes like turbulent mixing of the water body and subsequent dilution of CO in the surface layer can be excluded from the considerations. Moreover, molecular diffusion which is responsible for the exchange of these gases between surface waters and air is too small to explain the rapid decrease of the CO concentration at 2- to 3-m depth. Therefore, the CO concentration in surface waters must result from a dynamic equilibrium between CO production and CO consumption processes.

Since the CO and H_2 concentrations are comparable in magnitude in larger areas of the oceans, we conclude that supersaturation on the average is a significant global property of the ocean surface waters. The supersaturation results in a net flux of CO and H_2 from the ocean into the atmosphere. Using the "stagnant film layer model" developed by Broecker and Peng (1971) and an average supersaturation of 30 for CO, the global average net flux is calculated as $0.2-1.2 \times 10^{14}$ g/yr. Similarly, for H_2 the supersaturation is 2.4 on the average, leading to a net flux of $0.1-0.7 \times 10^{13}$ g/yr. Due to the uncertainties of the parameters involved in this model, the given atmospheric CO and H_2 production rates from the oceans may be uncertain by ±50%. The CO production rates would increase considerably, should it be true that the extremely high CO concentrations recently found in the northern Atlantic Ocean (Figure 5) are a widespread occurrence in ocean surface waters.

Soil

In contrast to the oceans, soil generally acts as a sink for CO and H_2. With the method M4, the CO and H_2 uptake rates are calculated from the equation:

$$P = \frac{V}{F \times t} \ln \frac{m_o - m_1}{m(t) - m_1} \quad [cm/sec]$$

where V = volume of the glass vessel
  F = exposed soil surface in the glass vessel
  t = time of exposition
  m_o = initial CO/H_2 mixing ratio of the test atmosphere
  m_1 = CO/H_2 equilibrium value
  $m(t)$ = CO/H_2 mixing ratio after the time of exposition

For method M5 this equation changes into:

$$P = \frac{R}{F} \quad \ln \frac{m_o - m_1}{m(t) - m_1} \quad [cm/sec]$$

where R = flow rate of the carrier gas through the glass vessel. The CO and H_2 uptake rates are given in terms of deposition velocities with the dimension cm/sec. This presentation makes the data independent of the CO and H_2 mixing ratios employed in the experiment.

Some of the CO and H_2 deposition velocities observed for different types of soil and different seasons are summarized in Table III. Also listed are data on the type of vegetation on the soil under test, the soil temperature at 0.5 cm-depth and the carbon content of the soil in the surface layer. At temperatures ranging from 3-27°C, the deposition velocities observed for the different soils show a surprisingly good agreement with values of 2-7 x 10^{-2} cm/sec for CO and 4-9 x 10^{-2} cm/sec for H_2. Comparable values were observed for these soils in spring and autumn for both CO and H_2 even at soil temperatures up to 48°C. In summer with temperatures higher than 45°C in 0.5-cm depth, the CO deposition velocities decreased with increasing temperature. At temperatures higher than 50°C, the properties of the soil changed from net consumption to net production of carbon monoxide. The CO equilibrium values increased accordingly. The H_2 deposition velocities, however, remained the same even at soil temperatures up to 55°C.

The difference in soil behavior in summer with respect to the CO uptake compared with the other seasons may be explained by the different vertical temperature distribution in the upper layer of the soil. In spring and autumn, the temperature decreased rapidly with depths from 40°C at the surface to ± 18°C below 10 cm. In summer only relatively small temperature gradients were observed in the upper soil layer. During sunny weather, the temperature at the 10-cm depth often reached values of more than 38°C. Considering the observed dependence of the CO equilibrium values on soil temperature and assuming that a functional relationship exists at all depths down to 1 m, CO production is expected to occur in spring and autumn only at the soil surface whereas CO is consumed at depths some millimeters below the surface. This interpretation has been supported by the measurements of vertical CO profiles which show a rapid decrease of CO occurring just below the surface in spring and autumn (Liebl and Seiler, 1976). At depths below 2 m, the CO mixing ratios reached values of less than a few ppb indicating a net CO consumption on these layers. Due to the generally higher soil temperatures in summer, the soil apparently acts as a source of CO throughout the entire upper soil layer.

Table III

Summary of Some CO and H_2 Deposition Velocities Obtained over Five Different Types of Soil

Type of Soil	CO Deposition Velocity (x 10^{-2} cm/sec)	H_2 Deposition Velocity (x 10^{-2} cm/sec)	Soil Temp. (°C)	Vegetation	Carbon Content (%)
Eolian sand	1.6-4.0	4.0-8.4	3-27	None	<2
Eolian sand	4.2	6.4	3	Grass	<2
Eolian sand	6.1-6.7	9.0-11.5	5	Pine woods	7.4
Clay	3.0	6.0	3	None	3.1
Loess loam as water-logged soil	3.5-4.2	6.5-7.6	5-13	Beech trees	5.6
Tschernosem	3.8-4.2	5.6-6.9	8-21	None	3.9
Brown soil	4.8-5.2	6.6-7.2	6	Grass	1.2
Loess loam as ground water soil	2.9-5.6	4.2-7.2	5-11	Grass	2.4

This conclusion is in agreement with the measured vertical
CO distribution in soil given in Figure 10 which shows CO
mixing ratios larger than 1 ppm exceeding considerably those
measured in the air above.

Recent studies by Ingersoll *et al*. (1974) indicate
that the CO consumption in soil is due to microbial activities.
It could be shown that a number of fungal species isolated
from the soil were capable of removing CO. Similar observations
are reported by Jones and Scott (1939), Kluyver and Schnellen
(1947), Kistner (1954), and Yagi (1958). The existence of
CO-consuming microbial processes would explain the behavior
of soil with respect to the CO uptake after heating to 45°C,
and the observed regeneration within an incubation time of
14 days. Apparently microbial processes are also capable of
removing hydrogen.

The existence of CO and H_2 equilibrium values indicates
that CO and H_2 must also be produced. This is clearly demonstrated by field experiments with different test atmospheres,
one containing CO and H_2 mixing ratios of 1 ppm and one
containing essentially no CO and H_2. As shown in Figure 13,
the same final CO values were reached after an exposition time
of 4 hours regardless of which test atmosphere was employed.
Similar observations were made for H_2, indicating that a balance
is set up between the simultaneous production and destruction
of both CO and H_2 in soil.

Using all data available at present, the mean CO and
H_2 deposition velocities averaged over the seasons are 4 x 10^2
cm/sec for CO and 7 x 10^{-2} cm/sec for H_2. If we assume that
these CO and H_2 deposition velocities are representative for
global conditions and the CO and H_2 consumption behaves like a
first-order reaction, the global CO and H_2 consumption can
be calculated by

$$g = m \times \zeta \times p \times A$$

where   m = atmospheric mixing ratios of CO and H_2
          ζ = densities of CO and H_2 (1 atm, 20°C)
          p = deposition velocities
          A = surface area of the continents active for the
             CO and H_2 uptake

If we take into account that larger parts of the continental
areas are covered by ice for several months, the CO consumption
results in 2.4 x 10^{14} g/yr and the H_2 consumption in 1.2 x
10^{14} g/yr. These rates are based on atmospheric CO mixing
ratios of 0.15 ppm in the northern hemisphere and 0.5 ppm in
the southern hemisphere (Seiler, 1976) and a H_2 mixing ratio
of 0.58 ppm (Schmidt, 1974). These values derive from measurements in unpolluted marine air masses. If we use CO mixing

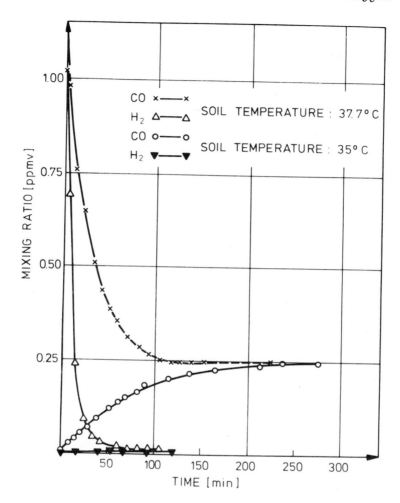

Figure 13.   Variations of the CO and H_2 mixing ratios in the
glass vessel as a function of time starting with
CO and H_2 mixing ratios of 1 ppm and with a CO-
and H_2-free air.

ratios observed over the continents which are higher by a
factor of two, the global CO consumption by microbial processes in soil would increase to about 5×10^{14} g/yr.

Plants

        The laboratory experiments and the *in situ* measurements
indicate also a considerable influence of plants on carbon
monoxide. Hydrogen, however, does not seem to be affected.
Since the glass sphere used for the experiments itself had
no influence on the carbon monoxide mixing ratio, the higher

CO mixing ratios observed at the outlet of the glass sphere
containing a plant can only be explained by CO production of
the plant under test. The production rates are calculated
in the following manner:

$$P = \frac{\Delta CO \times F \times \zeta}{B}$$

where ΔCO = difference of the CO mixing ratios at the
inlet and the outlet of the glass sphere
F = flow rate of the carrier gas through the
glass sphere
B = leaf area of the plant
ζ = density of CO (1 atm, 20°C)

Figure 14 summarizes the production rates as functions of the
radiation fluxes obtained by laboratory experiments and by
in situ measurements. The CO mixing ratios of the carrier
gas were varied for the individual experiments between 110 ppb
and 270 ppb, representing typical atmospheric background values
for continental air. The CO production rates increase in a
linear manner with increasing radiation fluxes. Maximum
values are 30 x 10^{-13} g/sec per cm^2 leaf area at a radiation
flux of 50 x 10^{14} erg/cm^2 sec. With radiation fluxes similar
to the global average solar flux, one calculates a mean CO
production rate of 3 x 10^{-13} g/sec per cm^2 leaf area. Due
to the similar results obtained for the different plants we
may expect similar production rates for other plants of the
C$_3$-type.
None of our laboratory experiments or *in situ* measurements have indicated a CO uptake by plants, although our method
would allow the detection of uptake rates somewhat less than
0.3 x 10^{-13} g/sec per cm^2 leaf area. This observation is in
complete contrast to the data given by Bidwell and Fraser
(1972) who found uptake rates of 23-47 x 10^{-3} g/cm^2 sec.
These values are two orders of magnitude above our detection
limit. Even if one takes into account that the data given by
Bidwell and Fraser (1972) were obtained for CO mixing ratios
of 1-2 ppm and extrapolates the CO uptake rates to CO mixing
ratios of 200 ppb as used here, the consumption rates would
still extend our detection limit by more than one order of
magnitude and, consequently, could not have escaped detection.
We believe that this difference in results is due to
the different methods employed by the different investigators.
The C^{14} method as used by Bidwell and Fraser (1972) allows
very sensitive measurements of the CO uptake rates, but is
not suitable for the determination of low production rates.
Our method, on the other hand, indicates the net influence
of the total ecological system of the plant, including the
gas exchange by the plant and/or by microbial processes on the
inner and outer leaf surfaces. It is, however, not appropriate

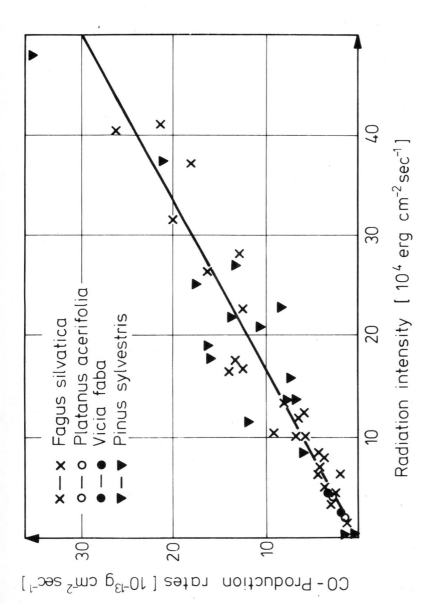

Figure 14. CO production rates by plants as a function of the radiation intensities. Data are obtained using the *Vicia faba*, *Platanus acerifolia*, *Fagus silvatica* and *Pinus sylvestris*.

for measurements of the individual production and destruction rates. The controversial results may, therefore, be explained by the simultaneous production and destruction of CO, probably by different processes occurring in the ecological system of the plant. As shown by our experiments, the net effect of higher plants is a production of CO.

At present, we do not know which processes are involved. The results found by Bidwell and Fraser (1972) showing an incorporation of CO into the plant material during daytime and the oxidation of CO into CO_2 during nighttime seem to indicate microbial processes on the leaf surface transforming CO into CO_2 which is then used by plant photosynthesis during irradiation. This assumption, however, is in contradiction to the observation of Bidwell and Fraser (1972) who found a completely different incorporation pattern into the cell material for ^{14}CO and $^{14}CO_2$.

The dependence of the CO production rates on the light intensity found in all our experiments seems to indicate a correlation between photosynthesis and CO production. Several tests with increasing CO_2 mixing ratios of the carrier gas up to 700 ppm showed an increase of the rates of the plant photosynthesis as we would expect. The CO production rates, however, remained constant, so that plant photosynthesis cannot be made responsible for the CO production processes. We assume tentatively that the observed CO production is due to the photodissociation of pigments in the plant material following irradiation. Corresponding tests are planned for the near future.

If we assume the CO production of 3×10^{-13} g/sec cm^2 leaf area to be representative for global average conditions, the global CO production rate due to plants is calculated as 1.3×10^{14} g/yr. This calculation is based on a total leaf area index of 5 and a plant growth period of 200 days. Because of the small number of measurements and the large uncertainties involved in the calculations, this value must be considered an order of magnitude estimate.

Contribution of Biospheric Processes to the
Global CO and H_2 Cycles

As a basis for the discussion of biosphere influence on the atmospheric cycles of CO and H_2, their main sources and sinks, together with the mean mixing ratios and residence times in the atmosphere, are summarized in Table IV. CO and H_2 are formed by a variety of processes including both natural and anthropogenic activities. The main H_2 sources are anthropogenic H_2 production by industry and automobiles (Seiler and Zankl, 1976), and photochemical H_2 production by the oxidation of methane (Warneck, 1976). The production rates for each of these sources are reported to be 0.2×10^{14} g/yr. Compared

Table IV
Summary of the Estimated Annual Global Production and
Destruction Rates of the Known CO and H_2 Sources and Sinks

	H_2	Author	CO	Author
SOURCES				
Anthropogenic	0.2	Seiler and Zankl (1975)	6.4	Seiler (1976)
Oceans	0.01-0.07	this paper	0.1-1.2	this paper
Bush Fires	–	–	0.6	Seiler (1974)
Oxidation of Hydrocarbons	–	–	0.6	Seiler (1974)
Plants	Negligible	this paper	1.3	this paper
Oxidation of Methane	0.2	Warneck (1975)	4.0	Seiler (1976)
TOTAL	0.4-0.5		13.1-14.1	
SINKS				
Uptake by Soil	1.2	this paper	5.0	this paper
Flux into the Stratosphere	Negligible	Schmidt (1974)	1.1	Seiler and Warneck (1976)
Oxidation by OH	0.1	Warneck (1975)	6.0	Seiler (1976)
TOTAL	1.3		13.1	
Mean Mixing Ratio (ppmv)	0.56	Schmidt (1974)	00.11	Seiler (1976)
Residence Time (year)	1.5-4.0	Seiler and Schmidt (1977)	0.3-0.4	Seiler and Schmidt (1977)

Emission rates are given in 10^{14} g/yr.

with these sources are biospheric H_2 production by microbial activities in the surface waters contributes on a global basis about 15% of the total H_2 production. For the atmospheric CO budget, biospheric processes, namely the microbial CO production in the oceans and CO production by plants, accounts for 20% of the total CO production, which is estimated to be about 14×10^{14} g/yr. About 75% of the total CO production is due to anthropogenic and photochemical CO production with production rates of 6×10^{14} g/yr, respectively.

A considerably higher influence of the biosphere was found for the sinks of atmospheric CO and H_2 where microbial CO consumption on the soil contributes about 40% of the total CO destruction. Considering the H_2 cycle, the H_2 uptake by soil even represents the dominant sink for atmospheric H_2.

Whereas the CO cycle using the production and destruction rates as given in Table IV is in balance, the H_2 destruction rates exceed the H_2 production rates by nearly a factor of 3. Therefore, we have to assume either higher total H_2 production rates perhaps involving additional H_2 sources or a lower consumption rate due to the microbial processes. Our *in situ* measurements indicate comparable H_2 deposition velocities for different types of soil. In addition, the H_2 deposition velocities were found to be independent of the soil temperature up to 60°C. Therefore, the first possibility is more likely.

Although Table IV summarizes only the net production and destruction rates of the biospheric processes instead of the individual rates, it becomes evident that the biosphere has a great influence on the CO and H_2 budget in the atmosphere. This statement applies also to the isotopic compositions of these two gases. Considerable caution must be exercised if one wishes to use the measured isotopic compositions of CO and H_2 for the estimates of the total CO and H_2 production rates as has been attempted by Weinstock (1969) and Stevens *et al.* (1972).

ACKNOWLEDGMENTS

I am indebted to Prof. Warneck and Dr. Bauer for discussions and Mssrs. Giehl, Liebl and Bunse for their help. This work has been performed as part of the program of the "Sonderforschungsbereich 73" receiving partial funds through the DFG.

REFERENCES

Barham, E.G., and I.W. Wilton. "Carbon Monoxide Production by a Bathypelagic Siphonophore," *Science* 144:860-862 (1964).

Bidwell, R.G.S., and D.E. Fraser. "Carbon Monoxide Uptake and Metabolism by Leaves," *Can. J. Bot.* 50:1435-1439 (1972).

Broecker, W.S., and T.H. Peng. "The Vertical Distribution of Radon in the Bomex-Area," *Earth Planet. Sci. Lett.* 11:99-108 (1972).

Chapman, D.I., and R.D. Tocher. "Occurrence and Production of Carbon Monoxide in Some Brown Algae," *Can. J. Bot.* 44:1438-1442 (1966).

Ingersoll, R.B., R.E. Inman and W.R. Fischer. "Soil's Potential as a Sink for atm Carbon Monoxide," *Tellus* 26:151-158 (1974).

Jones, C.W., and G. Scott. "Carbon Monoxide in Underground Atmospheres. The Role of Bacteria in its Elimination," *Ing. Eng. Chem.* 31:775-778 (1939).

Junge, C., W. Seiler, R. Bock, K.D. Greese and F. Radler. "Uber die CO-Produktion von Mikroorganismen," *Naturwissenschaften* 58:262-263 (1971).

Junge, C., W. Seiler, U. Schmidt, R. Bock, K.D. Greese, F. Radler and H.J. Rueger. "Kohlenoxid- und Wasserstoff-Produktion mariner Mikroorganismen in Nährmedium mit synth. Seewasser," *Naturwissenschaften* 59:514-515 (1972).

Kistner, A. "Conditions Determining the Oxidation of Carbon Monoxide and Hydrogen by Hydrogenomonas Carboxy Dovorans," *Proc. Koninkl. Ned. Akad. Wetenschap.* 57:186-195 (1954).

Kluyver, A.J., and CH.G.T.P. Schnellen. "On the Fermentation of Carbon Monoxide by Pure Cultures of Methane Bacteria," *Arch.Biochem.* 14:57-70 (1947).

Langdon, S.C. "Carbon Monoxide in the Pneumatocyst of Nereo-cystis," *Puget Sound Marine Station Publ.* 1:237-247 (1916).

Liebl, K.H., and W. Seiler. "CO and H_2 Destruction at the Soil Surface," in *Microbial Production and Utilization of Gases,* H.G. Schlegel, G. Gottschalk and N. Pfennig, Eds. (Gottingen: E. Goltze K.G., 1976), pp. 215-230.

Loewus, M.W., and C.C. Delwiche. "Carbon Monoxide Production by Algae," *Plant Physiol.* 38:371-374 (1963).

Radler, F., K.D. Greese, R. Bock and W. Seiler. "The Formation of Traces of Carbon Monoxide by Saccharomyces Cerevisiae and Other Microorganisms," *Arch. Microbiol.* 100:243-252 (1974).

Schmidt, U., and W. Seiler. "A New Method for Recording Mole-cular Hydrogen in atm Air," *Geophys. Res.* 75:1713-1716 (1970).

Schmidt, U. "Molecular Hydrogen in the Atmosphere," *Tellus* 26:78-90 (1974).

Seiler, W., and C. Junge. "Carbon Monoxide in the Atmosphere," *J. Geophys. Res.* 75:217-225 (1970).

Seiler, W. and U. Schmidt. "Dissolved Nonconservative Gases in Sea Water," *The Sea* 5, E.D. Goldberg, Ed. (New York: Wiley and Sons, 1974), pp. 219-243.

Seiler, W., and P. Warneck. "Decrease of Carbon Monoxide Mixing Ratio at the Tropopause," *J. Geophys. Res.* 77:3204-3214 (1972).

Seiler, W. "The Cycle of CO in the Atmosphere," *Proc. ICESA--Conference, 22* (New York: Inst. of Electrical and Electronics Engineers, 1976) 35/4/1-9.

Seiler, W., and H. Zankl. "Die Spurengase CO and H_2 über München (Carbon Monoxide and Hydrogen over Munich)," *Umschau* 75:284-285 (1975).

Seiler, W., K.H. Liebl, W. Th. Stoehr and H. Zakosek. "CO and H_2 Abbau am Boden," *Ztschr. f. Pflanzenernährung und Bodenkunde* (1977a).

Seiler, W., H. Giehl and G. Bunse. *The Influence of Plants on Atmospheric Carbon Monoxide and Dinitrogen Oxide* (Sent to *Planta*, 1977).

Stevens, C.M., L. Krout, G. Walling, A. Venters, A. Engelkemeir and L.E. Ross. "The Isotopic Composition of Atmospheric Carbon Monoxide," *Earth Planet. Sci. Lett.* 16:147-165 (1972).

Warneck, P. "The Role of Chemical Reactions in the Cycle of atm Trace Gases, Especially CH_4," in *Microbial Production and Utilization of Gases*, H.G. Schlegel, G. Gottschalk and N. Pfennig, Eds. (Gottingen: E. Goltze K.G., 1976), pp. 53-62.

Weinstock, B. "Carbon Monoxide: Residence Time in the Atmosphere," *Science* 166:224-225 (1969).

Wilson, D.F., J.W. Swinnerton and R.A. Lamontagne. "Production of Carbon Monoxide and Gaseous Hydrocarbons in Sea Water: Relation to Dissolved Organic Carbon," *Science* 168:1 77-1579 (197

Wittenberg, J.B. "The Source of Carbon Monoxide in the Float of Physalia Physalis, the Portuguese Man of War," *J. Exptl. Biol.* 37:698-705 (1960).

Yagi, T. "Enzymic Oxidation of Carbon Monoxide," *Biochim. Biophys. Acta* 30:194-195 (1958).

CHAPTER 63

CONTRIBUTION OF OXYGEN ISOTOPE FRACTIONATION DURING THE TRANSPIRATION OF PLANT LEAVES TO THE BIOGEOCHEMICAL OXYGEN CYCLE

H. FÖRSTEL

Institute of Chemistry 2
Nuclear Research Centre (KFA), P.O.B. 1913
D 5170 Jülich, Federal Republic of Germany

INTRODUCTION

The ^{18}O enrichment of the present atmospheric oxygen, as stated by Dole (1935), is an interesting tool for studying the geochemical oxygen cycle. The enrichment is related to the ^{18}O content of the oxygen bound in sea water, the main type of free water on the earth's surface, and shows only small variations of its $^{18}O/^{16}O$ ratio. The main source of unbound oxygen is the atmosphere (3.8×10^{19} moles), where no differences in the $^{18}O/^{16}O$ ratio could be found. Only 2.5×10^{17} moles of unbound oxygen are dissolved within the ocean. The turnover of the atmospheric oxygen by biological processes is very slow (turnover rate: 10^{16} moles per year), but the nonbiological processes are even slower (*e.g.*, present combustion by energy production: 3×10^{14} moles per year). A nonbiological source may be the photolytic oxygen production within the higher atmosphere; the lighter hydrogen is able to escape to the space. The weathering and combustion processes are the main nonbiological oxygen sinks.

Under present conditions, the biosphere remains within a stationary state. This means that the oxygen produced during photosynthesis is used at the same rate during respiration to recycle the organic material. Because of that condition, the fractionation factors of oxygen isotopes themselves can be used directly to get the part of the single processes and steps within the oxygen cycle in the ^{18}O enrichment of the atmosphere.

The respiratory processes mainly contribute to the atmospheric ^{18}O enrichment. The contribution of the photosynthetic processes is still open. The oxygen, produced by the marine algae, shall have practically the same ^{18}O content as that of the water surrounding them (Vinogradov *et al.*, 1960), *i.e.*, the sea water. A certain sample of sea water is the basis of the ^{18}O measurements and has by definition an enrichment of zero (Craig, 1961). Therefore, the marine algae will not contribute to the atmospheric ^{18}O enrichment. On the other hand, the photosynthesis of the land plants may play an important role in the ^{18}O enrichment (Dongmann *et al.*, 1972). The idea has been published that leaf water of transpiring plants shows a distinct ^{18}O enrichment (Gonfiantini *et al.*, 1965; Dongmann *et al.*, 1974; Förstel *et al.*, 1974). Under the assumption that the ^{18}O content of the photosynthetic oxygen will have the same isotopic composition as the water in the leaves, the land plants shall produce an ^{18}O-rich oxygen. The data, published formerly, can be considered an approximation only. In this paper, more relevant data shall be discussed.

The interest in the $H_2{}^{18}O$ enrichment of land plants was also stimulated by the new productivity data. In former times (*e.g.*, Rabinowitch, 1945), the marine biomass production had been overestimated. More modern data show that the total land production compared to that of the sea is higher by a factor of 1.6 (Lieth, 1974), instead of the land-to-sea area ratio of 0.4 to 1.

METHODS

To estimate global data, two strategies may be applied. Establish a dense network of sampling stations that must work for at least one year. The IAEA precipitation sampling network is not satisfactory, for there are problems with the continuous service at the stations, the amount of samples and resulting global isotope pattern (IAEA, 1971; Förstel *et al.*, 1974), but fortunately, we can get a worldwide overview of the distribution of the hydrogen and oxygen isotopes. The best known global network is established to get climate data which are readily available. However, one tends to study a phenomenon at a single location and to develop a general model. This model shall contain only parameters which are globally well-known.

Our assumption is that the photosynthetic oxygen has the same ^{18}O content as the water in the leaves, which we believe to be a well-mixed water compartment. In order to get a global estimate of the mean $H_2{}^{18}O$ content in leaf water, we started to study the naturally occurring enrichment in some plants at Jülich. Then we looked for the reasons behind that enrichment, *i.e.*, the transpiration of plants. After observation, we made a model and tried to verify it at the laboratory. Afterwards we used global data of the ^{18}O content in the precipitation, of the humidity and of the productivity to calculate a global mean of the $H_2^{18}O$ enrichment in leaf water.

The $H_2^{18}O$ content of leaf water from three trees was estimated: from a spruce (*Picea abies* KARST), from a birch (*Betula pubescens* EHRH.), and from a larch (*Larix decidua* MILL.). The three species represent an evergreen conifer, a summergreen conifer and a summergreen broadleaf tree. They grow at the location of the Nuclear Research Centre Jülich (KFA) within some meters at the border of a young, dense forest under identical environmental conditions, including solar radiation. The test was made on a hot and clear day. Samples of leaves and branches were immediately enclosed in vacuum-tight vessels and stored at -18°C. The water is gained by vacuum distillation from about 20°C into a liquid nitrogen-cooled trap. This water from the plant material has some odor and some organic material. The organic material may be oxidized by the help of potassium permanganate without any influence on the $^{18}O/^{16}O$ ratio. Water from atmospheric humidity was collected into three traps, cooled with an acetone/solid carbon dioxide mixture (-77°C) out of the streaming air (0.45 m^3/hr). To avoid disturbing isotopic fractionation effects, the water vapor must freeze out completely. This method has been tested carefully.

One milliliter of water is shaken with about five torrliter carbon dioxide at least overnight. Afterwards, the carbon dioxide is measured against a laboratory standard by the help of a mass spectrometer "micromass 602 C" (vacuum generators, Winsford, U.K.). The data are reported as δ values in per mil related to Vienna-SMOW. Only $^{18}O/^{16}O$ ratios are reported. It is important to note that the model experiments in the laboratory are related to that water which was used to cultivate the plants.

The model experiments have been done by the help of a Siemens climate cuvette, and a self-constructed small wind channel. The climate cuvette is fed by a constant air stream of certain temperature, humidity and $H_2^{18}O$ content of the humidity. The water, which is transpired by the plant, is frozen out within a bypass. The knowledge of the air volume per time and of the dew point of that bypass enables us to calculate the amount of transpired water. Difficulties arise from the condensation processes at the dew point traps: every condensation may alter the isotopic composition of the humidity. Another difficulty arises from the plants (radishes, *Raphanus sativus* L. *var. sativus*) themselves. They must be kept under certain conditions. To start transpiration, they were brought

suddenly into lower humidity and light. The plants responded
to that stress with some physiological effects.

The small tubular wind track allowed work in an air
stream of constant climate and $H_2^{18}O$ content at flow velocities
up to 5 m/sec (mean at Jülich: 3 m/sec). The wind track is
constructed in a manner so the plant could be kept in a turbulent air stream of equal velocity profile. Young small oak
trees (*Quercus robur* L) were kept in a nutrient solution and
was irradiated. The leaves have been harvested after at
least a threefold turnover of the leaf water—that means after
they are close to the stationary state of the ^{18}O enrichment.

The model used (Dongmann *et al.*, 1974) will be discussed
in the next chapter. The global patterns of $H_2^{18}O$ and of productivity were determined with the help of two computer programs (Förstel *et al.*, 1974): the SYMAP program, which will
transform a network of data points into a global pattern, and
the MAPCOUNT program, which enables us to get a quantitative
interpretation of the maps.

RESULTS AND DISCUSSION

Figure 1 presents the results of a comparison between
three species of trees. The water in the branches reflects the
average of the $^{18}O/^{16}O$ ratio of the precipitation at Jülich,
and this means also that it reflects the mean of the soil
water. The $^{18}O/^{16}O$ ratio of the air humidity is lower by 7
per mil, related to the branch water. It does not show a
diurnal tendency. Such a difference is observed during warm
weather conditions. Longtime measurements at Jülich (Durm and
Förstel, 1977) have reported that the difference between soil
water (*i.e.*, precipitation) and air humidity is about 10 per
mil. This is in agreement with the hypothesis that the soil
water and the air humidity are at an isotopic equilibrium.
The results from Jülich are generalized. The diurnal ^{18}O
enrichment curve of the leaves and needles is drawn by a least
square fit, using a polynomial function. The scattering is
caused by the methodological necessity that each measurement
requires a separate set of leaves or needles. Looking at
Figure 1, a rapid enrichment during the morning until the
afternoon can be seen. During the evening, and the night,
there is a slow decline of that enrichment. The three curves
of $^{18}O/^{16}O$ ratios in leaf water are parallel. Such a shift
may be caused by physiological reasons. There is an apparent
correspondence between the courses of ^{18}O enrichment and temperature. The temperature directly influences the relative
humidity and the water loss of plants by transpiration. In
summary, under natural conditions, high ^{18}O enrichments are
possible.

The reason for the ^{18}O enrichment is studied by examining
radish plants which are brought suddenly into new climate

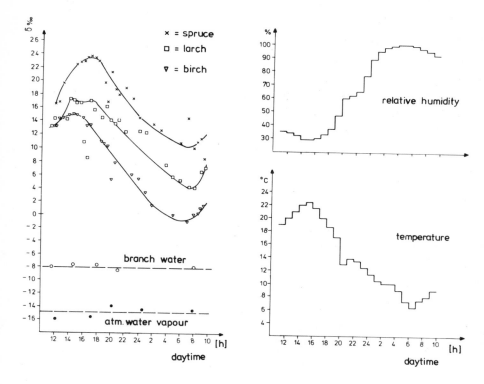

Figure 1. ^{18}O enrichment of the water of needles and leaves relative to Vienna-SMOW (left side). Three species have been observed at the same place during a whole day, while the weather was warm and clear. At the right side, the corresponding data of temperature and relative humidity are shown.

(from darkness to light, from 100 to 60% relative humidity at 18°C). The water turnover of the plants was measured by the Siemens cuvette. Figure 2 illustrates that after a sudden change in environmental conditions, a new stationary state is established during the turnover (transpiration) of the leaf water pool. The scattering of the values is caused mainly by the way of measurement: to get a value one must harvest the plant. The deviation from the theoretical curve, *i.e.*, from the exponential increase of the enrichment, is caused by the reaction of the plants to the sudden climate change: directly after the change there is a period of enhanced transpiration.

Under natural conditions, the water turnover of the leaves is rapid. Therefore, one may expect that the $^{18}O/^{16}O$ ratio of the leaf water is close to the stationary state. This assumption is supported by the shape of the exponential function. Starting the experiment by a climate step, the most

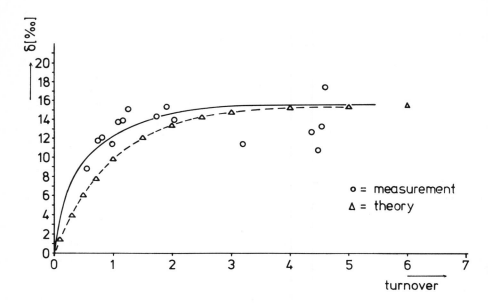

Figure 2. ^{18}O enrichment of radish plants (relative to the
initial water), which were brought at the beginning
of the experiment from darkness and 100% relative
humidity to irradiation and 60% humidity. The
plants immediately start to transpire. A new
stationary state is reached during the water turnover. The water flow through the plant is given
as turnover (g water transpired per g leaf water).

intense derivation of the $^{18}O/^{16}O$ ratio is found during the
first water turnover. Another support of the assumption is
given by the shape of the diurnal enrichment curve. During
the morning, the enrichment may be below the stationary state
and during the afternoon and evening above.
     The following formula describes the ^{18}O enrichment at
the stationary state δ_∞ (Dongmann et al., 1974):

$$\delta_\infty = \varepsilon_{eq} + \varepsilon_k(1 - h) + \delta_a h + \delta_s \qquad (1)$$

where ε_{eq} = equilibrium fractionation value of water
            evaporation
      ε_k = kinetic fractionation value of water
            evaporation
      δ_a = $^{18}O/^{16}O$ ratio of air humidity relative to
            the soil water
      δ_s = $^{18}O/^{16}O$ ratio of the soil water relative
            to the Vienna-SMOW
      h   = relative humidity (between 0 and 1).

All of the δ and ε values are stated in per mil. The ε values are constants derived from the fractionation factor α

$$\varepsilon = 1 - \alpha \qquad (2)$$

The validity of the model was confirmed within the experimental scattering by studying young oak trees in a wind track. The possibility to vary the air humidity was limited by the physiological behavior of the oaks. All of the data, as demonstrated in Figure 3, represent leaf samples after a manifold turnover of their water pool; that means the $^{18}O/^{16}O$ ratio of the leaf water is at a stationary state. The $^{18}O/^{16}O$ ratios are related to the initial water, which was used for humidity control as well as for the water supply of the plants. Therefore, during this experiment δ_a equalled $- \varepsilon_{eq}$. Because of the turbulent air stream condition, the following data were taken as theoretical values: ε_{eq} equal 9 per mil, ε_k equal 16 per mil.

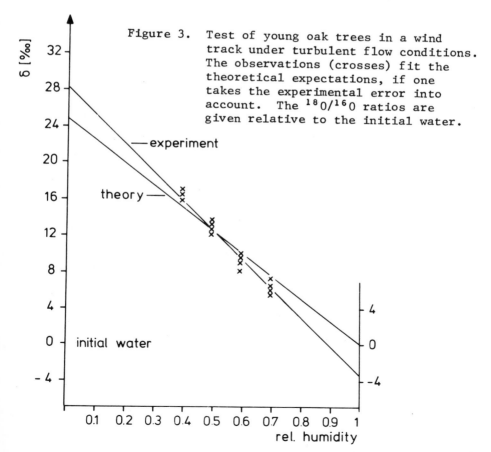

Figure 3. Test of young oak trees in a wind track under turbulent flow conditions. The observations (crosses) fit the theoretical expectations, if one takes the experimental error into account. The $^{18}O/^{16}O$ ratios are given relative to the initial water.

ε_{eq} and ε_k are constants, which depend on the environmental conditions. ε_{eq} depends on the temperature:

10.2 per mil at 10°C
9.2 per mil at 20°C
8.3 per mil at 30°C

The most varying parameter is ε_k, which is dependent on the air stream condition close to the water-air surface. At the leaf surface, there is an adjacent boundary layer across which the water vapor must diffuse into the free air. If the water vapor diffuses into a turbulent air, one can expect a value of 16 per mil. Under the conditions of laminar flow 21 per mil and during the diffusion into an air at rest 32 per mil can be obtained. From our experiments we got an impression of the variation of ε_k. Table I summarizes our results, which show a broad range between the lower limit of the theory (turbulence), and the medium value (laminar flow). This seems reasonable, if one looks to the open-air conditions. Table I also demonstrates that there is large variability even within a species during the day. Especially this variation within a day may

Table I

Kinetic fraction value ε_k (in per mil) of different species under various conditions. The values are reached by extrapolating the measurements at various humidities relative to zero humidity by the help of regression lines.

Conditions	Species	Daytime	ε_k (per mil)
Wind track[a,c]	Oak	–	23
Open-air[b]	Oak	9:00–11:30	20
		11:00–20:30	14
	Birch	9:00–11:30	21
		17:00–20:30	13
Open-air[a]	Birch	–	18
	Larch	–	17
	Spruce	–	24
	Range		13–24

[a]This work.
[b]Förstel *et al.*, 1974.
[c]The experimentally found ε_{ea} has been used.

be strengthened by the method of calculation: the ε_k values are obtained by the extrapolation of the measured values to a relative humidity of zero. For the calculation of this paper, four values of ε_k shall be considered: the two limits out of our open-air experiments, and the two theoretical limits.

The global value for the mean stationary enrichment of ^{18}O in the leaf water, which shall represent the photosynthetic oxygen under the assumptions mentioned above, is calculated in the following manner. At first $-\varepsilon_k$ is substituted for δ_a (Durm and Förstel, 1977). This results in Equation 3:

$$\bar{\delta}_\infty = (\varepsilon_{eq} + \varepsilon_k)\,(1 - \bar{h}) + \bar{\delta}_s \qquad (3)$$

The parameters $\bar{h}$ and $\bar{\delta}_s$ shall be the global averages, which are weighted by the local productivity pattern. For these calculations, the earth has been subdivided into equal zones of 15° latitude. Figure 4 shows the percentage of total continental productivity in each zone (Lieth, 1975; Box, 1975). Half of the productivity is situated at ± 15° latitude around the equator. Therefore, data from this area are very important.

Well-distributed information on the diurnal course of the relative humidity are not common. We used the maps of the USSR Academy of Sciences (Gerasimov, 1964) which contained only the averages of the whole days. These averages show a

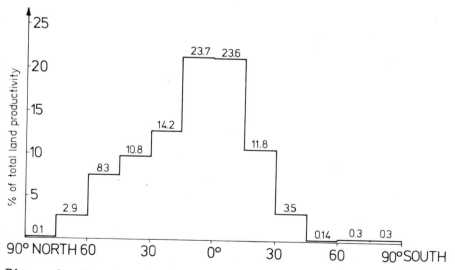

Figure 4.   Percent continental productivity within 15° latitude zones of the earth (data after Lieth, 1975).

relative humidity of 85% between 15° S and 15° N around the
equator, and 70% for all other continental areas. To get the
relative humidity of the time of photosynthetic activity
only – the mean relative humidity from the morning to the evening – we compared data of 25 tropical stations taken in early
morning and at noon. A mean difference of about 15% (lower
data at noon) was observed, but for calculation the mean values
were lowered by 10% only (Air Ministry U.K., 1958). The
following estimates of the relative humidities at the time of
the photosynthetic activity have been used:

$$h \text{ (15° N to 15° S)} = 75\%$$
$$h \text{ (elsewhere)} \quad = 60\%$$

For the global mean of the $^{18}O/^{16}O$ ratio, the precipitation of the soil water can be calculated from the histogram
in Figure 5. A world map of the $^{18}O/^{16}O$ ratio pattern was
produced with the help of 59 stations, and the average of each
15°-latitude section was calculated. By weighting these values
by the productivity of each section, a global mean of -5.1
per mil relative to Vienna-SMOW was obtained.

Therefore, one can now calculate the global $^{18}O/^{16}O$
ratio of leaf water, *i.e.*, of oxygen from the land plant community. The average annual temperature (Budyko, 1975), weighted by the productivity histogram, is 20° C. The important
tropical regions show only small seasonal variation. The ε_k

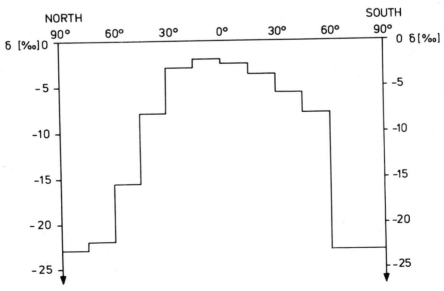

Figure 5.   Histogram of the $^{18}O/^{16}O$ ratios of precipitation
relative to Vienna-SMOW within 15° latitude zones
of the earth (data from IAEA, 1971).

values are given as a range. Table II presents the results of the calculation (Equation 2). The range of photosynthetic oxygen produced by the land plants may vary between the limits 2 to 6 per mil (taking the theoretical limits) relative to Vienna-SMOW. If one takes into account a rapid exchange across the sea surface, the values must be lowered according to the land-sea productivity ratio.

As a result, one can expect that the contribution of photosynthesis by the land plants to the Dole effect does not exceed 5 to 6 per mil, but it must be lower if one regards the marine algae. Including the ocean productivity, the upper limit may not exceed 3 to 4 per mil.

Three sources of error must be taken into account:

1. The ε_k values seem to have the most uncertain parameter. They vary not only because of different flow conditions, but also because of physiological differences between the species at various states. It is necessary to look at a possible variation of ε_{eq} under natural conditions.
2. The $^{18}O/^{16}O$ ratio of the air humidity in tropical forest must be known.
3. More ^{18}O enrichment curves from various plant communities, especially from the tropical rain forests, should be known.

Nevertheless, as a general rule, one is able to say that the contribution of land plants to the Dole effect is a limited one, but may explain the gap between the results of the fractionation measurements during respiration and the total atmospheric ^{18}O enrichment.

Table II

Values and Final Calculation of the Global Stationary $^{18}O/^{16}O$ in Leaf Water (per mil relative to Vienna-SMOW). All per mil values are given in whole numbers.

ε_{eq} (per mil)	ε_k (per mil)	h (percent)	δ_s (per mil)	Result of Land Plant Only (per mil)	Result Including Sea[a] (per mil)
9^b	Experimental limits 13	0.67	-5	2	1
	24			6	4
	Theoretical limits 16			3	2
	21			5	3

[a] Land-to-sea ratio by Lieth (1974).

[b] At 20°C.

REFERENCES

Air Ministry U.K., Meteological Office. *Tables of Temperature, Relative Humidity and Precipitation for the World, Part I-VI* (London: Air Ministry U.K., 1958).

Box, E. "Quantitative Evaluation of Global Primary Productivity Models Generated by Computer Maps," in *Primary Productivity of the Biosphere*, H. Lieth and R.H. Whittaker, Eds. (Berlin, Heidelberg, New York: Springer, 1975), pp. 265-283.

Budyko, M.I. *Climate and Life* (New York, London: Academic Press, 1974), p. 243.

Craig, H. "Standard for Reporting Concentrations of Deuterium and Oxygen-18 in Natural Waters," *Science* 133:1833-1834 (1961).

Dole, M. "The Relative Atomic Weight of Oxygen in Water and in Air," *J. Am. Chem. Soc.* 57:2731 (1935).

Dongmann, G., H. Förstel and K. Wagener. "^{18}O-Rich Oxygen from Land Photosynthesis," *Nature New Biology* 240:127-128 (1972).

Dongmann, G., H.W. Nürnberg, H. Förstel and K. Wagener. "On the Enrichment of $H_2^{18}O$ in the Leaves of Transpiring Plants," *Rad. Environ. Biophys.* 11:41-52 (1974).

Durm, A., and H. Förstel. "$^{18}O/^{16}O$ Ratios of Atmospheric Water Vapour During the Year/Measurements at Jülich 1973," *Rad. Environ. Biophys.* (1977).

Förstel, H., H. Bernhardt and G. Schleser. *Tagesgang der $H_2$$^{18}O$-Anreicherung im Blattwasser von Eiche und Birke. Jül-1139-PC* (1974).

Förstel, H., A. Putral, G. Schleser and H. Lieth. "The World Pattern of ^{18}O in Rainwater and its Importance for the Biogeochemical Oxygen Cycle," *IAEA Symposium on Isotope Ratios as Pollutant Source and Behavior Indicators* (Vienna: IAEA, 1974), pp. 3-20.

Gerasimov, I.P., Ed. *Fisiko-geografitscheskij Atlas Mira* (Moscow: Akademija Nauk SSSR, 1964).

Gonfiantini, R., S. Gratziu and E. Tongiorgi. "Oxygen Isotopic Composition of Water in Leaves," in *Use of Isotopes and Radiation in Soil Plant Nutrition Studies* (Vienna: IAEA, 1965), pp. 405-410.

IAEA. "Environmental Isotope Data No. 3: World Survey of Isotope Concentration in Precipitation 1966-1967," *IAEA Tech. Rep. Ser.* 129 (1971).

Lane, G.A., and M. Dole. "Fractionation of Oxygen Isotopes During Respiration," *Science* 123:574-576 (1956).

Lieth, H. "Modelling the Primary Productivity of the World," in *Primary Productivity of the Biosphere*, H. Lieth and R.H. Whittaker, Eds. (Berlin, Heidelberg, New York: Springer, 1975), pp. 237–263.

Lieth, H. "Basis und Grenze der Menschheitsentwicklung: Stoffproduktion der Pflanzen," *Umschau* 74:169–174 (1974).

Rabinowitch, E.I. *Photosynthesis and Related Processes*, Vol. 1 (New York: Wiley-Interscience, 1947), p. 10.

Vinogradov, A.P., V.M. Kutyurin, M.V. Ulembekova and I.K. Zadoroshny. "Isotopnij sostav kisloroda fotosyntesa i duchanie," *Doklady AN SSSR* 134:1486–1489 (1960).

CONTRIBUTION OF THE RESPIRATORY OXYGEN ISOTOPE FRACTIONATION TO THE ^{18}O BUDGET OF THE ATMOSPHERE

G.H. SCHLESER

Institute of Biophysical Chemistry
ICH 2, Nuclear Research Center Jülich
5710 Jülich, Federal Republic of Germany

INTRODUCTION

The starting point of the present investigation was the established fact that atmospheric oxygen is enriched in ^{18}O relative to ocean water. Though this difference in the isotopic composition of oxygen has been known for some decades, and was first reported by Dole (1935), Morita (1935), and Morita and Titani (1936), the cause of this effect is not yet fully understood. From the beginning it was clear, however, that essential contributions can only be expected during the turnover of oxygen within the biocycles. This led to investigations of isotope fractionation during the uptake of oxygen, *i.e.*, during respiration and the release of oxygen by photosynthesis.

The $^{18}O/^{16}O$ ratio of atmospheric oxygen has been determined in the course of this work to be $\delta^{18}O = 23.65°/_{oo}$. δ is the per mil enrichment of ^{18}O relative to the SMOW-standard (SMOW = standard mean ocean water) (Craig, 1961).

The contribution of photosynthesis on land to the enhanced ^{18}O content of the atmosphere was calculated to be $\delta^{18}O = 4.5 °/_{oo}$. This determination was based on experimental data from Dongmann (1972), and Durm and Förstel (1977), together with a model of Dongmann and Wagener (1974) on the enrichment in $H_2^{18}O$ of transpiring leaves and the assumption of Ruben (1941) and Vinogradov (1947), that photosynthetic oxygen contains the same isotopic composition as oxygen bound in leaf water. In relation to the ^{18}O enrichment of the atmosphere, this value leads to the conclusion that the respiratory processes have to be far more important than photosynthesis. Measurements of oxygen isotope fractionation factors during respiration of typical biological systems revealed much higher values (Lane and Dole, 1956). The large differences in the fractionation factors for various biological systems make it rather difficult, however, to determine the total contribution of the respiratory oxygen isotope fractionation on land to the ^{18}O budget of the atmosphere. Soil microorganisms especially showed rather large differences.

Soil respiration, however, accounts for almost 75% of the global respiration on land. Therefore it seemed justified to center the investigations on soil respiration, *i.e.*, soil microorganisms (fungi, bacteria), which are by far the most important community with respect to respiration. Under the assumption that organisms of the same class, like fungi or bacteria, show identical oxygen isotope fractionation factors if equal respiration rates are compared, a bacterial culture and a yeast culture were investigated as representative strains of their classes.

By calculating a mean global respiration rate and correlating this figure with the corresponding respiration rates of the investigated cultures, it is possible to extract a mean global oxygen isotope fractionation factor for respiration on land.

NOTATIONS AND DEFINITIONS

The investigations were carried out with the help of steady-state cultures. This procedure provides the possibility of maintaining fixed conditions within a culture independent of time. In this context a number of quantities are important and will be defined subsequently.

The uptake of oxygen in mg/hr related to the biomass (mg dry weight) of the culture is denoted as specific respiration rate and will be designated by Q:

$$Q = (1/N) \times (\Delta O_2 / \Delta t) \quad [1/hr]$$

The specific growth rate μ is designated by μ and stands for the increase in biomass (mg dry weight) per hour related to the biomass of the culture:

$$\mu = (1/N) \times (\Delta N / \Delta t) \quad [1/hr]$$

In the steady state, the specific growth rate is equal to the dilution rate D, defined as the ratio of the medium flow rate to the culture volume, *i.e.*, the number of complete volume changes per hour.

$$D = f/v \quad [1/hr]$$

The oxygen isotope fractionation factor α for respiring organisms is given as the ratio of the ^{18}O-mole fraction X_3 of respired oxygen to the initial ^{18}O-mole fraction X_1 (see Figure 1).

$$\alpha_r = X_3/X_1$$

Heeding the mass balance for oxygen and the ^{18}O-mole fraction, this leads to a fractionation factor of:

$$\alpha_r = (R_1/R_3) \times [1 - (R_2/R_1) \times (X_2/X_1)] \qquad \text{(see Figure 1)}$$

This leads to a value of $\alpha < 1$ and, therefore, a definition by Dole (1956) is commonly used in literature. In this case, α is defined as the percentage ratio of ^{18}O in the oxygen of the air in contact with the organisms to the percentage of ^{18}O in the oxygen being consumed by the organism at any moment.

$$\alpha = X_2/X_3 \qquad \text{(see Figure 1)}$$

Both values will be used in this paper.

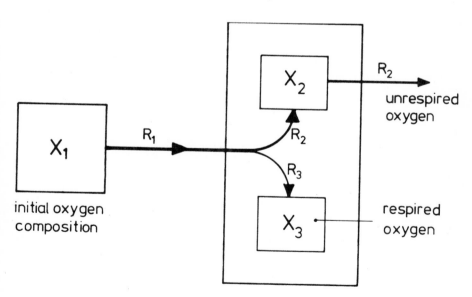

Figure 1. Diagram of the oxygen flow for the derivation of the isotope fractionation factor.

X_i: represents the steady-state ^{18}O-mole fraction of the ith reservoir

R_i: rate of oxygen from the ith or into the ith reservoir.

MATERIALS AND METHODS

Two different types of microorganisms were used for the experiments. A strain of *E. coli* K 12 Ymel λ-lysogen and a strain of *Torulopsis utilis* (ATCC 9256).

The bacterial strain was grown in a medium of the following composition: 0.03 M KCl, 0.001 M MgCl$_2$ x 6 H$_2$O, 0.09 M Na$_2$HPO$_4$ x 2 H$_2$O, 0.03 M NaH$_2$PO$_4$ x H$_2$O, 0.015 M (NH$_4$)$_2$ SO$_4$, 2.8 mM glucose filled up to 1 liter with distilled water. The pH value settled at roughly 7.15 and did not change throughout the experiments. Glucose was the growth-limiting component, all other components being present in excess.

The yeast was grown in a medium of the following composition: 0.072 M NaH PO$_4$ x 2H$_2$O, 0.0123 M (NH$_4$)$_2$SO$_4$, 0.013 M KCl, 0.001 M MgSO$_4$ x 7H$_2$O, 0.17 mM CaCl$_2$ x 2H$_2$O, 0.012 mM ZnSO$_4$ 7H$_2$O, 0.0064 mM Fe(NH$_4$)$_2$(SO$_4$)$_2$ x 6H$_2$O, 0.5 μM CuSO$_4$ x 5H$_2$O, 0.044 μM MnSO$_4$ x H$_2$O, 0.07 μM CoSO, 0.017 μM Na$_2$MoO4 x 2HO, 0.02 μM biotin. Either glycerol or glucose was the growth-limiting component, all other components being used present in excess. The pH value was kept at 4.5 throughout the the experiments.

A small laboratory-type chemostat (BRAUN, Melsungen, Typ Biostat, FRG) with a working capacity of 2.5 liter was used for all experiments. Aeration is accomplished by a vane-disk stirrer mounted on a central shaft, with baffles attached to the outer part of a cylindrical heating unit surrounding the stirrer. The level of liquid in the vessel is maintained constant by two membrane pumps which control the in- and out-flow of nutrient solution.

The flow system of air is shown in Figure 2. Control of the flow rate is achieved by a flow meter (Rota App. u. Maschinenbau, Oeflingen, Typ Rota L 0.63/33-3887, FRG).

Gas samples were taken from sampling units at the input and output side of the flow system (Figure 2). Their preparation - *i.e.*, the conversion of its oxygen content to carbon dioxide for isotope ratio measurements - necessitates the separation of oxygen from all other components (CO$_2$, H$_2$O, N$_2$) which are present in the sampling units. Carbon dioxide and water were separated with the help of cooling traps, using isopentane of 120K as coolant. To make sure that the cooling system retains all of the carbon dioxide evolved by microorganism of the chemostat, every sample was checked for its carbon dioxide content. A liquid column closes the end of the gas line to prevent back flow of laboratory air into the system. The whole system is gastight in order to avoid distortions of the oxygen isotope composition. A gas chromatographic column filled with 5 Å molecular sieve is used to separate oxygen from nitrogen before the oxygen gas is converted to carbon dioxide. For technical details, see the publication by

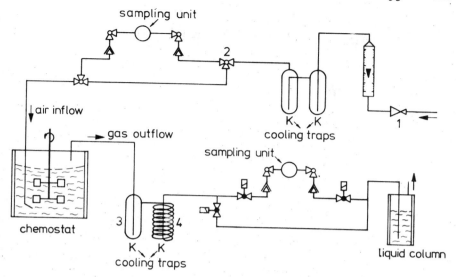

Figure 2. Schematic view of the air flow through the culture
vessel and the sampling units.

Förstel *et al.* (1976). The oxygen isotope ratio measurements
were performed with a precision double collector mass spectrometer (VG Micromass, Winsford, type Micromass 602C, England).
       Gas samples were taken only when the chemostat culture
proved to be in a steady state. This is necessary in order
to guarantee fixed physiological conditions for which only
constant oxygen uptake rates can be expected. Steady-state
conditions were checked by measuring the turbidity every
third hour and controlling the protein content of the culture.
Figure 3 illustrates the steady-state concentrations (biomass
as dry weight) calculated from turbidity data at three different
specific growth rates, $D = \mu$, of the chemostat population.
       For each steady state, the fractionation factor α
was determined and related to the corresponding oxygen uptake
rate of the culture. The oxygen uptake rate was determined by
interrupting the inflow of air into the culture and reducing
the agitation to 50 rpm. The following decrease of the dissolved oxygen concentration in the cutlure against time is
plotted in Figure 4 for different specific growth rates. With
simultaneous determination of the biomass (dry weight), the
specific respiration rate for each specific growth rate was
obtained (see also Schleser and Förstel , 1975).

RESULTS AND DISCUSSION

       Measurements of oxygen isotope fractionation factors
have been carried out for a large number of different specific
respiration rates Q. For *E. coli* K 12 the specific respiration

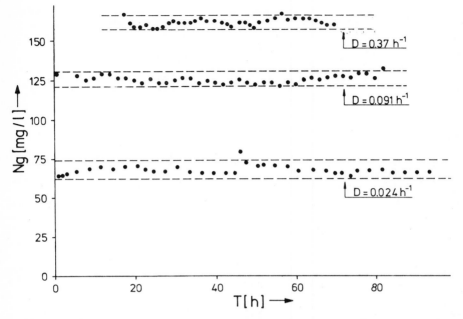

Figure 3.   Steady-state biomass concentration (dry weight) of
            E. coli K 12 for three different dilution rates D.
            The dotted lines represent the 95% fiducial limits.

rate was varied from Q = 0.025 hr^{-1} to 0.43 hr^{-1}. For *Torulop-sis utilis*, Q was varied from Q = 0.125 hr^{-1} to Q = 0.31 hr^{-1}.
The corresponding fractionation factors α are plotted in Figure
5. In the case of *E. coli*, it is seen that α depends very much
on the specific respiration rate, but levels off to a fixed
value of about $\alpha \simeq 1.011$ for very low values of Q. Contrary
to the bacterial culture, the yeast culture only shows a weak
functionality of the fractionation factor α with Q. The lowest values range in the order of $\alpha \simeq 1.018$ and latest measurements indicate that no significant decrease in α towards lower
specific respiration rates is to be expected.

      Assuming that these results are representative for
soil microorganisms, *i.e.*, bacteria and fungi, it is possible
to derive a mean global value of the oxygen isotope fractionation factor during respiration on land, if a global specific
respiration rate Q is known. The above measured fractionation
factors of the appropriate specific respiration rate can then
be correlated to this value.

      The global specific respiration rate was obtained in
the following way: the majority of soil microorganisms are
chemoorganotrophic organisms which obtain their energy through
the oxidation of organic H-donors. This means that the
oxidation is coupled to the primary productivity via

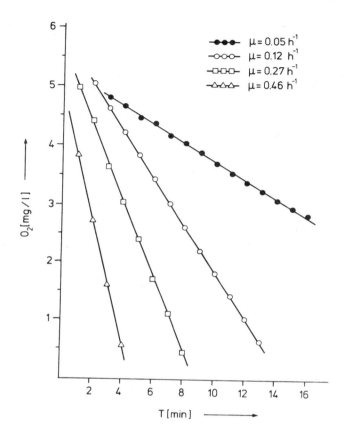

Figure 4. Oxygen consumption of *E. coli* K 12 for different
specific growth rates, measured as the time-
dependent decrease of the dissolved oxygen within
the nutrient solution (carbon source: succinic
acid; pH = 7.0; T = 37°C).

photosynthesis. Therefore, the oxygen consumption of soil
microorganisms on the earth should follow from the net primary
productivity, assuming that the ecosystems under consideration
are in steady state.

For a first approach, it may be accepted that all
the oxygen is used to decompose glucose. Thus, from the productivity data of the continents follows an estimate of the
overall respiratory activity Q:

$$Q = \frac{f}{365 \times 24} \times \frac{<P>}{B \times <V>}$$

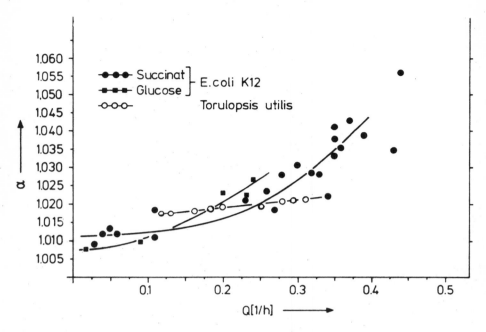

Figure 5.   Oxygen isotope fractionation factor α plotted
versus the specific respiration rate Q.

The conversion factor f gives the correlation between glucose
and oxygen, <P> stands for the mean global productivity and
<V> stands for the average vegetation period in years.   The
averaged biomass is given by B.   For the assessment of a mean
continental productivity figure, data from Lieth (1974) were
used.   With the productivity $P(A_\nu)$ given in all areas A_ν of
the earth, the continental productivity <P> amounts to:

$$<P> = \frac{\Sigma P(A_\nu) \times A_\nu}{\Sigma A_\nu} \times 672.4 \text{ g/m}^2/a$$

The mean vegetation period <V> has been calculated using the
vegetation periods of all productivity areas.   The productivi-
ties with the corresponding areas have been taken as weighting
factors.

$$V = \frac{\Sigma A_\nu \times P(A_\nu) \times V(A_\nu)}{\Sigma A_\nu \times P(A_\nu)} = 0.73 \text{ a}$$

For a biomass $B = 265$ g/m^2 (calculated from Brauns, 1968), the following respiration rate Q is evaluated:

$$Q = 0.42 \text{ g/kg/hr}$$

The respiratory activity as calculated above can only be taken as a crude estimate. This average value is very low compared to laboratory measurements of individual species and indicates that fractionation factors α have to be chosen which correspond to even lower specific respiration rates than reported here. The experiments show, however, that for extremely low specific respiration rates, no further decrease in the fractionation factor is to be expected.

All experiments have been run at optimum temperatures for the respective microorganisms. This implies higher temperatures than normally will be encountered in nature. Measurements at various temperatures have shown, however, that a slight increase in α with decreasing temperature is found (Schleser, 1977). As the most active soil respiration is expected in tropical areas for which an average temperature of 24°C has been assumed, appropriate temperature corrections for α lead to the following oxygen isotope fractionation factors:

$$\alpha = 1.01295 \quad \text{contribution of } E.\ coli$$
$$\alpha = 1.01995 \quad \text{contribution of } T.\ utilis$$

According to Anderson and Domsch (1973), the ratio of the respiratory activity between fungi and bacteria within the soil amounts to about 7:3. Heeding this ratio, the contribution of soil respiration to the enhanced ^{18}O concentration of the atmosphere results in:

$$\alpha = 1.01764$$

For representation of the whole biological oxygen cycle with its two contributions to the enhanced ^{18}O content of the atmosphere, it is more convenient to cite the fractionation factor α_r which is easily calculated to be:

$$\alpha_r = 0.9824$$

Figure 6 summarizes the results. From this diagram, it is seen that the respiratory oxygen isotope fractionation is the most important contribution to the enhanced ^{18}O budget of the atmosphere.

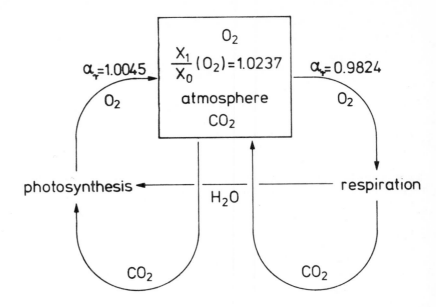

Figure 6.   The ^{18}O fractionation factors α_r for the continental oxygen cycle. X_1/X_0 represents the steady-state ^{18}O enrichment of the atmosphere relative to SMOW.

REFERENCES

Anderson, I.P.E., and K.H. Domsch. "Quantification of Bacterial and Fungal Contributions to Soil Respiration," *Acta Bio.* 7:113 (1973).

Brauns, A. *Praktische Bodenbiologie* (Stuttgart: G. Fischer Verlag, 1968).

Craig, H. "Standard for Reporting Concentrations of Deuterium and Oxygen-18 in Natural Waters," *Science* 133:1833 (1961).

Dole, M. "The Relative Atomic Weight of Oxygen in Water and in Air," *J. Am. Chem. Soc.* 57:2731 (1935).

Dongmann, G. "Die $H_2{}^{18}O$-Anreicherung in den Blättern transpirierender Pflanzen und ihre Bedeutung für die stationäre ^{18}O-Überhöhung in der Atmosphäre," Ph.D. Thesis, Aachen (1972).

Dongmann, B., H.W. Nürnberg, H. Förstel and K. Wagener. "On the Enrichment of $H_2{}^{18}O$ in the Leaves of Transpiring Plants," *Rad. Environ. Biophys.* 11:41 (1974).

Durm, A., and H. Förstel. "$^{18}O/^{16}O$ Ratios of Atmospheric Water Vapour During the Year - Measurements at Jülich 1973," *Rad. Environ. Biphys.* (1977).

Förstel, H., B. Weiner and G. Schleser. "Preparation of Oxygen Samples for $^{18}O/^{16}O$ Measurements by a Combined Gas Chromatography-Burning Technique," *Int. J. Appl. Rad. Isot.* 27:211 (1976).

Lane, G.A., and M. Dole. "Fractionation of Oxygen Isotopes During Respiration," *Science* 123:574 (1956).

Lieth, H. "Basis und Grenze der Menschheitsentwicklung: Stoffproduktion der Pflanzen," *Umschau* 74:169 (1974).

Morita, N., and T. Titani. "The Difference in the Isotopic Composition of Oxygen from the Atmosphere and from Water," *Bull. Chem. Soc. Japan* 11:36 (1936).

Morita, N. "The Increased Density of Air Oxygen Relative to Water Oxygen," *J. Chem. Soc. Japan* 56:1291 (1935).

Ruben, S., A. Randall, M. Kamen and J.L. Hyde. "Heavy O (^{18}O) as a Tracer in the Study of Photosynthesis," *J. Am. Chem. Soc.* 63:877 (1941).

Schleser, G. "Die Isotopenfraktionierung des Sauerstoffs bei der Respiration: Untersuchungen an dem Bakterienstamm *E. Coli* K 12 und der Hefe *Torulopsis utilis*," Ph.D. Thesis, Aachen (1977).

Schleser, G., and H. Förstel. "Geochemical Importance of Isotopic Fractionation During Respiration," *Proc. of the 2nd International Conference on Stable Isotopes*, E.R. Klein and P.D. Klein, Eds. (Argonne: Argonne National Laboratory, 1975).

Vinogradov, A.P., and R.V. Teis. "Isotope Composition of Oxygen of Different Origins," *Doklady Acad. Sci. USSR* 56:59 (1947).

SECTION III

BIOGEOCHEMISTRY AND GEOMICROBIOLOGY OF METALS WITH
SPECIAL REFERENCE TO MANGANESE NODULE ENVIRONMENTS

CONDITIONS FOR BACTERIAL PARTICIPATION IN THE INITIATION OF MANGANESE DEPOSITION AROUND MARINE SEDIMENT PARTICLES

H. L. EHRLICH

Department of Biology
Rensselaer Polytechnic Institute
Troy, New York 12181 USA

INTRODUCTION

Bacteria have been detected on ferromanganese nodules and in deep sea sediments. These bacteria have the ability to oxidize Mn(II) after it is first bound to Mn(IV) oxide (Ehrlich, 1963, 1968; Ehrlich *et al.*, 1972). These bacteria appear unable to oxidize free Mn^{2+} ion. The nodules on which the bacteria reside may form around nuclei that may be pumice, altered basaltic rock or glass, clays, tuffaceous material, silica (as in diatom frustules or radiolarian tests), carbonate (as in foraminiferal, coccolith or pteropod remains), or phosphorite (Burns and Burns, 1975; Crerar and Barnes, 1974), or something as spectacular as a shark's tooth or an ear bone of a whale, none of which normally contain Mn(IV) but which can adsorb Mn^{2+}. This raises the question whether the Mn(II)-oxidizing bacteria can catalyze the oxidation of Mn(II) adsorbed to something other than Mn(IV) oxide and thus help in the initiation of ferromanganese nodule formation. The following experiments were designed to seek an answer to this question.

MATERIALS AND METHODS

Culture

The bacterial culture employed for these experiments was isolated from a Pacific ferromanganese nodule. It was designated strain BIII 45 and may be related to *Oceanospirillum* (Krieg, 1976). The culture was grown either on slants of

sea water-nutrient agar (Difco) or slants of diluted sea
water-nutrient agar (0.8 g nutrient broth, Difco, 15 g agar,
1000 ml natural sea water). Roux bottle slants were used to
prepare cell inocula for experiments. Incubation was at
15° C for 24 hr. Cells were harvested, washed three times
in sterile, natural sea water, and resuspended in sterile
natural sea water to a concentration of about 10^9 cells per
ml, determined by turbidity measurement of a tenfold diluted
sample.

Sediments

Sediment samples from the Atlantic (A_1-A_5) and the
Pacific Oceans (P_1 and P_2), collected in 1962 and 1970,
respectively, were used. The sediment samples had been stored
in a freezer. Samples A_1, A_2, A_4 and A_5 appeared sterile
when portions were tested in sea water-nutrient broth at the
time of the present experiments, although they harbored
bacteria at the time of their collection. The Atlantic samples
were obtained with a gravity corer, while the Pacific samples
were obtained with a box corer. Table I lists the origin of
these samples. Sediment samples from gravity cores were

Table I
Sources of Sediment Samples

Sample Number	Approximate Sediment Depth (cm)	Nature of Sediment	Location Latitude	Longitude
A_1	15	red clay	27° 10.2'N	65° 42' W
A_2	surface	red clay	25° 29' N	66° 43' W
A_3	surface	red & blue clay	26° 59' N	72° 12.5'W
A_4	138	red & blue clay	23° 31' N	70° 2.5' W
A_5	77	red clay	27° 10.2'N	65° 42' W
P_1	surface	red clay	Eastern Pacific north of equator	
P_2	surface	red clay	Eastern Pacific north of equator	

obtained with a sterile cork borer with which subcores were taken by lateral penetration through the core liner. Only the uncontaminated portion of each subcore was used for study. Sediment samples from box cores were obtained with sterile glass tubes.

Manganese Removal Test

Manganous ion removal by sediment was tested in 50-ml Erlenmeyer flasks, each containing 0.2 g of a given sediment sample. Each condition was run in duplicate. To measure Mn^{2+} removal in the absence of added bacteria, each of two flasks received 8 ml sterile, natural sea water (pH 7.5), 1 ml 0.04 M $MnSO_4 \cdot H_2O$, and 1 ml of 0.114 M $NaHCO_3$ (pH 7.5). To measure Mn^{2+} removal in the presence of bacteria, each of two flasks received 7 ml sterile natural sea water (pH 7.5), 1 ml 0.04 M $MnSO_4 \cdot H_2O$ and 1 ml washed cell suspension of bacterial strain BIII 45.

When the effect of pretreatment with iron was to be tested, four flasks with sediment received 7 ml sterile, natural sea water (pH 7.5) and 0.2 ml 0.0019 M $FeCl_3 \cdot 6H_2O$. The flasks were then incubated overnight at 15° C. On testing for Mn(II)-oxidation the next day, the following solutions were added to the solution already in the four flasks: 1 ml 0.04 M $MnSO_4 \cdot H_2O$ and 1 ml 0.114 M $NaHCO_3$ (pH 7.5). Two of the flasks then received 1 ml sterile sea water and the remaining two received 2 ml washed cell suspension. All flasks were then incubated for 4 hr at 15° C, after which 3.5-ml aliquots were removed from each flask, centrifuged at 4500 x g for 5 min, and two 1-ml aliquots of the supernatant fluid assayed for residual dissolved manganese by the persulfate assay (Ehrlich, 1963).

To check the initial manganese concentration, two sets of duplicate flasks were set up without sediment, each containing 8 ml sterile, natural sea water (pH 7.5), 1 ml of 0.04 M $MnSO_4 \cdot H_2O$, and 1 ml 0.114 M $NaHCO_3$ (pH 7.5). One set also received 0.2 ml 0.0019 M $FeCl_3 \cdot 6H_2O$ solution. Two 1-ml aliquots from all four flasks were immediately assayed for dissolved manganese after centrifuging at 4500 x g.

RESULTS

All sediments tested caused Mn^{2+} removal from solution in the absence of bacteria during four hours of incubation at 15° C. The presence of bacterial strain BIII 45 did not increase the amount of Mn^{2+} removed by the sediment in a reaction mixture that was free of added iron or to which ferric chloride had been added at the start of the Mn^{2+} removal test (Table II, columns 2 and 3). Only when a sediment sample had been preincubated overnight in the presence of 5.27 x 10^{-5}

Table II
Effect of Fe(III) on Mn^{2+} Removal by Sediment
in the Presence of Bacteria

Sediment Sample[a]	ΔMn^{2+} Removed in 4 hr due to Bacteria (nmol/ml)[b]		
	No Fe Pretreatment[c]	Mn+Fe Mixture[d]	Fe Pretreatment[e]
A_1	0	+10	-40
A_2	+10	+10	-30
A_3	+10	0	0
A_4	+10	0	-20
A_5	0	0	-40
P_1	ND[f]	ND	-30
P_2	0	ND	0

[a] Inocula for sediment samples A_1 through A_4, P_1 and P_2 were grown on dilute sea water nutrient agar. Inoculum for A_5 was grown on undiluted sea water nutrient agar.

[b] ΔMn^{2+} equals nanomoles Mn/ml removed in 4 hr in the absence of bacteria minus nanomoles Mn/ml removed in 4 hr in the presence of bacteria. Negative values indicate that more Mn^{2+} was removed in the presence than in the absence of bacteria. Positive values indicate that more Mn^{2+} was removed in the absence than in the presence of bacteria. A zero value indicates that equal amounts of Mn^{2+} were removed in the presence and absence of bacteria.

[c] Experiment without iron-pretreatment.

[d] Experiment with Fe and Mn added concurrently.

[e] Experiment involving overnight pretreatment with ferric chloride.

[f] Not determined.

M ferric chloride, did bacteria enhance its ability to remove Mn^{2+} from solution (Table II, column 4). The increase in the amount of Mn^{2+} removed in 4 hr by iron-pretreated sediment due to bacterial activity ranged from about 1 to 11 percent.

In the absence of bacteria, two iron-pretreated sediments (A_1 and A_4) removed more Mn^{2+} from solution than unpretreated sediment (Table III). One (A_1) did so even in a Mn+Fe mixture. However, in the presence of bacteria, the pretreated sediments removed even more Mn^{2+} (1180 and 1540 nmol/ml, respectively). On the other hand, of sediments A_2 and A_3, which without bacteria did not remove more Mn^{2+} after pretreatment with iron, sediment A_2 showed increased

Table III
Mn^{2+} Removal by Sediments in the Absence of
Bacteria under Various Conditions

Sediment Sample[a]	ΔMn^{2+} Removed in 4 hr $(nmol/ml)$[b]		
	No Fe Pretreatment[c]	Mn+Fe Mixture[d]	Fe Pretreatment[e]
A	1120	1140	1140
A	1270	1250	1250
A	1410	1380	1380
A	1510	1500	1520
A	1250	1180	1190
P	--	--	620
P	800	--	440

[a] See Table II.

[b] ΔMn^{2+} equals the difference between initial Mn^{2+} concentration and final Mn^{2+} concentration after 4 hr in the absence of bacteria.

[c] See Table II.

[d] See Table II.

[e] See Table II.

Mn^{2+} removal after pretreatment with iron (1280 nmol/ml) when tested with bacteria, while sediment A_3 did not. Sample P_2 after pretreatment with iron also did not show enhanced Mn^{2+} removal in the presence of bacteria.

DISCUSSION

The removal of Mn^{2+} from solution by sediment involves mainly adsorption and is assumed to follow the reaction sequence described by Ehrlich (1975). Autoxidation of Mn^{2+} under the conditions of the experiments is negligible. The role of the bacteria in Mn^{2+} removal by sediment is to promote oxidation of adsorbed Mn^{2+} to Mn(IV) oxide, which can then scavenge additional Mn^{2+} which, in turn, can be oxidized by bacteria. Thus it is the oxidizing activity of the bacteria that increases the number of adsorption sites by generating Mn(IV) oxides and thereby increasing the amount of Mn^{2+} removed from solution by sediment in a given amount of time. This is in contrast to the situation in which bacteria are absent. Few or no new adsorption sites are created on the sediment because of the negligible autoxidation of adsorbed Mn(II). The observation that the increase in Mn^{2+} removal due to bacterial action ranges from only 1 to 11 percent is consistent with the observation that Mn^{2+} adsorption is much more rapid than subsequent oxidation of adsorbed Mn^{2+} in our experiments.

As the experiments in the present work have shown, direct adsorption of Mn^{2+} by sediment is not sufficient to permit bacterial action. Only if sediment is preincubated with ferric iron are the bacteria able to cause increased Mn^{2+} removal by it at all. But even then, not every type of pretreated sediment responds to the bacteria. Since no detailed analysis of the sediment samples used is available, it is not possible to say what accounts for these differences in behavior of the sediments. A more extensive study with larger sediment samples is needed to resolve this question.

The present work suggests that bacteria can assist in the initiation of ferromanganese nodule formation around nuclei other than those consisting of ferromanganese, but only after prior reaction with iron, which would not have been necessary if Mn(IV) oxide had been the adsorbent. What the role of the iron is relative to the bacterial activity remains to be elucidated.

Burns and Burns (1975) have proposed that crystal structure relationships exist between host Mn(IV) oxide and hydrated iron oxide. They have observed a hydrated iron oxide phase at the boundaries between nodule nuclei and ferromanganese oxide layers. They attribute the iron oxide precipitation to locally high pH due to the dissolution and hydrolysis of carbonate, silicate, or phosphate anions from the nuclei. They view the hydrated ferric oxide as a template for laying down specific minerological forms of Mn(IV) oxide by epitaxial growth. While Burns and Burns seem to view the initial deposition of ferric oxide on nodule nuclei as a universal requirement for initiation of nodule growth, Morgan (1975) has restricted this need to silicate nuclei. Although these observations and conclusions may help in the mineralogical explanation of nodule growth initiation, they do not help in explaining the effect of the iron on the bacterial action based on the present information, since active bacteria have been shown to oxidize Mn(II) adsorbed to Mn(IV) oxide in the absence of added iron (*e.g.*, Ehrlich, 1968).

ACKNOWLEDGMENTS

The expert technical assistance of Alice R. Ellett is gratefully acknowledged. This work was supported by research grant No. DES73-06583 from the National Science Foundation.

REFERENCES

Burns, R. G. and V. M. Burns. "Mechanism for Nucleation and Growth of Manganese Nodules," *Nature* (London) 255:130–131 (1975).

Crerar, D. A. and H. L. Barnes. "Deposition of Deep-Sea Manganese Nodules," *Geochim. et Cosmochim. Acta* 38:279–300 (1974).

Ehrlich, H. L. "Bacteriology of Manganese Nodules. I. Bacterial Action on Manganese in Nodule Enrichments," *Appl. Microbiol.* 11:15–19 (1963).

Ehrlich, H. L. "Bacteriology of Manganese Nodules. II. Manganese Oxidation by Cell-Free Extract from a Manganese Nodule Bacterium," *Appl. Microbiol.* 16:335–359 (1968).

Ehrlich, H. L., W. C. Ghiorse and G. L. Johnson. "Distribution of Microbes in Manganese Nodules from the Atlantic and Pacific Oceans," *Dev. Ind. Microbiol.* 13:57–65 (1972).

Krieg, N. R. "Biology of the Chemoheterotrophic Spirilla," *Bacteriol. Rev.* 40:55–115 (1976).

Morgan, C. L. "Nucleation and Accumulation of Marine Ferromanganese Deposits," Ph.D. dissertation, The University of Wisconsin, Madison, Wisconsin (1975).

CHAPTER 66

THE ISOLATION AND CHARACTERIZATION OF MARINE BACTERIA WHICH CATALYZE MANGANESE OXIDATION

KENNETH H. NEALSON

Scripps Institution of Oceanography
University of California in San Diego
La Jolla, California 92093 USA

INTRODUCTION

It is now generally accepted that microorganisms participate in the mediation of a variety of biogeochemically
important processes. With regard to manganese this generali-
zation is less well proven than with other metals, although
there is no doubt that organisms exist that catalyze both
the oxidation (Beijerink, 1913; Bromfield, 1950; Ehrlich, 1968;
Johnson, 1966; Krumbein, 1971; Schweisfurth, 1972; Tyler, 1967;
Van Veen, 1972; Zavarzin, 1962) and the reduction (Ghiorse,
1974; Trimble, 1968 and 1970) of manganese. Furthermore, the
distribution of manganese bacteria in nature has suggested to
some authors their importance in the mediation of both manganese precipitation and remobilization (Ehrlich, 1972; LaRock,
1975; Silverman, 1964). It is the intent of this chapter
to present preliminary findings and observations from our
laboratory that bear on the question of the role(s) of bacteria
in the cycling of manganese in the marine environment. To
this point, our studies have dealt only with organisms that
catalyze the oxidation of Mn^{2+} to MnO_2.

RESULTS AND DISCUSSION

Isolation of the Bacteria

Over 150 bacterial isolates that catalyze manganese
oxidation were obtained from a variety of marine environments
by direct plating and by enrichment cultures. It was the
object of the isolations to obtain a diverse and representative group of organisms. For enrichment cultures, 10-200 ppm
manganese was added to the samples and they were incubated

at 10° - 18° C. In all, 35 enrichments were made as shown
in Figure 1 (top). Platings from the enrichments were done at
monthly intervals on six different media described in Table
I. K medium, a modified medium of Krumbein, was found to be
the best general medium.

When first set up, both the water and sediment were
examined for the presence of manganese oxidizers. With only
one exception (Table II) all tubes were negative; fourteen
months later, all were positive. The time course data
presented in Table II make it apparent that enrichment for
manganese oxidizers is not a rapid process, and that all
samples must contain some manganese oxidizers that are eventually enriched. In most of the enrichments more than one
type was found.

The courses of sediments and water samples for the
enrichments were varied, although with one exception (the
RS samples) all were marine. Samples 1-53 were from marine
sediments offshore (coast of southern California) to 30
meters near San Diego. Samples 54-60 were obtained from
manganese nodules and deep sea sediments. Material was
removed aseptically from a box core immediately after retrieval
and inoculated into enrichment cultures. Samples 61-67 were
from offshore sediments at a variety of intermediate depths.
The RS strains were obtained by direct plating from manganese-
coated rocks obtained from a dark freshwater cave.

For each location, other enrichments were made. In
those samples to which no manganese was added, no oxidizers
appeared, and in every case in which organics (glucose,
acetate, succinate or glycerol) were added, rapid bacterial
growth occurred and no manganese oxidizers were ever observed.
The same was true for amino acid and protein (peptone and
tryptone) additions. For the sake of continuity and simpli-
city, all fungi capable of manganese oxidation were discarded,
although there were many of these organisms in the enrichments.

Identification of the Manganese Oxidizers

Strong or very active manganese oxidizers can be
visualized easily on K medium by brown precipitates on the
bacterial colonies. However, many oxidizers are not so
active as to be visually detected without staining. So, in
every instance a manganese oxidation was determined with
Feigl's benzidinium reagent (1958), which produces a dark
blue color upon reaction with manganese dioxide. Before
addition of this toxic reagent, replica plates were made so
that positive colonies could be identified and subcultured.
Platings from several enrichment cultures are shown in Figure
1 (B, C and D).

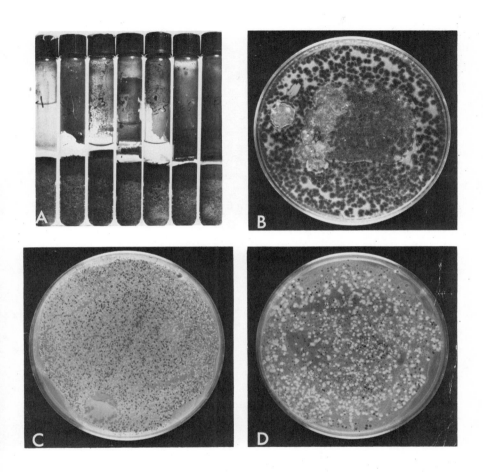

Figure 1.   Enrichment and plating of manganese bacteria.
Samples of marine sand or mud (or manganese nodules) plus
overlying water were collected and placed in tubes as shown.
They were enriched with 200 ppm of divalent manganese. The
tubes shown in A have been enriched for 14 months. A sterile
pipet was used to remove 0.1-ml samples, which were plated;
colonies grew as shown in B, C and D. The plates are
stained with Feigl's reagent, which reacts with MnO_2 to
produce a blue (dark) color.

Table I
Media Used for Isolation
of Manganese Bacteria from Enrichment Cultures

Ingredients	A	B	C	K	R	Z
Dist. Water	1L	1L			1L	1L
75% Sea Water	1L		1L	1L		
NaCl		30			30	30
$MnSO_4$ · 4H O		0.05		0.2	0.2	
$Mn(CH_3COO)_2$	0.1					0.1
Mn Bicarbonate Solution			100 ml			
$FeSO_4$ · $7H_2O$				0.001		
$MgSO_4$ · $7H_2O$		0.02	0.01			0.05
(NH_4) · $_2SO_4$		0.1	0.1			1
$KHCO_3$			0.1			
K_2HPO_4		0.05	0.01			0.1
Fe CO_3						0.05
$Ca(NO_3)_2$ · $4H_2O$						0.02
$Ca_3(PO_4)_2$		0.1				
Peptone	2			2		
Yeast Extract	0.5	0.5		0.5	0.5	
Agar	15	15	15	15	15	15

Liquid medium - leave out agar

Soft agar - 8 g/l agar

In all cases, 75 percent sea water can be substituted for 3 percent NaCl.

For nonmarine types, add 1-5 g/l NaCl.

Characterization of the Manganese Oxidizers

Once isolated as pure cultures, the manganese bacteria display good growth on a variety of media. In many respects they appear to be a heterogenous group of Gram-Negative heterotrophic bacteria that lend themselves quite well to laboratory study. No example of an obligate autotrophic or even an obligate manganese-requiring organism has yet been obtained by our methods.

Table II
Appearance of Maganese Bacteria in Enrichments[a]

Time (months)	Water[b] Positives/Total	% Positive[d]	Sediment[c] Positives/Total	% Positive
0	0/35	0	1/35	3
2	0/35	0	1/35	3
6	0/35	0	3/35	9
12	1/35	3	30/35	86
14	3/35	9	35/35	100

[a]All other enrichments (no manganese, amino acids or sugars) were all negative, and so are not included in this table.

[b]0.1-ml samples of the sea water 1 cm above the sediment were removed and plated onto the 6 media.

[c]0.1-ml samples of interstitial water were similarly plated.

[d]Tubes were scored as positive if one or more of the colonies that grew on the plates were positive for manganese oxidation.

Characterization was begun with 172 strains, many of which were obvious duplicates. As the study progressed, duplicates were eliminated until 45 strains remained. A list of the tests performed on these strains is presented in Table III. With the generous help of Dr. R. R. Colwell, the properties of these strains were subjected to computer analysis, which grouped them according to the scheme shown in Table IV. It is clear from these preliminary data that a variety of bacterial types have been obtained that have in common the ability to oxidize manganese. The morphological and DNA base ratio data make it possible to equate some of these groups to known organisms, as indicated in Table IV. Work is still in progress to identify some of the organisms for which it has not yet been possible to make specific generic assignments.

Morphological Characteristics

Morphological characterization serves more than one purpose, and from the taxonomic survey we have been able to get a "feel" for these organisms. Table V presents the major generalizations that can be derived from morphological data. It also presents some of the unusual features of the manganese bacteria, the discussion of which will follow.

Table III
Tests Performed on all Strains of Maganese Oxidizers

Morphology	Colony shape, size, thickness, edges Cell shape, size, Gram strain Flagella number and location
Physical Effects on Growth	Temperature, pressure, salinity pH, O_2
Nutrient Effects on Growth	Autotrophic growth Heterotrophic growth Phototrophic growth Fermentative vs. aerobic growth

Biochemical Tests	Oxidase, catalase
	Storage products: PHB, glycogen, starch
	Extracellular enzymes: amylase,
	  protease, cellulase, alginase,
	  chitinase, lipase
	NO_3-reduction, NO_2 reduction
	SO_4-reduction
	Gas production, acid production
	Acetoin production
	Deamination of phenylalanine
	Indole utilization
	Arginine dihydrolase
	Antibiotic sensitivity (8 antibiotics)
	Hydrocarbon utilization

Effects on Maganese Oxidation	Temperature, pH, salinity, O_2 Glucose, cyclic AMP

Most isolates have a Na^+ requirement as determined by the method of Reichelt and Baumann (1974), and all are Gram-negative, motile rods that are oxidase and catalase positive. Beyond these similarities they represent a great diversity of physiological (morphological) traits.

The individual organisms exhibit a truly versatile life potential. They are tolerant of extremes of temperature, pressure, salinity and pH. The ability of these organisms to withstand extremes is interesting in terms of assessing meaning to their presence (*e.g.*, their ability to survive wide extremes predicts that they will be present in many environments regardless of their funtional activity). Their ability to grow under a wide variety of conditions, including high pressure and low temperature, make them candidates for organisms of significance at the benthic boundary layer.

Table IV
Taxonomic Analysis of Maganese Oxidizers

Group	No. of Strains	DNA (G&C Content)[a]		Designation[b]
I	20	52.5 – 57.6	(3)	Pseudomonas
II	11	39.3	(1)	Flavobacterium
III	3	–		?
IV	3	57.6	(1)	?
V	2	38.6	(1)	?
VI	2	52.2	(1)	Aeromonas
VII	1	41	(1)	Cytophage
VIII	1	48.8	(1)	(Deep Sea–unnamed of RR Colwell)
IX	1	–		?
X	1	59	(1)	?
		45		

[a]Numbers in parentheses indicate the number of strains tested. Others in progress.

[b]Designations are best guesses on basis of comparative numerical taxonomy.

? Indicates assignment not yet established.

Factors Affecting Manganese Oxidation

Although all factors have not yet been tested, some general impressions are possible at this time; a summary is presented in Table V. With regard to temperature and salinity, any conditions that allow for growth also allow manganese oxidation. A pH of 9.0 or above inhibits manganese oxidation, but not growth for most strains. Manganese oxidation for many strains is favored by low oxygen levels (microaerophilic) while growth is favored by high oxygen levels. This is true despite the fact that molecular oxygen is presumably a sub-strate for the reaction.

Nutrients exert complex and diverse effects. Of 40 strains tested, 10 continue to catalyze manganese oxidation irrespective of the medium used. For the others, manganese oxidation is strongly inhibited by the presence of glucose or other metabolites. For 14 of the inhibited strains, the inhibition can be reversed by cyclic AMP. This effect is shown in Figure 2. It is interesting to note that many of the strains originally identified as weak oxidizers on K

Table V
Characteristics of Manganese Oxidizers

Taxonomic Characters	
Usual	Unusual
Oxidize Mn^{2+} MnO_2	Temperature Tolerance 4–45°C
Gram-negative, motile rods	Pressure Tolerance 1–1000 ATM
Catalase and oxidase positive	Salt Tolerance 10 mM 3–4M NaCl
Require Na^+	pH Tolerance 5–9 pH

Effects on Manganese Oxidation	
Temperature	No effect, oxidation at all temperatures
Salt	No effect, oxidation with growth
Pressure	Not tested under growing conditions
pH	High pH (9.0 or greater) inhibits oxidation but not growth for most strains
Nutrients	Glucose represses oxidation but not growth Repression reversed by cyclic AMP
Oxygen	Manganese oxidation favored by low oxygen, high oxygen appears to favor growth

medium are scored as very strong in the presence of cyclic AMP (Strain III, Figure 2). Table VI shows that four patterns of response to glucose and cyclic AMP exist among our isolates, indicating that this area will require careful and complete study in the future. Catabolite repression as a control mechanism is often taken as evidence that the function which is being controlled is of advantage under nutrient-limiting conditions (LaRock and Ehrlich, 1975; Silverman and Ehrlich, 1968). It is not unreasonable to postulate that at least some of the manganese oxidizers do in fact gather energy from the oxidation, and that this process is under the control of catabolite repression. This aspect of the manganese bacteria, which is currently under study, will be of great importance in assessing the role(s) of these organisms in the environment.

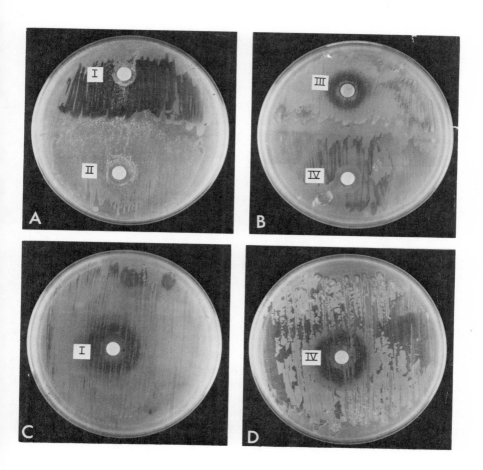

Figure 2. Catabolite repression of manganese oxidation. A and B show four different cultures grown on K medium with a disk of cyclic AMP added. Culture I is positive for manganese oxidation and inhibited in its growth by high c-AMP concentrations. Culture II is a negative control. Culture III is negative, even on K medium unless c-AMP is added. Culture IV is like I. C and D show the effect of adding glucose to the K medium; manganese oxidation is inhibited. However, for both cultures I and IV, this inhibition is reversed by c-AMP.

Table VI
Classes of Response to Glucose and Cyclic AMP

		No Addition	C-AMP	Glucose	Glucose + C-AMP
Weak Oxidizers	A	±	+	±	++
	B	±	+	-	++
Strong	C[b]	++	++	++	++
	D[c]	++	++	-	-
	E[c]	++	++	-	++

[a]All strains were tested on K medium, which contains a low amount of amino acid nutrients. Apparently some strains are repressed even by this medium.

[b]Some strains exhibit strong oxidation, regardless of the medium.

[c]These strains show strong glucose repression, some (group E) being reversed by the addition of c-AMP, and others not.

SUMMARY

Considering our results at this point in time, very little can be put forth in the form of a model for bacterial activity on manganese in the oceans. The present facts are: (1) that manganese bacteria have been isolated from all marine environments so far examined, including the benthic ones, (2) that these bacteria are a varied group, consisting of several different types, (3) that their properties are consistent with survival and activity under nearly any condition found in the ocean, and (4) that nutrient level and type profoundly influence the manganese-oxidizing activity of many of the strains.

ACKNOWLEDGMENTS

The technical assistance of John Amish and Judeye Garfield is acknowledged. This research was supported by the NSF-IDOE manganese nodule program; grant No. OCE76-04253.

REFERENCES

Beijerinck, M. W. "Oxydation des mangan-carbonates durch bakterien und schimmel pilze," *Folia Microbiologica* 3:123-134 (1913).

Bromfield, S. M. and V. B. D. Skerman. "Biological Oxidation of Manganese in Soils," *Soil Sci.* 69:337-349 (1950).

Ehrlich, J. L. "Bacteriology of Manganese Nodules. II," *J. Bacteriol.* 16:197-202 (1968).

Ehrlich, H. L., W. C. Ghiorse and G. L. Johnson II. "Distribution of Microbes in Manganese Nodules from the Atlantic and Pacific Oceans," in *Devel. in Indust. Microbiol.* Am. Inst. Biol. Sci., Washington, D. C. (1972) pp. 57-65.

Feigl, F. *Spot Tests in Inorganic Analysis* (New York: Elsevier, 1958).

Ghiorse, W. C. and H. L. Ehrlich. "Effects of Seawater Cations and Temperature on Manganese Dioxide-Reductase Activity in a Marine Bacillus," *Appl. Microbioo.* 28:785-792 (1974).

Johnson, A. H. and J. L. Stokes. "Manganese Oxidation by *Sphaerotilus discophorus*," *J. Bacteriol.* 91:1543-1547 (1966).

Krumbein, W. F. "Manganese Oxidizing Fungi and Bacteria in Recent Shelf Sediments of the Bay of Biscay and the North Sea," *Die Naturwissenschaften* (1971).

La Rock, P. and H. L. Ehrlich. "Observations of Bacterial Microcolonies on the Surface of Ferromanganese Nodules from Blake Plateau by Scanning Electron Microscopy," *Microbiol Ecology* 2:84-96 (1975).

Magasanik, B. "Catabolite Repression," *Cold Spring Harbor Symposium on Quantitative Biology* 26:249-256 (1962).

Magasanik, B. "Glucose Effects: Inducer Exclusion and Repression,' in *The Lac Operon*, J. R. Beckweith and D. Zipser, Eds. (Cold Spring Harbor, New York, 1970), pp. 189-219.

Reichelt, J. L. and D. Baumann. "Effect of Sodium Chloride on Growth of Heterotrophic Marine Bacteria," *Arch. Microbiol.* 97:329-345 (1974).

Schweisfurth, V. R. "Manganoxydierende Mikroorganismen in Trinkwasserversorgungsanlagen," *Gwf-wasser/abwasser* 113: 562-572 (1972).

Silverman, M. P. and H. L. Ehrlich. "Microbial Formation and Degradation of Minerals," in *Advances in Applied Microbiology*, Volume 6, W. W. Umbreit, Ed. (New York: Academic Press, 1964), pp. 153-206.

Trimble, R. B. and H. L. Ehrlich. "Bacteriology of Manganese Nodules. III. Reduction of MnO_2 by Two Strains of Nodule Bacteria," *Appl. Microbiol.* 16:695-702 (1968).

Trimble, R. B. and H. L. Ehrlich. "Bacteriology of Manganese Nodules. IV," *Appl. Microbiol.* 19:966-972 (1970).

Tyler, P. R. and K. C. Marshall. "Hyphomicrobia - A Significant Factor in Manganese Problems," *J. Am. Water Works Assoc.* 59:1043-1048 (1967).

Van Veen, W. L. "Factors Affecting the Oxidation of Manganese by *Sphaerotilus discophorus*," *Ant von Leeuw* 38:623-626 (1972).

Zavarzin, G. A. "Symbiotic Oxidation of Manganese by Two Species of Pseudomonas," *Mikrobiologiya* 31:586-588 (1962).

CHAPTER 67

TRACE ELEMENTS IN THE PORE WATER AND SEA WATER IN THE RADIOLARIAN OOZE AREA OF THE CENTRAL PACIFIC AS RELATED TO THE GENESIS OF MANGANESE NODULES

CHRISTIAN SCHNIER

Gesellschaft für Kermemergieverwertungin Schiffbau
und Schiffahrt m. b. H. (GKSS)
Geesthacht, Federal Republic of Germany

HEINRICH GUNDLACH
VESNA MARCHIG

Bundesanstalt für Geowissenschaften und Rohstoffe (BGR)
Hannover, Federal Republic of Germany

INTRODUCTION

Sediments, manganese nodules and sea water were sampled during two cruises (1972 and 1976) of the German research vessel "Valdivia." The sediments were pressed out to obtain the pore water. The investigation area was the manganese nodule-rich area between the Clarion and Clipperton Fracture Zones in the central Pacific Ocean southeast of Hawaii. The ubiquitous sediment facies was "radiolarian ooze" consisting of clay, opaline tests (mostly radiolarians), some micro-nodules, and volcanic glass. This chapter will present the results of the investigation of the Mn and Cu concentrations in the pore water and in a sea water column.

METHODS

Sediment samples were taken by a box corer, which took sediment cores of 30 x 40 cm down to about 40 cm from the sediment surface. Immediately after being brought on board the sediment column was divided into four parts: 0-5 cm, 5-15 cm, 15-25 cm, 25-35 cm from the sediment surface. Samples

were pressed out using Teflonized[1] Sartorius filter presses
at a maximum pressure of 4 atm using filters of 0.45 μm pore
diameter. The amount of Cu or Mn in the pore water sample
is therefore the sum of the dissolved part and that colloidal
part having a particle diameter of less than 0.45 μm. Filters
of the same size were used for the sea water samples. As
the 0.45 μm filter size is the one usually used in oceanography,
the analyses of our pore water and sea water samples can
easily be compared with the average for sea water samples
from the literature.

The pure water and sea water samples were freeze-dried
immediately after being pressed out or filtered in order to
avoid reaction in the samples, *i.e.*, precipitation or reactions
with the material of the bottles. Neutron activation analysis
(NAA) was used to determine Mn and Cu in our laboratories on
land. A solvent extraction procedure was used to eliminate
Na radiation interference (Gundlach, Marchig and Schnier, 1977).

DISCUSSION OF THE RESULTS

Figure 1 shows the distribution of Mn in pore water
and sea water with depth. The higher concentration of Mn in
pore water compared with sea water is readily apparent.
There is also some enrichment in the sea water compared to
the mean value for sea water (Riley and Skirrow, 1975). The
Mn concentration in the pore water has a maximum in the 5-15
cm core section. We assume that Mn is dissolved in the
sediment column, transported upward through the pore water
and precipitated again at or near the sediment surface in
the form of manganese nodules or micronodules.

A decrease of organic matter with depth (Figure 2) is
found in the same sediments. The distribution of Mn in
pore water and the distribution of organic matter in the
sediment are in agreement with our previous investigations,
which show that Eh (redox-potential) and the number of manganese micronodules decrease with depth in the sediment
(Marchig and Gundlach, 1976), as shown in Figures 3 and 4.
This means that the oxidation of organic matter causes the
Eh decrease, which in turn causes the dissolution of Mn
micronodules deeper in the sediment. The process of Mn
transport upwards through the pore water in the sediment
column must be much stronger in the radiolarian oozes than
in other types of deep sea sediments because of the greater
porosity of this type of sediment.

Pore water also has a higher concentration of Cu when
compared with the literature value for Cu in sea water (Figure
5). Cu may be mobilized by the dissolution of radiolarian

---

[1]Registered trademark of E. I. duPont de Nemours and Company,
Inc., Wilmington, Delaware.

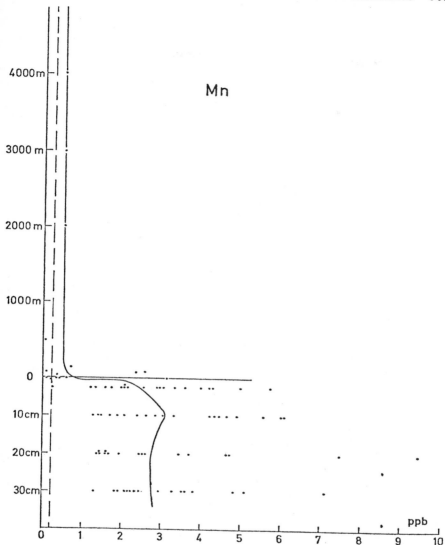

Figure 1. Manganese content plotted against depth in sea
   water and pore water from the 1976 cruise.
     points: manganese-values in ppb
     horizontal line: contact sea water/sediment
     vertical dashed line: manganese in sea water, after
        Riley and Skirrow, 1975
     curved line: connected geometric mean values of
        manganese contents for each depth

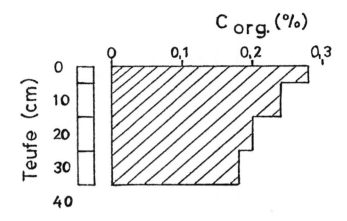

Figure 2.   Organic matter in the sediments from the 1976
   cruise.   Arithmetic mean values for each depth.

tests and not only by the dissolution of manganese micronodules in the sediment.   Cu does not show a maximum concentration in the samples between 5 and 15 cm as does Mn, but
increases continuously to the top of the sediment column.
The absolute concentrations of Mn and Cu in pore waters are
of the same order of magnitude (Figure 6).   The absolute
concentration of Mn in nodules and micronodules is one order
of magnitude greater than that of Cu.   If one assumes that
Mn from pore water is precipitated at the sediment surface,
the newly formed manganese nodules and micrododules will be
able to incorporate only a part of the Cu available.   Thus
most of the Cu will not be incorporated into the manganese
nodules, but will diffuse to the bottom-near sea water and
lead to the higher Cu concentrations sometimes found in sea
water.   Investigations of the behavior of other trace elements
important to the growth of manganese nodules are being
worked on and are not yet finished.
       Our hypothesis is that this process of remobilization
of Mn and Cu and perhaps some other trace elements is
qualitatively and quantitatively favored by the radiolarian
ooze type of sediments.   Thus the manganese nodules formed
there are better as ores and occur more frequently than
those growing on other substrata.   These processes are by
no means the only ones responsible for the growth of manganese nodules.   In general, an important part of the material
for the growth of manganese nodules must be precipitated
directly from the sea water.   This is especially true for
the iron-rich nodules as found on seamounts, with a thin
sediment cover or without it.

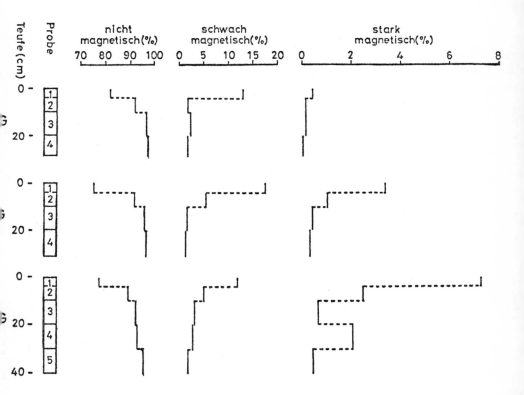

Figure 3. Percentages of three fractions of differing magnetism, contained in the size fraction >63 μm, plotted against depth in the sediment for three cores from the 1972 cruise.(Marchig and Gundlach, 1976).

nonmagnetic fraction   –   radiolarian tests
weakly magnetic fraction   –   radiolarian tests encrusted with Mn-Fe-oxides and some volcanic glass
strongly magnetic fraction–   manganese micronodules and some volcanic glass.

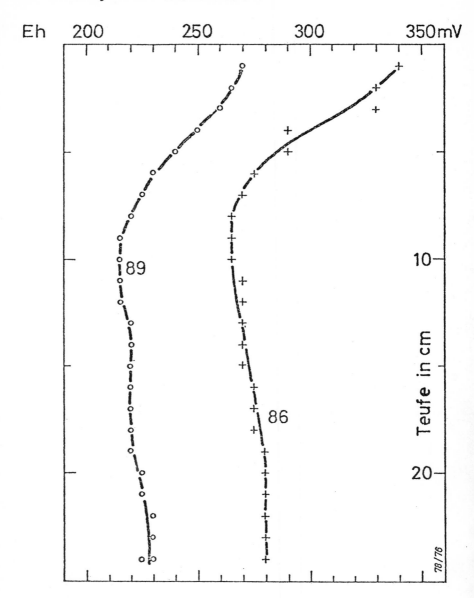

Figure 4.   Uncorrected Eh values plotted against depth in the top 25 cm of two cores from the 1972 cruise (Marchig and Gundlach, 1976).

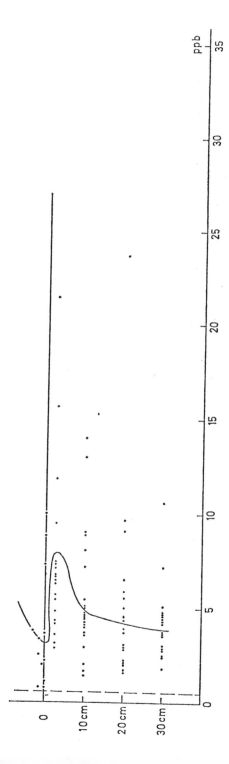

Figure 5. Copper content plotted against depth in pore water and bottom–near sea water from the 1976 cruise.
  points: copper values in ppb
  horizontal line: contact sea water/sediment
  vertical dashed line: contact sea water, after Riley and Skirrow, 1975
  curved line: connected geometric mean values of copper contents for each depth

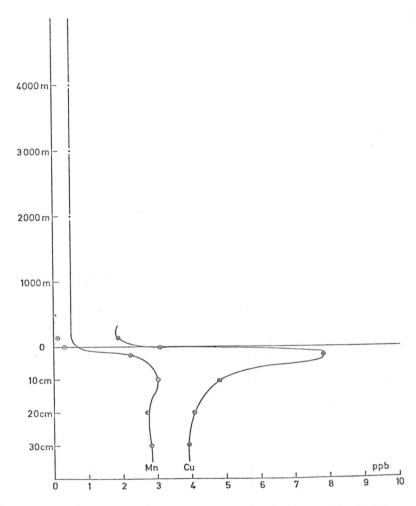

Figure 6.   Geometric mean values of manganese and copper plotted against depth.

    • = single Mn-content
    ⊙ = Mn geometric mean value of appropriate depth
    ⊗ = Cu geometric mean value of appropriate depth
    — = contact sea water/sediment

REFERENCES

Gundlach, H., V. Marchig and C. Schnier. "Zur Geochemie von Manganknollen aus dem Zentralpazifik und ihrer Sedimentunterlage: 2. Porenwasser und Meereswasser," *Geol. Jb.* D 23 Hannover (1977).

Marchig, V. and H. Gundlach. "Ein Hinweis auf die Auflösung des Mangans innerhalb des Sediments als Materialquelle fur die Bildung von Manganknollen," *Geol. Jb.* D 16:79-83 Hannover (1976).

Riley, J. P. and G. Skirrow. *Chemical Oceanography* (2nd Edition) 2 Volumes 606 and 647 pp. (London, New York, San Francisco: Academic Press, 1975).

CHAPTER 68

DISTRIBUTION AND IDENTIFICATION OF MANGANESE-PRECIPITATING BACTERIA FROM NONCONTAMINATED FERROMANGANESE NODULES

C. SCHÜTT
J. C. G. OTTOW

Institut für Bodenkunde und Standortslehre
Universitat Hohenheim, Stuttgart - Hohenheim
Emil Wolff Strasse 27
Federal Republic of Germany

INTRODUCTION

The genesis of ferromanganese nodules on the deep sea bottom of most oceans has been the object of chemical (Schweisfurth, 1971; Hubred, 1975) as well as microbiological speculations (Ehrlich, 1972; 1975; 1976). But so far, the mechanisms of Mn(II) and Fe(II) precipitation and/or oxidation and subsequent accretion are still far from solved. Since nearly all nodules contain nuclei of minerals, clays, remnants of bones, teeth and various other components (Hubred, 1975), these nuclei are thought to be the starting point for the Mn - Fe precipitation and accumulation processes. The precipitation as well as the continuous accretion of the Mn(IV) and Fe(III) oxides may have been caused by chemical oxidation and/or by the activity of manganese-"oxidizing" microorganisms. The specific role of microorganisms in nodulation has been stressed before (Morgenstein and Felsher, 1971; Ehrlich, 1972; Heye, 1975), but so far only a few manganese-oxidizing bacteria have been detected (4-18 percent of the total bacterial count) (Ehrlich *et al.*, 1972) rather than abundantly *in* or *on* such structures.

However, if manganese-precipitating bacteria are indeed catalyzing the genesis of nodules, these organisms should (1) be ubiquitously occurring in deep sea regions and (2) belong to common, heterotrophic bacterial taxa in order to explain the world-wide distribution of the ferromanganese nodules.

Aware of the facts that

1. nodules from the deep sea sediment are easily contaminated while being transported to the surface,
2. long storage of even appropriately taken samples may change the autochthone microflora both qualitatively and quantitatively (see Ehrlich *et al.*, 1972), and
3. the success in the enumeration of manganese-precipitating bacteria depends greatly on the type and choice of the medium selected

we decided to investigate the microbial flora of only a restricted number of nodules that were both excluded from contamination and studied as soon as possible after sampling. In this chapter, some of the results obtained with freshly and aseptically taken nodules are presented and compared with the flora of associated sediments and sea water samples.

MATERIALS AND METHODS

Origin of Nodules

Five elipsoidal to spheroidal (E/S-type) manganese nodules (*ca.* 50 x 30 x 30 mm and 30-50 g each) and one spheroidal intergrown polynodule (Kg-type) were examined. These nodules were collected by one of us (C.S.) during the "Valdivia" cruises (January 1976) in the central Pacific Ocean. Samples were obtained by coring the sea bottom with a spade corer. In this way, undisturbed surface layers containing noncontaminated nodules could be observed. Sediment samples were taken by spade- and box-coring (for technical details, consult Kollwentz, 1973). Immediately after sampling, each nodule or sediment sample was collected aseptically, placed into sterile bags and stored at 5-6° C.

Preparation of Nodules for Microbiological Examination

Within four weeks after sampling, the top side (T zone) and bottom side (B zone) of each nodule were scraped off aseptically and the material crushed to powder in a sterile mortar. One g of each sample was shaken (30 min) in 9 ml 0.13% Na-pyrophosphate solution as a dispersing agent and the entire suspension thus obtained was diluted serially with 90 ml Ringer solution (1/4 conc.) up to 10^{-8}. One-milliliter samples of each dilution were used to inoculate three parallel plates or tubes with appropriate differential media in order to evaluate the various groups of microorganisms. Details on the methods and media used will be published elsewhere (Schütt and Ottow, 1977).

Evaluation of Mesophilic and Psychrophilic Mn(II)-Precipitating Bacteria

From each positive tube of Pepton-Yeast Extract-Glycero-phosphate broth used to evaluate total bacterial population (30° C) and the psychrophilic population (5-6° C), several MnCO₃-agar plates (Mulder and van Veen, 1963) were streaked and incubated for ten days (30° C) and four weeks (5-6° C), respectively. Brown colonies or those showing an intensive blue color with benzidine-acetic acid reagent (Bromfield, 1956) were regarded as manganese-precipitating bacteria and evaluated semiquantitatively.

Identification of Mesophilic Manganese-Precipitating Bacteria

Brown colonies were restreaked on the same medium until a microscopic pure culture was obtained and collected on slants. In total, cultures were isolated and identified according to the methods of Stanier *et al.*, (1966), except for the O/F-test (glucose) (Hugh and Leifson, 1953) and the detection of orginine-dihydrolase system (Thornley, 1960). The isolates were allocated according to the diagnostic criteria of *Bergey's Manual of Determinative Bacteriology* (1974).

RESULTS

Flora of Top Side (T), Bottom (B) and Center (C)

Table I presents a survey of the bacterial flora recorded in the top side, bottom and center of five different E/S- and one Kg-type nodules. From Table I the following general conclusions may be drawn. First, nodules from the Pacific Ocean are inhabited by a large bacterial population, the greater part being either psychrophilic and/or halophilic. Second, the nodule surface, its subside or center are populated to nearly the same extent. Third, mesophilic manganese-precipitating bacteria are abundantly inhabited among the indigenous flora of the various nodules. In addition, the study with one of the manganese nodules (nr. 11, Table I) showed, among a total number of *ca.* 10^5 psychrophilic bacteria, at least 10^4 to be capable of precipitating manganese after a three- to four-week (5-6° C) incubation period. If some of the strains were restreaked on the same MnCO₃-yeast extract-Citrate agar and incubated at 30° C, growth failed entirely. This suggests the presence of obligate psychro-philic, manganese-precipitating bacteria on nodules. This is interesting, since temperatures recorded at the sea bottom ranged between 2-3°C! Both quantitative and qualitative studies on this group of psychrophilic bacteria are con-tinued.

Table I

Survey of Various Groups of Bacteria Determined on the Top Side (T), Bottom (B) and in the Center (C) of Ferromanganese Nodules Collected from the Pacific Ocean Floor[a]

Bacterial Groups Tested	Top Side (T)		Bottom (B)		Central Core (C)	
	E/S-Type(5)	Kg-Type(1)	E/S-Type	Kg-Type	E/S-Type	Kg-Type
A. Dilution Tube Method (MPN/g)						
Total Number of Aerobic Bacteria(30°)	$5.4 \times 10^5 - 3.1 \times 10^7$	3.1×10^6	$9.5 \times 10^5 - 5.4 \times 10^6$	NT	$1.2 \times 10^5 - 5.4 \times 10^6$	1.2×10^6
Psychrophilic Bacteria (5-6°)	$3.1 \times 10^4 - 3.1 \times 10^5$	1.2×10^6	$1.2 \times 10^5 - 5.4 \times 10^5$	NT	$1.2 \times 10^5 - 5.4 \times 10^5$	5.4×10^4
Halophilic Bacteria(+20%NaCl)	$1.2 \times 10^3 - 3.1 \times 10^5$	5.4×10^5	$1.2 \times 10^3 - 5.4 \times 10^5$	NT	$5.4 \times 10^3 - 5.4 \times 10^4$	3.1×10^5
Denitrifying Bacteria (37°C)	$1.2 \times 10^2 - 5.4 \times 10^3$	1.2×10^3	$2.0 \times 10^2 - 3.1 \times 10^3$	NT	$1.2 \times 10^2 - 5.4 \times 10^3$	1.2×10^2
Fe(III)-NH$_4$-Citrate Precipitating Bacteria (synthetic medium; 30° C)	$0 - 1.2 \times 10^2$	0	$0 - 3.1 \times 10$	NT	$0 - 1.2 \times 10^2$	0
Total Number of Anaerobic Bacteria	$1.2 \times 10^3 - 5.4 \times 10^4$	1.2×10^3	$1.2 \times 10^2 - 1.2 \times 10^4$	NT	$5.4 \times 10^2 - 3.1 \times 10^4$	3.1×10^3
B. Semiquantitative Method = highest dilution with positive test on Mn(IV) when streaked on MnCO$_3$-yeast extract-citrate agar, Mulder and Van Veen, 1973						
Mn(II)-Precipitating Mesophilic (30°) Bacteria	10^4-	10^5	10^4- 10^6	NT	10^3- 10^6	NT

[a] Numbers (highest and lowest values recorded) are expressed in MPN/g oven-dry material.

Comparison with Sediment and Sea Water

In Table II, a comparison is made between the flora of manganese nodules and samples of the sediment surface as well as of associated sea water. Table II shows that, although some variation occurs between the various groups of organisms, no significant differences could be ascertained within the manganese-precipitating group of bacteria.

Identification of Manganese-Precipitating Bacteria

All 67 strains examined were Gram-negative, aerobic, oxidase- and catalase-producing rods that failed to produce soluble exopigments (phenazine or fluorescent types). None produced indol, nor gave a positive result on the methylred and acetoin test (except for strains 35, 37, 65, 66 and 67) nor produced Arginine dihydrolase (except the strains 60 and 64). All strains developed well at 5 percent NaCl; most of them (70 percent) grew still at 15% NaCl. So far, 30 percent of the isolates revealed an *ortho*-ring fission mechanism with chinate as inducer; *meta*-cleavage was not recorded.

Based on the O/F-test (glucose), the isolates may be separated into three groups:

group A: O/F = +/- (33 strains)
group B: O/F = +/+ (4 strains)
group C: O/F = -/- (30 strains).

Table III presents a tentative allocation based on four properties of high diagnostic value.

DISCUSSION

From the present comparative study on the bacterial flora of noncontaminated ferromanganese nodules, sediment material and sea water, the following general conclusions may be drawn:

1. The microflora of manganese nodules may be regarded as a continuous part of the indigenous sea bed flora.
2. The bacteria are neither restricted nor concentrated on the surface or bottom region, but occur at about the same density throughout the entire nodule. This holds true also for manganese-precipitating organisms.
3. Mesophilic manganese-precipitating bacteria are not restricted to nodules only, but are found at similar densities in the surrounding sediment material and in the associated sea water.
4. Manganese-precipitating bacteria are common heterotrophic organisms classified into the genera *Pseudomonas* and *Aeromonas*.

Table II

Survey of Several Groups of Bacteria Enumerated with Ferromanganese Nodules, Sediment Material and Associated Sea Water Compared to a Garden Soil[a]

Groups of Bacteria	E/S-Type Manganese Nodules (5)	Sediment Samples (2) (0-1.0 m depth)	Sea Water (2) (1 m of Sediment Surface)	Garden Soil (Hohenheim)
Total Number of Bacteria (30°)	$5.4 \times 10^5 - 3.1 \times 10^7$	$1.6 \times 10^8 - 2.9 \times 10^8$	$4.0 \times 10^6 - 9.0 \times 10^6$	2.8×10^7
Psychrophilic Number of Bacteria (5 - 6° C)	$3.1 \times 10^4 - 3.1 \times 10^5$	7.6×10^6	$2.3 \times 10^5 - 4.0 \times 10^5$	1.1×10^3
Halophilic Bacteria (+20% NaCl)	$1.2 \times 10^3 - 3.1.10^5$	$5.3 \times 10^6 - 7.6 \times 10^7$	$2.3 \times 10^5 - 4.0 \times 10^5$	2.8×10^3
Denitrifying Population	$1.2 \times 10^2 - 5.4 \times 10^3$	0	$0 - 7.6 \times 10^5$	5.3×10^3
Fe(III)-NH₄-Citrate Precipitating Bacteria (synthetic medium 30°)	$0 - 1.2 \times 10^2$	$9.2 \times 10 - 7.6 \times 10^5$	$9.2 \times 10^2 - 4.0 \times 10^4$	2.8×10^5
Mn(II)-Precipitating Bacteria (semiquantitatively, 30° C)	$10^4 - 10^5$	$10^3 - 10^7$	$10^5 - 10^6$	10^4

[a] The numbers given (MPN/g oven-dry material or per ml) represent the population range limited by the highest and lowest number determined.

Table III

A Tentative Classification of 67 Polarly-Flagellated,
Gram-Negative, Mesophilic Manganese-Precipitating
Bacteria Isolated from Noncontaminated Ferromanganese Nodules

Group O/F	Starch	Gelatin	Egg Yolk	Denitrification	Isolate Number	
A1	-	+	+	+	1,5,7,12,16	P. fluorescens (?)
A2	-	-	+	+	4,6,8,9,11,13,17,18,19, 20,21,22,23,59	P. acidovorans (?)
A3	-	+	-	+	3,10	P. aeruginosa (?)
A4	-	-	-	+	14	P. medocina (?)
A5	-	+	-	+	15	P. fluorescens (?)
A6	-	+	-	-	24	P. pseudoalcaligenes (?)
A7	+	-	-	-	35	P. saccoarophilia (?)
A8	-	-	+	-	54,55,57,58,62,64	P. acidovorans (?)
A9	-	+	+	-	60	Pseudomonas sp.
A10	-	-	-	-	63	Pseudomonas sp.
B1	-	+	-	-	61,65,66,67	Aeromonsd sp. (anaerogenic)
C1	-	+	+	+	2	P. fluorescens-biotype (?)
C2	-	-	-	-	25,26,27,30,31,32,33, 34,36,37,38,39,40,41, 42,46,47,48,52,56,	P. lemoignei (?)
C3	+	-	-	-	28,29	Pseudomonas sp.
C4	-	+	+	-	43,44,45,51,53	Pseudomonas sp.
C5	+	-	+	-	50,49	Pseudomonas sp.

These findings differ in certain respects from those reported by Ehrlich and his group (1972).

Thus several of the nodules examined by Ehrlich and co-workers (1972) revealed bacteria concentrated primarily on the surface region of the manganese nodules and only very few in the center. It should be recalled here that the differences in results between Ehrlich and his co-workers and those reported here need not to be explained in terms of thesis against antithesis, but may be easily explained through differences in type of nodules, their porosity and age or by the medium and technique applied during the investigations.

Nevertheless, if manganese-precipitating bacteria are indeed involved in the genesis of ferromanganese nodules, the *ecological conditions* rather than the presence of such bacteria need to be considered, since manganese-precipitating bacteria seem to occur throughout the entire sea bottom region. So far, little is known of the ecological conditions of the deep sea bottom, but the presence of oxygen, organic matter and intensive mineralization processes, at least in subsediments, seem to occur (Volkov *et al.*, 1975). This is reflected by the high number of bacteria found by us in the sediments. The continuous supply of soluble $Mn(II)$ from the continent or from the subsediments on one side and the presence of large amounts of organic ligands (chelates, complexes, humic acids) on the other guarantee the formation of organometal chelates. We believe that if these common manganese-precipitating bacteria should be involved in nodule genesis, the manganese-precipitating and mineral accretion process is

1. displayed particularly at exposed sites of active bacterial mineralization (teeth, clay minerals) and
2. the result of Mn-precipitation through the metabolism of organomineral chelates and complexes rather than by specific enzymatic oxidation (with ATP-gain).

The start rather than the subsequent oxidation and mineral accretion is thought to be of microbial origin.

ACKNOWLEDGMENTS

This research is supported by the Deutsche Forschungsgemeinschaft, Bad Godesberg, West Germany.

REFERENCES

Bergey, D. H., R. E. Buchanan and N. E. Gibbons. *Bergey's Manual of Determinative Bacteriology*, 8th ed. (Baltimore: The Williams and Wilkins Company, 1974) pp. 217-253.

Bromfield, C. M. "Oxidation of Manganese by Soil Microorganisms," *Aust. J. Biol. Sci.* 9:238-254 (1956).

Ehrlich, H. L. "The Role of Microbes in Manganese Nodule Genesis and Degradation," in *Ferromanganese Deposits on the Ocean Floor*, D. R. Horn, Ed. (Washington, D. C.: The Office of Intern. Decade Ocean Expl. Mat. Sci. Found., 1972), pp. 63-70.

Ehrlich, H. L., W. C. Ghiorse and G. L. Johnson. "Distribution of Microbes in Manganese Nodules from the Atlantic and Pacific Oceans," *Devel. Ind. Microbiol.* 13:57-65 (1972).

Ehrlich, H. L. "The Formation of Ores in the Sedimentary Environment of the Deep Sea with Microbial Participation: The Case for Ferromanganese Concretions," *Soil Sci.* 119: 36-41 (1975).

Ehrlich, H. L. "Manganese as an Energy Source for Bacteria," in *Environmental Biogeochemistry*, Vol. 2, *Metals Transfer and Ecological Mass Balances.*, J. O. Nriagu, Ed. (Ann Arbor, Michigan: Ann Arbor Science Publishers, Inc., 1976), pp. 633-644.

Heye, D. "Wachstumsverhaltnisse von Manganknollen," *Geol. Jb.* E 5:3-122 (1975).

Hubred, G. "Deep-Sea Manganese Nodules: A Review of the Literature," *Minerals Sci. Eng.* 7:71-85 (1975).

Hugh, R. and E. Leifson. "The Taxonomic Significance of Fermentative Versus Oxidative Metabolism of Carbohydrates by Various Gram Negative Bacteria," *J. Bact.* 66:24-26 (1953).

Kollwentz, W. "The Marine Nodules Project: Exploration Methods and Techniques/Experiments with R/V Valdivia," in *The Origin and Distribution of Manganese Nodules in the Pacific and Prospects for Exploration*, M. Morgenstein, Ed. (1973), pp. 85-92.

Morgenstein, M. and M. Felsher. "The Origin of Manganese Nodules: A Combined Theory with Special Reference to Palagonitization," *Pacific Sci.* 25:301-307 (1971).

Mulder, E. G. and W. L. Van Veen. "Investigations on the Sphaerotilus-Leptothrix Group," *Antonie van Leeuwenh. J. Ser. Microbiol.* 29:121-153 (1963).

Schweisfurth, R. "Manganknollen im Meer," *Naturwiss.* 58: 344-347 (1971).

Schütt, C. and J. C. G. Ottow. "Mesophilic and Psychrophilic Manganese-Precipitating Bacteria in Manganese Nodules of the Pacific Ocean," *Z. Allg. Mikrobiol.* (in press).

Stanier, R., M. J. Palleroni and M. Doudoroff. "The Aerobic Pseudomonads: A Taxonomic Study," *J. Gen. Microbiol.* 43: 159-271 (1966).

Thornley, M. J. "The Differentiation of Pseudomonads from Other Gram-Negative Bacteria on the Basis of Arginine Metabolism," *J. Appl. Bact.* 23:37 (1960).

Volkov, I. I., A. G. Rozanov and V. S. Sokolov. "Redox Processes in Diagenesis of Sediments in the Northwest Pacific Ocean," *Soil Sci.* 119:28-35 (1975).

CHAPTER 69

MECHANISMS OF FERROMANGANESE NODULE FORMATION IN THE SEDIMENT-WATER INTERFACE OF THE DEEP SEA

J. C. G. OTTOW

Institut für Bodenkunde und Standortslehre
Universitat Hohenheim
7 Stuttgart-Hohenheim
Emil Wolff Strasse 27
Federal Republic of Germany

INTRODUCTION

Ferromanganese nodules are mineral accretions distributed abundantly (with an average of 10 kg/m^2) and widely (at 25-50 percent of deep sea bottom) on the floor of most oceans (Schweisfurth, 1971; Hubred, 1975). Most nodules are scattered over the sediment surface, although some of them may be covered by sediment material. Because of their high Mn and Fe content (11-28 percent and 4-20 percent, respectively) and particularly because of the elements Ni(0.5-1.4 percent), Cu(0.5-1.2 percent), Co(0.01-0.7 percent), Zn(ca. 0.1 percent) and Pb(0.05-0.25 percent), these nodules become increasingly important as potential resources for economical exploration (Friedrich et al., 1973; Greenslate et al., 1973; Hubred, 1975). The growth rate of these nodules is quite different (0.001-10 mm/1000 yr) and this slow rate of development presents a certain problem: the upward growth of these accretions may be one or two orders of magnitude slower than the average deposition rates of most sediments in the deep sea area (Menard and Shipek, 1958).

CONDITIONS OF FORMATION

Although the conditions and mechanisms of genesis are still open for discussion, some essential knowledge and information has been compiled that should be considered while seeking an explanation for the genesis of these mineral accretions. Thus, there is little doubt on the origin of the Mn and Fe compounds. The greater part is derived from continental weathering and is supplied to the deep sea as colloidal material, chelated to organic matter or in their reduced forms (Morgenstein and Felsher, 1971; Ehrlich, 1975; Hubred, 1975).

It is this hydrogenous continental supply of organic material that is responsible for the creation of three different sedimentation zones on the deep sea bottom. The first zone consists of sediments with strong reducing conditions (caused by the decay of organic matter) along the continental slope. This zone passes over into a second zone of transitional sediments (with little organic matter) of the marginal oceanic region. A third fully oxidized core of pelagic sediments (red oozes) is found in the center of the deep sea (Greenslate *et al.*, 1973; Volkov *et al.*, 1975). In the small reducing zone, Mn(IV) and Fe(III) compounds are dissolved by reduction and may be redistributed. This is in contrast to the transitional sediments, in which both oxidizing and reducing conditions alternate, resulting in sharp fluctuations of the Eh and the presence of both Mn^{2+}/Mn^{4+}- as well as Fe^{2+}/Fe^{3}-couples.

In the sediment-water interface of the central core, organic matter is low (0.3-0.5 percent), and iron and manganese occur in low concentrations (in their oxidized state or chelated to organic ligands). Particularly in these red oozes, ferromanganese nodules, crusts and ores are found (Logvinenko *et al.*, 1972; Hubred, 1975; Ehrlich, 1975; Volkov *et al.*, 1975). In the surface sediments with erosional unconformities, in strong bottom currents and in water with a relatively high biological productivity, conditions are suitable to promote nodule formation as judged from the distribution of developing micronodules (Margolis, 1973).

MECHANISMS OF ACCRETION

In explaining the genesis of formation, it should be recalled that most nodules contain nuclei of petrefacts, clay particles, volcanic debris, remnants of bones and teeth (Ehrlich, 1975; Hubred, 1975) or develop on siliceous microfossils (Margolis, 1973). This role of nuclei in the formation of ferromanganese nodules is quite significant, since high accretion rates of Fe- and Mn-oxides are generally associated with high accumulation rates of terrigenic minerals in an oxidizing environment (Greenslate *et al.*, 1973).

Several mechanisms of nodule formation have been proposed (Schweisfurth, 1971; Ehrlich, 1975; Hubred, 1975), two of which are discussed here as supplementary processes rather than alternatives.

Nodulation as a Chemical Accretion Process

According to this mechanism nodule formation is initiated in those sediment-water interfaces that have low or moderate iron and manganese concentrations in the presence of aerobic, oxidizing conditions (Goldberg and Arrhenius, 1958; Schweisfurth, 1971; Greenslate *et al.*, 1973; Heye, 1975). Readily precipitated, positively charged $(Fe(OH)_3$-particles become spontaneously attached to the negatively charged nuclei (such as clays, weathered minerals, phosphates of decaying bones). Subsequently, reaction, negatively charged MnO_2-particles are adsorbed and precipitated, incorporating other elements by coadsorption. It is not certain if these processes are true catalysis or simple sorption and oxidation reactions. It is assumed that both Mn(II) and Fe(II) ions are also produced in deep sediment layers and transported by diffusion and exchange reactions upward into the oxidizing zone (Ehrlich, 1975). According to Bender (1971), the major part of Mn(II) is delivered by the water phase. Based on nodule analysis it has been suggested that the initial development processes proceed much more rapidly than the subsequent accretions.

Nodulation by Microbial Catalysis

If microorganisms are involved in the accumulation of Mn and Fe oxides, these organisms should be (1) ubiquitously distributed in the sediment-water interface, (2) of aerobic rather than anaerobic nature and (3) capable of precipitating soluble Mn and Fe compounds (divalent forms or as metallo-organic ligands). Nodules are indeed populated by a dense bacterial flora (10^5-10^6/g) at the top surface, its subside as well as in the core (Schütt and Ottow, 1977). This indigenous population on the nodule surface has been shown by electron micrographs (LaRock and Ehrlich, 1975). Ehrlich and co-workers (1972) studied freshly taken nodules from the Pacific and Atlantic Oceans and found bacteria concentrated at the nodule surface rather than in the core.

Recent population studies by Schütt and Ottow (1977), however, showed a dense bacterial flora throughout the nodules, with only minor differences. Among these bacteria, a large population of mesophilic (up to 10^5/g) as well as psychrophilic (*ca.* 10^4/g) manganese-precipitating bacteria were found. The same amount of bacteria was also found in the sediment and surrounding water. Apparently, the ecological conditions at the initial sites of genesis rather than the presence of these manganese-precipitating bacteria should be considered, if such bacteria are regarded as catalysts. The actual accumulation of Mn(IV) oxides may be interpreted by either one of the following mechanisms.

1. Accretion by Enzymatic Oxidation of Adsorbed Mn(II) Ions

This mechanism was introduced by Krauskopf (1957) and developed by Ehrlich (1963, 1966, 1975). In this process, manganese accretion is composed of two steps, a nonbiological adsorption of Mn(II) by preexisting, negatively charged Mn(IV) oxides (H_2MnO_3) and a subsequent enzymatic oxidation through Mn(II)-oxidizing bacteria. In this way, new adsorption sites for further adsorption reactions are produced (with affinities for Fe, Cu, Ni, Co):

$$H_2MnO_3 + Mn(II) \xrightarrow[\text{adsorption}]{\text{chemical}} MnMnO_3 + 2H^+$$

$$MnMnO_3 + 2H_2O + 1/2 \ O_2 \xrightarrow[\text{oxidation}]{\text{enzymatic}} (H_2MnO_3)_2$$

Such an oxidizing, catalytic activity has been found in cell-free preparations (Ehrlich, 1968) and is related to a mechanism of ATP-generation (Ehrlich, 1976). Direct proof, however, must await further enzymatic experiments.

2. Accretion by Unspecific Heterotrophic Mn Precipitation and/or Oxidation

It should be recalled that all Mn(II)-oxidizing bacteria isolated so far from different sources (Ehrlich, 1966; Schweisfurth, 1973/74, 1975; Schütt and Ottow, 1977) have been identified as common, heterotrophic bacteria of the genus *Pseudomonas* (Schweisfurth, 1973; Schütt and Ottow, 1977). These bacteria grow only in the presence of organic compounds. Based on these facts, a mechanism is visualized in which Fe and Mn organic compounds (supplied by the continent and/or from sediment sublayers) are mineralized by prototrophic bacteria, resulting in a precipitation and/or oxidation of the liberated Mn(II) and Fe(II) ions. According to our view, most active sites of mineralization of the sea floor are those vulcanic debris, clay minerals and bones that are exposed mainly to the bottom currents (O_2 and organic supply) and that provide charges for adsorption of the precipitated iron and manganese oxides. Thus, the accumulation of Mn(IV) and Fe(III) oxides is regarded as a side product of common heterotrophic metabolism and of unspecific oxidation reactions.

The mechanisms summarized here are still open for discussion and proof must await further studies and experiments.

ACKNOWLEDGMENTS

Studies on the biological mechanism of nodule formation are supported by a research grant of the Deutsche Forschungs-gemeinschaft, Bonn - Bad Godesberg, Germany.

REFERENCES

Bender, M. L. "Does Upward Diffusion Supply the Excess of Manganese in Pelagic Sediments?" *J. Geophys. Res.* 76: 4212-4215 (1971).

Ehrlich, L. L. "Bacteriology of Manganese Nodules. I. Bacterial Action on Manganese in Nodule Enrichments," *Appl. Microbiol.* 11:15-19 (1963).

Ehrlich, H. L. "Reactions with Manganese by Bacteria from Manganese Marine Ferromanganese Nodules," *Devel. Ind. Microbiol.* 7:279-286 (1966).

Ehrlich, H. L. "Bacteriology of Manganese Nodules. II. Manganese Oxidation by Cell-Free Extract from a Manganese Nodule Bacterium," *Appl. Microbiol.* 16:197-202 (1968).

Ehrlich, H. L., W. C. Ghiorse and G. L. Johnson. "Distribution of Microbes in Manganese Nodules from the Atlantic and Pacific Oceans," *Develop. Ind. Microbiol.* 13:57-65 (1972).

Ehrlich, H. L. "The Formation of Ores in the Sedimentary Environment of the Deep Sea with Microbiol Participation: The Case for Ferromanganese Concretions," *Soil Sci.* 119: 36-41 (1975).

Ehrlich, H. L. "Manganese as an Energy Source for Bacteria," in *Environmental Biogeochemistry*, Vol. 2, *Metals Transfer and Ecological Mass Balances*, J. O. Nriagu, Ed. (Ann Arbor, Michigan: Ann Arbor Science Publishers, Inc., 1976), pp. 633-644.

Friedrich, G. H., H. Kunzendorf andW. L. Pluger. "Geochemical Investigations of Deep Sea Manganese Nodules form the Pacific on Board R/V Valdivia. An Application of the EDX-Technique," in *The Origin and Distribution of Manganese Nodules in the Pacific and Prospects for Exploration*, M. Morgenstein, Ed. (Honolulu, Hawaii: 1973), pp. 31-44.

Goldberg, E. D. and G. Arrhenius. "Chemistry of Pacific Pelagic Sediments," *Geochim. Cosmochim. Acta* 13:153-212 (1958).

Greenslate, J. L., J. Z. Fracer and G. Arrhenius. "Origin and Deposition of Selected Transition Elements in the Sea Bed," in *The Origin and Distribution of Manganese Nodules in the Pacific and Prospects for Exploration*, M. Morgenstein Ed. (1973), pp. 45-68.

Heye, D. "Wachstumsverhältnisse von Manganknollen," *Geol. Jb.* E 5:3-122 (1975).

Hubred, G. "Deep-Sea Manganese Nodules: A Review of the Literature," *Minerals Sci. Eng.* 7:71-85 (1975).

Krauskopf, K. B. "Separation of Manganese from Iron in Sedimentary Processes," *Geochim. Cosmochim. Acta* 12:61-84 (1957).

LaRock, P. A. and H. L. Ehrlich. "Observations of Bacteria Microcolonies on the Surface of Ferromanganese Nodules from Blake Plateau by Scanning Electron Microscopy," *Microbiol. Ecol.* 2:84-96 (1975).

Logvinenko, N. V., I. I. Volkov and E. G. Sokolova. "Rhodochrosite in Deep Water Sediments of the Pacific Ocean," *Dokl. Akad. Nauk SSSR* 203:204-207 (1972).

Margolis, S. V. "Manganese Deposits Envountered During Deep Sea Drilling Project Leg 29," in *Origin and Distribution of Manganes Nodules in the Pacific and Prospects for Exploration,* M. Morgenstein, Ed. (Honolulu, Hawaii, 1973), pp. 109-115.

Menard, H. W. and C. J. Shipek. "Surface Concentrations of Manganese Nodules," *Nature* 182:1156-1158 (1958).

Morgenstein, M. and M. Felsher. "The Origin of Manganese Nodules: A Combined Theory with Special Reference to Palagonitization," *Pacific Sci.* 25:301-307 (1971).

Schütt, C. and J. C. G. Ottow. "Distribution and Identification of Manganese-Precipitating Bacteria from Ferromanganese Nodules," in *Third International Symposium on Environmental Biogeochemistry,* Wolfenbüttel, Abstracts ISEB III (1977).

Schweisfurth, R. "Manganknollen im Meer," *Naturwiss.* 58:344-347 (1971).

Schweisfurth, R. "Manganoxidierende Bakterien. I. Isolierung und Bestimmung einiger Stämme von Manganbakterien," *Z. Allg. Mikrobiol.* 13:341-347 (1973).

Schweisfurth, R.   "Manganoxidierende Bakterien," *Zentr. bl. Bakt., Parasitenkde., Infektionskr. Hyg. Abt. I,* Referate 233:257-270 (1973/74).

Volkov, I. I., A. G. Rozanov and V. S. Sokolov.   "Redox Processes in Diagenesis of Sediments in the Northwest Pacific Ocean," *Soil Sci.* 119:28-35 (1975).

CHAPTER 70

THE FAUNAL ENVIRONMENT OF MANGANESE NODULES
AND ASPECTS OF DEEP SEA TIME SCALES

H. THIEL

Institut für Hydrobiologie und Fischereiwissenschaft
der Universität Hamburg
2 Hamburg 50, Palmaille 55
Federal Republic of Germany

INTRODUCTION

During recent years the contribution of organisms to
the growth of manganese nodules in the deep sea has been
widely discussed. Most controversies centered around microbial and fungal activities and concerned the questions of
active precipitation and of environmental conditioning
(Ehrlich, 1978; Ghiorse, 1978; Nealson, 1978; Ottow, 1978;
this volume).

Larger organisms, protozoans through megafauna, constitute the faunal environment of manganese nodules. After
summarizing briefly our knowledge on the abundance of benthic
organisms, this chapter describes the interaction between
fauna and nodules and discusses aspects of deep sea time
scales.

FAUNAL STANDING STOCK IN THE DEEP SEA

Manganese-iron concretions show a wide distribution in
the sea, especially in the deep sea, where most of the exploit-
able nodule fields are encountered. Interaction with organisms
depends on the density and behavior of the organisms, and
varies with the different organisms size classes.

Investigations during the last 30 years confirmed the
very low standing stock in the deep sea (Thiel, 1975). Most
research was done on macrofauna. Densities range from
0.05 g/m^2 in central regions to 0.5 g/m^2 in the peripheral
deep sea of the Pacific Ocean (Filatova, 1969). The general
pattern of biomass distribution depends on surface plankton

productivity, on distance from continents and on water depth.
Highly productive zones in the oceans are the coastal and
shelf areas, while production is lowest in central oceanic
parts.   Zenkevitch, Filatova, Belyaev, Lukyanova and Suetova
(1971) provide a general view of the world ocean benthos and
point to the higher standing stock, *e.g.*, below the upwelling
areas off California, Chile and Peru, as well as below the
eastern part of the equatorial region, with higher productivity in surface waters and a higher standing of the benthos.
A similar general pattern is to be expected in the other
oceans, too.   This view is supported by at least some results
from other areas (Thiel, 1975).

Little is known about quantitative aspects regarding
the smaller invertebrates (meiofauna: > 1 mm).   In central
oceanic regions numbers per 10 cm^2 sediment area range between
50-200 specimens, with total weights of about 0.05-0.2 g/m^2
and higher values near the continents.   Benthic foraminifera
may contribute 10-20 percent to this size order of organisms.
While they contain a small volume of protoplasm, their tests
are fairly large.   Other protozoans, such as *Sarcodina* of
the orders *Proteomyxida* and *Amoebida*, were counted by
Burnett (personal communication).   Below the North Pacific
central gyre he calculated about 2 x 10^4 individuals/cm^2.
Ciliates are known from the deep sea, but they seem to be
rare.

The results on micro-, meio-and macrofauna suggest
that "with increasing depth small organisms gain importance
in the total metabolism of benthic deep sea associations"
(Thiel, 1975, p. 594).   This hypothesis is biased by the low
total number of samples taken from the deep sea and by the
fact that sampling was not accomplished in coordinated programs.   Most quantitative work on macrofauna was done in the
Pacific Ocean; meiofauna is mainly collected in the Atlantic
Ocean, and only a few preliminary figures are available for
the microfauna.

Little is known on the production of deep sea benthic
associations.   First results on metabolic rates by substrate
degradation through bacteria were given by Jannasch, Eimhjellen,
Wirsen and Farmanfarmaian (1971) and by Jannasch and Wirsen
(1973).   Production in the deep sea seems to be 100-1000
times less than in shallow waters.   Smith and Teal (1973)
give some data on total community respiration measured in a
depth of 1830 m, and Smith and Hessler (1974) present preliminary data on fish respiration at 1230 m depth.   They found
comparably low values.   However, the change of permeability
in the oxygen electrodes under high pressure has not been
investigated.

So far, organisms of those size orders are considered
that can be quantitatively investigated using grab samples.
No quantitative data are available for larger organisms

(megafauna: readily visible on photographs). Any type of dredge or trawl prohibits quantitative sampling, and comparison within gear types is limited by varying catching capacity on different types of sediment.

Considering a deep benthic food web directed from smaller to larger organisms, one would predict a much lower standing stock for megafauna than for the groups of smaller organisms. However, megafaunal species, having the ability to swim, are also capable of using other food sources. Baited camera experiments (*e.g.*, Dayton and Hessler, 1972) showed a fast concentration of fishes and decapods around the bait and its total destruction within a few hours. Those species seem to be able to locate large food parcels and carcasses that fall down from upper ocean layers. No direct indication of this type of food source is known, but the immediate reaction of some species to the bait below the camera suggests an adaptation to this food source.

Some megafaunal species exploit the bathypelagic food reservoirs through vertical migration. During recent years, stomach contents of macrourids were found to consist of pelagic prey (*Decapoda, Mysidacea, Euphausiacea, Cephalopoda,* fish) to variable percentages (Haedrich and Henderson, 1974; Pearcy and Ambler, 1974). Haedrich (1974) reports the capture of one supposedly demersal macrourid species 1440 m off the bottom, and Pearcy (1976) reports another species more than 850 m above the sea floor. Considering a pure benthic food chain, these megafaunal species function in food transfer, using allochthonous food materials themselves and constituting the final step in the ladder of vertical migration (Vinogradova, 1962). By digestion they prepare the organic material as a food source suitable for deposit feeders that dominate the deep benthic associations. Regarding the groups of smaller organisms, nothing is known about biological activity, *i.e.*, growth patterns, food consumption, metabolic rates, life span, reproductive potentials and generation times. The interaction of the deep sea organisms with manganese nodules can be observed and deduced from photographs, but no values for its intensity can be given.

THE RELATIONSHIP BETWEEN MANGANESE NODULES AND FAUNA

The relationship between manganese nodules and fauna varies according to organism size and density. The very low standing stock of the deep sea fauna suggests its rather limited influence on the nodules. However, time scales for the growth of manganese nodules and for sedimentation have to be taken into account. Both rates are very slow: metal oxide precipitation ranges between 1 and 10 mm within 10^6 years, and sedimentation rates are approximately a few millimeters per 1000 years. Manganese nodules sit in the sediment surface for centuries, *i.e.*, there is time enough for countless generations of fauna to pass by and to interact with the nodules. The deep sea's time scales and the activity of fauna compared to the growth of nodules may thus result in relatively frequent interactions between nodules and fauna. The physical environment is most stable, while environmental disturbance is caused by the fauna. The interaction between fauna and nodules may be considered under two aspects: (1) the disturbance of the nodules and their environment by faunal activities and (2) the nodules as hard substrates for sedentary organisms and their metalliferous and nonmetalliferous contribution to nodule growth.

The Disturbance of Nodules and Their Environment by Faunal Activities

Bioturbation through macro- and megafauna has pronounced effects on shallow water sediments. Crawling on the sediment surface or within the sediment column, digging, burrowing and tube dwelling are all accompanied by some sediment shifting and transportation, resulting in surface tracks and breaks, in mounts and craters. Rowe (1974) summarized observations on bioturbation from shallow waters and deduced the effects on deep sea sediments. Deep sea photographs frequently show activity marks. In nodule fields, especially those with high densities, many nodules are partly or totally covered by mud that has been shifted over them by the animals' behavior. Sediment feeders, holothurians and arcon worms take up vast amounts of mud and defecate it in often characteristically structured fecal masses. These as well may bury nodules.

Larger in- or epifaunal species may even move the nodules from their position, they may be tilted and in some rare cases even be turned over. Bottom-feeding fish sometimes plough the sediment surface during food searching and this may similarly shift the nodules or cover them with sediment. Only in vigorous swimming and in severe fights for food, which one can imagine from monster camera photos (Dayton and Hessler, 1972) and from movie records of baited trap experiments using the Remote Underwater Manipulator (RUM) (Thiel and Hessler, 1974), may nodules be turned over. However, no evidence has been presented for rolled nodules. Frequent growth of sessile foraminifera on the lower side of the nodules is no sufficient criterion for nodules having been turned over. Vagile foraminifera, living not attached to a substrate, do not exclusively inhabit the sediment surface. They are frequently encountered residing in deeper layers of the sediment (Thiel, 1975; Coul *et al.*, 1977), and sessile foraminifera may be expected to have the same ability of growing buried in the sediment.

Most deep sea photographs show some sign of biological activity. The German "Arbeitsgemeinschaft meerestechnisch gewinnbare Rohstoffe" (AMR) kindly entrusted to me for biological evaluation 520 exposures, taken at a depth of about 5100 m in the central North Pacific between Clarion and Clipperton fracture zones. Each frame covered an area of 5 m². Only 2 percent of the photos exhibited no fecal material. Animal tracks were much less abundant. The density of epifauna amounted to only one specimen in 50 m². Animal groups occurring are *Enteropneusta, Holothuria, Ophiuroidea, Asteroidea, Crinoides, Actinaria, Gorgonaria, Porifera* and *Decapoda Natantia.* Only the first four groups are active in bioturbation and the first two may have some effect on the nodules by pushing, sediment shifting and fecal castings. Holothurians make up nearly 50 percent of the epifauna, resulting in one specimen interacting with the nodules in an area of 100 m². Paul (1976), using a similar method, arrived at about four times higher values for a depth of 4500 m some 1400 nautical miles to the northeast (14° 17.5' N, 126° 15.4' W) under waters with a higher surface productivity. All these figures are taken from records on epifauna, while the infauna is not recorded by photographic surveys. Their activity is seen only by sediment mounts and craters and by tracks close below the surface rifting the interface. Rowe (1974) speculates that 100 g of sediment may pass through a single holothurian per day, amounting to 1 g of sediment turned over per square meter per day. Actually, no quantitative data are available. Fecal masses are abundant; however, the rate of their production and destruction through other organisms and currents is unknown.

Biological deep sea processes are slow, although geological ones are much slower. Organism activity may gain in importance through the difference in biological and geological time scales. Assuming bioturbation reaches only 5 cm down into the sediment, the animals rework particles gathered at the ocean floor between the present and 5000 to 25,000 years ago.

Manganese Nodules as a Hard Substrate for Sessile Organisms, and their Metalliferous and Nonmetalliferous Contribution to Nodule Growth

No or very little bioturbation is caused by sessile organisms. In most deep sea areas a lack of hard substrates exists, prohibiting settlement and growth of larvae of sessile species on hard materials. Manganese nodules sitting in the sediment surface for times much longer than animal life spans provide a suitable substrate for foraminifera, *Porifera, Stephanoscyphus* (Scyphozoa), *Hydroida, Actinaria, Gorgonaria, Bryozoa, Brachiopoda, Polychaeta,* tube-living *Crustacea, Crinoidea* and *Ascidia.* They cover the nodule surface to a smaller or larger extent, presumably without any additional effect on the nodules during their lifetime. Greenslate (1975) observed an undescribed soft-bodied organism that occupied a hemispherical depression, which "may be considered as capable of redistributing previously deposited concretionary manganese." Total coverage, *e.g.*, by sponges, may prohibit the nodule's growth, but life processes near the nodule surface may result in different environmental conditioning. These last statements are highly speculative, and they should only point to the fact that still unknown interactions may exist.

As in the case of free-living organisms in the deep sea, the sessile ones have life spans of decades, which is still short compared to the growth and age of the nodules. This allows many generations of sessile organisms to settle on and to contribute to the growth of single nodules. While most of the skeletal structures extending into the overlying waters finally break away and decay, the basic parts cemented to the nodule surface are fairly stable and may get encrusted by newly precipitated oxides. Thus, the footplate or holdfast of *Stephanoscyphus, Gorgonaria* and the hydrocaulus of the *Hydroida* or other organic remnants may become incorporated into the nodule by the advancing oxide front and may contribute to their nonmetalliferous growth.

Shells of foraminifera and Polychaeta are other examples of organic structures on nodule surfaces. Their domes, tubes or irregularly shaped housings are glued to the nodule by their full length, often protected in impressions or crevices (Greenslate, 1975; Greenslate, Hessler and Thiel, 1974). If not mechanically disturbed, these structures are persistent for periods much longer than they are inhabited by their constructors. The most important group of nodule dwellers are the foraminifera. Many different species and forms of growth are observed, some of which are listed in Greenslate (1975). Their small biologically active body and their ability for asexual reproduction make them well suited for deep sea life under low food concentrations (Thiel, 1975). Many nodules show agglutinated foraminiferal encrustations, but no information is available on the number of structures occupied at one time. Carefully sampled with a grab, these crusts come up in their original construction, while in dredged samples most of them are broken and scraped away by the impact of the gear and by collision with other nodules. By further precipitation of metal oxides these organismic structures are encapsulated and filled, and are thus incorporated into the nodule matrix. Greenslate (1974, 1975) and Wendt (1974) encountered the embedded skeletal structures of protozoans and metazoans by leaching the metal oxides from the nodules, proving their nonmetalliferous contribution to nodule growth.

Additionally, some of the foraminifera, assembling their shells through agglutination of sediment particles (Figure 1), contribute to the metalliferous growth of manganese nodules. Together with mineral grains and biogenous particles

Figure 1. Different species of sessile, agglutinating
foraminifera on a manganese nodule (3x). ("Valdivia"
expedition 4, 1972, Pacific Ocean, 5120 m)

like the calearous shells of pelagic foraminiferans, the
siliceous ones of diatoms and of radiolarians and coccoli-
thophorids, manganese micronodules are collected by some
sessile foraminiferan species from the sediment in their
immediate vicinity with the aid of their pseudopodia. All
these particles are transported and glued to the edge of the
shelter for its enlargement. This behavior of agglutinating
foraminifera concentrates and fixes micronodules to a definite
position on or above the nodule's surface in the test
(Figure 2). These micronodules become incorporated into the
nodules through further precipitation of oxides covering the
foraminiferan shell, or the micronodules may act as crystallization centers for further precipitation. Thus, some of
the agglutinating foraminiferal species actively contribute
to the metalliferous growth of manganese nodules.

Figure 2. *Hormosina* spec. (foraminifera) with manganese
micronodules (black) incorporated into the test (20x).
("Valdivia" expedition 4, 1972, Pacific Ocean, 5135 m)

REFERENCES

Coull, B. C., R. L. Ellison, J. W. Fleeger, R. P. Higgins,
W. D. Hope, W. D. Hummon, R. M. Rieger, W. E. Sterrer,
H. Thiel and J. H. Tietjen. "Quantitative Estimates of
the Meiofauna from the Deep-Sea Off North Carolina, USA,"
Mar. Biol. 39:233-240 (1977).

Dayton, P. K. and R. R. Hessler. "Role of Biological
Disturbance in Maintaining Diversity in the Deep-Sea,"
Deep-Sea Res. 19:199-208 (1972).

Greenslate, J. "Microorganisms Participate in the
Construction of Manganese Nodules," *Nature* 249:181-183
(1974).

Greenslate, J. "Manganese-Biota Associations in Northeastern
Equatorial Pacific Sediments," Ph.d. Dissertation, University
of California at San Diego (1975).

Greenslate, J.,RR. R. Hessler and H. Thiel. "Manganese Nodules are Alive and Well on the Sea Floor," *Rep. Mar. Technol. Soc.*, *10th Annual Conference Proceedings*, 171-181 (1974).

Haedrich, R. L. "Pelagic Capture of the Epibenthic Rattail *Coryphaenoides rupestris*," *Deep-Sea Res.* 21:977-979 (1974).

Haedrich, R. L. and N. R. Henderson. "Pelagic Food of *Coryphaenoides armatus*, A Deep Benthic Rattail," *Deep-Sea Res.* 21:739-744 (1974).

Jannasch, H. W., K. Eimhjellen, C. O. Wirsen and A. Farmanfarmaian. "Microbial Degradation of Organic Matter in the Deep Sea," *Science* 171:672-675 (1971).

Jannasch, H. W. and C. O. Wirsen. "Deep-Sea Microorganisms: *in situ* Response to Nutrient Enrichment," *Science* 180: 641-643 (1973).

Paul, A. Z. "Deep-Sea Bottom Photographs Show that Benthic Organisms Remove Sediment Cover from Manganese Nodules," *Nature* 263:50-51 (1976).

Pearcy, W. G. "Pelagic Capture of Abyssobenthic Macrourid Fish," *Deep-Sea Res.* 23:1065-1066 (1976).

Pearcy, W. G. and J. W. Ambler. "Food Habits of Deep-Sea Macrourid Fishes off the Oregon Coast," *Deep-Sea Res.* 21:745-759 (1974).

Rowe, G. T. "The Effects of the Benthic Fauna on the Physical Properties of Deep-Sea Sediments," in *Deep-Sea Sediments. Physical and Mechanical Properties*, A. L. Inderbitzen, Ed. (New York and London: Plenum Press, 1974), pp. 381-400.

Smith, K. L. and R. R. Hessler. "Respiration of Benthopelagic Fishes: *in situ* Measurements at 1230 Meters," *Science* 184:72-73 (1974).

Smith, K. L. and J. M. Teal. "Deep-Sea Benthic Community Respiration: An *in situ* Measurements at 1230 Meters," *Science* 179:282-283 (1973).

Thiel, H. "The Size Structure of the Deep-Sea Benthos," *Int. Revue ges. Hydrobiol.* 60:575-606 (1975).

Thiel, H.   "Structural Aspects of the Deep-Sea Benthos," *Ambio,* suppl. Vol.

Thiel, H.   and R. R. Hessler.   "Ferngesteuertes Unterwasser- fahrzeug erforscht Tiefseeboden," *Umschau in Wiss, und Techn.* 14:451-453 (1974).

Vinogradova, N. G.   "Some Problems of the Study of Deep-Sea Bottom Fauna," *J. Oceanog. Soc. Jap.* 20th Ann. 724-741 (1962).

Wendt, J.   "Encrusting Organisms in Deep-Sea Manganese Nodules," *Spec. Publ. Intern. Assoc. Sediment* 1:437-447 (1974).

Zenkevitch, L. A., Z. A. Filatova, G. M. Belyaev, T. S. Lukyanova and I. A. Suetova.   "Quantitative Distribution of Zoobenthos in the World Ocean," *Bull. der Moskauer Ges. der Naturforscher, Abt. Biol.* 76:27-33 (1971).

CHAPTER 71

IRON AND MANGANESE DEPOSITION BY BUDDING BACTERIA

W. C. GHIORSE
P. HIRSCH

Institut für Allgemeine Mikrobiologie
University of Kiel
Federal Republic of Germany

INTRODUCTION

Deposition of iron and manganese oxides in neutral environments is frequently attributed to the activity of microorganisms. Bacteria of the *Sphaerotilus-Leptothrix* group, *Gallionella*, and the budding bacteria, *Metallogenium* and *Pedomicrobium*, are often cited as important metal precipitators in these environments (Aristovskaya and Zavarzin, 1961; Zavarzin, 1968; Glathe and Ottow, 1972). In addition, other less-known budding bacteria have been observed to deposit the oxides of these metals (Hirsch, 1974). A few *Pedomicrobium*-type budding bacteria have recently been isolated and studied in pure culture (Tyler and Marshall, 1967; Hirsch, 1968; Schweisfurth, 1972; Gebers, 1974). However, despite their known activity and apparent ubiquity, few attempts have been made to assess the significance of these bacteria in natural processes of iron and manganese deposition. Furthermore, except for the observations of Hirsch (1968), the mechanisms of oxide deposition by these bacteria have not been investigated.

In the present study, strains of budding bacteria were tested on various media for their iron- and manganese-depositing abilities. Observations are also reported concerning metal oxide deposition by the test-strains, expecially very active strains detected during this survey.

MATERIALS AND METHODS

Twenty strains of budding bacteria (Table I), originally isolated from a wide variety of aquatic and terrestrial habitats, were selected from the culture collection of our

Table I
Strains of Budding Bacteria Selected for Survey
of Iron- and Manganese-Depositing Ability

Strain	Original Designation	Source	Donor (Date)
ZV-580		Swamp, Russia	Zavarzin (1964)
854	T-37	Hydroelectric pipeline, Tasmania	Tyler (1968)
868	Hy-1	Temporary puddle, Michigan	Babinchack (1969)
869	Hy-2	" " "	" "
932	Hy-332	Thermal Spring, Austria	Schweisfurth (1976)
933	Hy-337	" " "	" "
938	Hy-343	" " "	" "
W54		Forest Pond, Germany	Wieczorek (1974)
FH-1		Forest Soil, "	Ghiorse (1976)
B-522		Soil, New Hampshire	Hirsch (1962)
NQ-521 gr Str.B		Elbe estuary, Germany	Mevius Jr. (1953)
SW-809		Brackish water, Connecticut	Hirsch (1966)
SW-812		" " "	" (1965)
SW-813		" " " "	" "
SW-815		" " " "	" "
SW-816		" " " "	" "
SW-819		" " " "	" "
SX-820		" " " "	" "
SX-821		" " " "	" "
SX-822		" " " "	" "

laboratory.   Since their isolation, these strains had been
maintained on a variety of artificial media; however, they
were all found to grow on PYGV-medium consisting of 0.025%
each of peptone, yeast extract and glucose plus vitamins,
basal salts and 1.5% agar (Staley, 1968; van Ert and Staley,
1971) make-up in either distilled water or, for the brackish
water strains, in artificial sea water (MacLeod *et al.*, 1954).
      To test these 20 strains for iron and manganese oxide
deposition, inocula from stock cultures were streaked on
PYGV-agar containing different inorganic sources and various
concentrations of the metals (Table II).   Normally, the metal
source, a soluble salt or an insoluble powder, was added to
the medium prior to autoclaving.   However, iron(II) sulfate
solution (2.5%) was sterilized by filtration and then added
to molten PYGV-agar.   Iron paper clips were first unfolded,
degreased with acetone and washed in 95% ethanol.   They were
then flame-sterilized and placed in sterile petri dishes and
PVGV-agar was poured over them.   The brackish water strains
were also tested on artificial sea water media containing
either 0.1% manganese(II) carbonate or a sterile paper clip
plus 0.337% methylamine hydrochloride and 1.8% agar.   This
medium was adjusted to pH 7.8 after autoclaving with sterile
NaOH.   Unless otherwise stated, all plates were incubated at
30° C in an incubator with methanol in the atmosphere.

Table II
Iron and Manganese Sources[a] Added to PYGV-Agar Media

Source	Concentration %	Final pH of PYGV-agar	
		Distilled Water	Artificial Sea Water
$FeSO_4 \cdot 7H_2O$	0.005	6.7	6.8
	0.01	6.8	7.2
Fe^o paper clip		6.8	7.8
Fe^o powder[b]	0.1	7.0	7.8
	1.0	7.0	7.8
FeS powder[c]	0.2	6.8	7.5
$MnSO_4 \cdot H_2O$	0.005	7.4	7.8
	0.02	7.1	7.7
	0.1	7.0	7.5
$MnCO_3$ powder	0.1	7.7	7.7
MnO_2 powder[d]	0.1	6.9	7.5

[a]All chemicals, except FeS powder, purchased from E. Merck, Darmstadt.

[b]Reduced iron powder (99.5% Fe).

[c]Riedel-de Häen AG, Seelze-Hannover (29% S).

[d]Pyrolusite (85-90% MnO_2).

After one, two and four weeks of incubation, plates were examined for growth and for metal oxide deposition. Iron(III) oxide was detected in colonies by adding a drop of 2% aqueous potassium ferrocyanide followed by a drop of 1.5 N hydrochloric acid (Prussian blue reaction = PB-reaction). Manganese(III and IV) oxides were detected by adding a drop of acidified (pH 3 to 4) 0.2% leucoberbelin blue solution (Berbelin blue reaction = BB-reaction) (Krumbein and Altmann, 1973).

Iron oxide deposition was studied in liquid cultures using 125- or 250-ml flasks containing a sterile paper clip and 25 ml of PYGV-medium or 50 ml of the sea water-methylamine medium. Microscopic observations along with the PB-reaction were used to detect iron deposition associated with bacterial growth. Manganese oxide deposition was studied in liquid cultures using test tubes containing 10 ml of PYGV-medium and various concentrations of manganese(II) sulfate.

Manganese oxides, deposited on cells and in cell clones growing in PYGV-liquid medium, were measured using a colorimetric method employing leucoberbelin blue (Altmann, 1972). In this method, appropriate amounts of suspension were diluted to 5.0 ml with distilled water and 0.05 ml 25% acetic acid and an equal amount of 4% leucoberbelin blue solution were added. After 30 min incubation at room temperature with occasional mixing, the absorbance at 623 nm was measured with a Hitachi 101 spectrophotometer. Standard curves were constructed using manganese-oxides freshly produced in alkaline solutions of manganese(II) sulfate. Protein concentration in the cell suspensions was determined with a biuret method (Herbert *et al.*, 1971), modified by the addition of 0.2 ml 1.5 N oxalic acid to remove manganese oxides from the centrifuged cells prior to boiling in 1 N NaOH. This method was chosen over the more sensitive Lowry method because it is much less affected by elevated concentrations of manganese (Hann and Makemson, 1976).

Light microscopic observations were made using a Zeiss photoscope. Electron microscopic observations of platinum-shadowed preparations were made with a Phillips 300 electron microscope.

RESULTS

Iron oxide deposition was considered to be proven when colonies turned blue when tested by the PB-reaction. By this criterion deposition was detected in 11 of the 20 test strains growing on PYGV-agar with an iron paper clip included (Tables III and IV). Seven of these strains (868, 869, 932, 933, 938, 854 and 809) were very active, producing brown colonies that turned deep blue in the presence of ferrocyanide and HCl. Four strains (FH-1, NQ-521 gr, SW-819 and SX-820) were weakly active on these media, producing opaque colonies that turned light blue when tested with ferrocyanide and HCl. Five of the very active strains deposited iron oxide when 0.1 percent of iron powder was included in the medium (Table III); however, when the concentration of iron powder was elevated to 1.0 percent, these strains either did not grow or were inactive, suggesting that high concentrations of iron inhibited growth and/or oxide deposition.

On the other hand, five other strains, two of which were inactive on all other sources, deposited iron from 1.0 percent iron powder. When iron(II) sulfide was included in PYGV-agar, the very active strains 868 and 869 deposited iron oxide, but their growth was inhibited, suggesting that this source contained toxic components. Other very active strains either did not grow on PYGV-agar containing iron sulfide or produced colonies that reacted weakly. Iron(II) sulfate at the low concentration normally found in PYGV-agar,

Table III
Iron Oxide Deposition by Selected Aquatic
and Terrestrial Budding Bacteria on Media
Containing Various Sources of Iron

| Strain | Iron Source Included in PYGV-Agar[a] | | | | | | |
	Fe^0 Paper Clip	Fe^0 Powder 0.1%	Fe^0 Powder 1.0%	FeS Powder 0.2%	FeSO$_4$·7H$_2$O 0.005%	FeSO$_4$·7H$_2$O 0.01%	None[b]
868	++	++	–	++[c]	–[c]	–[c]	+
869	++	++	–	++[c]	–[c]	–[c]	+
932[d]	++[c]	++[c]	0	0	0	0	+[c]
854	++	–	+	NT	–	+	–
ZV-580	–	–	+	–	–	–	–
B-522	–	–	+	–	–	–	–
FH-1	+	NT	+	NT	–	–	–
W54	–	NT	–	–	–	–	–
NQ-521 gr	+	–	+	–	–	+	–

[a]Made with distilled water.
[b]PYGV-agar contained 0.0005% FeSO$_4$ · 7H$_2$O
[c]Poor growth.
  0 = No growth.
 ++ = Colonies brown, strong PB-reaction.
  + = Colonies opaque, positive PB-reaction.
  – = Colonies opaque, negative PB-reaction.
 NT = Not tested.
[d]Strains 933 and 938 deposited iron like 932, but grew only on PYGV and PYGV+ paper clip.

provided enough iron for deposition by eight of the test strains (Tables III and IV). However, when higher concentrations of this compound were added to PYGV-agar, the ability of the very active strains to grow and/or deposit iron was eliminated or reduced, suggesting that elevated concentrations of iron(III), produced from iron(II) at neutral pH in the PYGV-agar, were inhibitory. This idea is supported by the frequent observation that the very active strains 868 and 869 grew poorly close to rusting paper clips in PYGV-agar where iron(III) concentrations would be expected to be highest.

Since most of the nine brackish water strains had previously been found to deposit iron in sea water-methylamine media (Hirsch, 1968) and since only three of these were presently found to be active on iron-containing PYGV-agar

Table IV
Iron Oxide Deposition by Brackish Water Budding Bacteria
on Media Containing Various Sources of Iron

Strain	Fe° Paper Clip	Fe° Powder 1.0%	FeS Powder 0.2%	FeSO$_4$·7H$_2$O 0.005%	FeSO$_4$·7H$_2$O 0.01%	None[b]
				Iron Source Included in PYGV-Agar[a]		
SW-809	++	−	+	−	+	+
SW-812	−	−	−	−	−	−
SW-813	−	−	−	−	−	−
SW-815	−	−	−	−c	−c	−
SW-816	−	−	−	−	−	−
SW-819	+	−c	−	+	+	+
SX-820	+	−	−	+	+	+
SX-821	−	−	−	−	−	−
SX-822	−	−	−	−c	−c	−

[a]Made with artificial sea water.

[b]PYGV-agar contained 0.0005% FeSO$_4$·7H$_2$O.

[c]Poor growth.

0 = No growth

++ = Colonies brown, strong PB-reaction.

+ = Colonies opaque, positive PB-reaction.

− = Colonies opaque, negative PB-reaction.

(Table IV), it was decided to test these strains in a liquid sea water-methylamine medium similar to that employed by Hirsch (1968). After 70 days incubation in such a medium with and without iron paper clips, only three of the strains had grown (Table V). Of these, only strain SW-809 grew well and became encrusted with iron(III) oxide. Strains SW-819 and SX-820 grew poorly but did accumulate oxide particles in cell clones. On the same medium containing a paper clip and solidified with agar, five of the nine brackish water strains formed colonies containing iron oxide. Furthermore, on this medium colonies closest to the iron paper clips gave the strongest color from the PB-reaction, suggesting that these strains, unlike the very active strains 868 and 869, but similar to the strains depositing iron oxide from 1 percent iron powder and 0.01 percent iron(II) sulfate (Table III), preferred higher concentrations of iron(III) for deposition.

Table V
Iron Oxide Deposition by Selected Brackish Water
Budding Bacteria in Artificial Sea Water-Methylamine
Medium with and without Iron Paper Clips

Strain	Fe^{0} Agar	Fe^{0} Liquid[a]	No Fe Liquid[a]
SW-809	+	++	−
SW-812	+	0	0
SW-813	+	0	0
SW-815	+	0	0
SW-816	0	0	0
SW-819	0	+[b]	−[b]
SX-820	+	+[b]	−[b]

[a]After 70 days of incubation.

[b]Poor growth.

0 = No growth.

++ = Cells encrusted with iron oxide.

+ = Colonies or cell clumps PB-positive. Colonies closest to paper clip showed stronger PB-reaction.

− = Colonies or cell clumps PB-negative.

These results indicate that most of the brackish water strains may still be active under the conditions employed by Hirsch (1968). However, after more than ten years of laboratory culture on artificial media, their ability to grow on sea water-methylamine media and, to some extent, their ability to deposit iron has been lost.

Fortunately, strain SW-809 still possesses both abilities. Light microscopic observations showed that in PYGV-liquid medium with an iron paper clip added, mother cells and hyphae became heavily encrusted with iron oxide much like those of iron depositors photographed by Hirsch (1968). Furthermore, on some cells, particles of iron oxide gave a beaded appearance to the hyphae. Interestingly, mother cells and hyphae of the very active strains 868 and 869 became similarly encrusted and beaded with iron oxide when growing in PYGV-liquid media containing iron paper clips.

Manganese oxide deposition was considered to be positive when colonies turned blue when tested by the BB-reaction. By this criterion manganese oxide deposition was detected in colonies of 5 of the 20 test strains growing on PYGV-agar

(Table VI). Furthermore, it is notable that the very active manganese-depositing strains were also very active iron depositors (Table III). In addition, except for slight accumulations of manganese oxide in the vicinity of colonies of strain SW-809 growing on manganese sulfate media, none of the brackish water strains displayed manganese-depositing activity (not illustrated).

The finding that no manganese oxide was deposited by strains 868 and 869 growing on PYGV-agar containing 0.02% and higher concentrations of manganese(II) sulfate (Table VI)

Table VI
Manganese Oxide Deposition by Selected Aquatic and
Terrestrial Budding Bacteria on Media
Containing Various Sources of Manganese

| | Manganese (II) Source Included in PYGV-Agar[a] | | | | | |
| | MnCO | MnO$_2$[b] | MnSO$_4$ ·H$_2$O | | | |
Strain	0.1%	0.1%	0.1%	0.02%	0.005%	None[c]
868	++	++	-[d]	-	++	+
869	++	++	-[d]	-	++	+
932[d]	++[e]	0	0	0	++[e]	+[e]
854	-	-	-	-	-	-
ZV-580	-	-	-	-	-	-
B-522	-	-	-	-	-	-
FH-1	-	NT	-	-	-	-
W54	-	NT	-	-	-	-
NO-521 gr	-	-	-	-	-	-

[a]Made with distilled water.

[b]Pyrolusite contained small amounts of absorbed Mn (II).

[c]PYGV-agar contained 0.0002% MnSO$_4$ ·H$_2$O.

[d]Strains 933 and 938 deposited Mn like 932 but grew only on PYGV and PYGV + 0.1% MnCO$_3$.

[e]Poor growth.

 0 = No growth.

++ = Colonies dark brown, strong BB-reaction.

 + = Colonies opaque, negative BB-reaction.

NT = Not tested.

raised a question as to the maximum concentration of this source that would allow for manganese oxide deposition. In experiments using PYGV-liquid medium, strain 869 deposited manganese oxide from 0.02 percent manganese(II) sulfate; however, in the same medium containing 0.03% of this source growth occurred with practically no deposition (Table VII). Similar results were obtained when strain 868 was grown in

Table VII
Initial Manganese (II) Concentration and Deposition
of Manganese Oxides by Strain 869 in PYGV-Liquid Medium

At Time of Inoculation		After 3 Weeks Incubation[a]		
$MnSO_4 \cdot H_2O$ Percent	Mn(II) (mg/l)	Mn(IV)[b] (mg/l)	Protein (mg/l)	mg Mn (IV) (mg Protein)
0.0002[c]	0.6	0.6	18	0.03
0.01	32.5	25.3	23	1.15
0.02	64.9	28.6	17	1.68
0.03	97.9	0.6	23	0.02

[a]At 30°C, without MeOH.

[b]Mn (IV) oxides assayed colorimetrically with leucoberbelin blue.

[c]Concentration in PYGV-liquid medium without added manganese.

PYGV-liquid medium containing manganese(II) sulfate. This indicates that the maximum limiting concentration in a liquid medium lies between 0.02 and 0.03% of manganese(II) sulfate. In PYGV-agar medium deposition was observed at 0.01% and lower concentrations of manganese(II) sulfate (not illustrated), suggesting that the effect of metal concentration on deposition may depend on the availability of a solid surface as well as on other microenvironmental factors.

Light and electron microscopy of strains 868 and 869 growing in PYGV-liquid medium revealed that mother cells occasionally produced multiple hyphae and that terminal buds were often attached with their long axes perpendicular to the hyphae. Also revealed were light-refractile, electron-dense particles on mother cells (Figure 1). The number and size of the particles increases as cell clones developed and they disappeared after treatment with oxalic acid or with acidified 0.2% leucoberbelin blue, indicating that the particles contained manganese oxides. When 0.005% of manganese(II) sulfate was included in the medium, cell clones accumulated large manganese oxide deposits with bare hyphae growing outward from them. In older cultures, a few mother cells and hyphae were observed to be encased in manganese oxide, but in most clones discrete particles were seen on mother cells

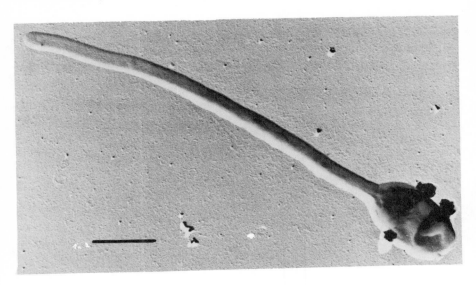

Figure 1.   Electron-dense particles thought to be metal
oxide deposits on mother cell of strain 868.   PYGV-liquid
medium.   Platinum-shadowed preparation.   Bar represents
1 μm.

and hyphae. These observations are consistent with the idea
that manganese oxide deposition begins as particles on mother
cells which increase in size and number as cell clones develop.
Ultimately in older cultures, oxide particles occur on hyphae
as well as on mother cells.

DISCUSSION

The media employed during this study revealed the
ability of 16 strains of budding bacteria to deposit iron
oxides and 5 strains to deposit manganese oxides. This
suggests that budding bacteria from a wide range of environments have the ability to deposit such metal oxides from low
concentrations of their soluble inorganic forms as existed
in our media. With these media it is now easily possible to
detect iron and manganese depositors among budding bacterial
strains. By using the iron and manganese sources tested in
this work, in combination with more selective mineral media,
it may also be possible to detect metal oxide-depositing
budding bacteria directly on dilution plates. Such techniques
were used successfully by Tyler (1970) and by Schweisfurth
(1972) to isolate manganese-oxidizing budding bacteria.
However, enumeration of budding bacteria on such media will
be hampered by the presence of other metal-depositing bacteria
that can grow on these media (Tyler, 1970).

The findings that the majority of the budding bacteria strains were able to deposit iron under some condition whereas only a few strains could deposit manganese, suggest that iron-depositing ability is more widespread amongst budding bacteria than manganese-depositing ability. It is interesting in this regard that all of the very active manganese-depositing strains were also capable of iron deposition. However, the opposite was not true. Strains SW-809 and 854, both very active iron depositors, did not deposit manganese in their colonies. Oddly enough, strain 854 was obtained as strain T-37 of Tyler and Marshall (1967) who originally isolated it from a ferromanganese deposit in a hydroelectric pipeline. This strain was originally reported to deposit manganese. For 10 years it has been kept in our culture collection on medium 337 (Hirsch and Conti, 1964). In addition, strain T-37, like many other manganese-depositing bacteria, showed spasmodic manganese-depositing ability after isolation and subculture (Tyler and Marshall, 1967). As far as the present authors know, strain T-37 has never been tested for iron deposition.

Morphologically, the very active strains 868 and 869 closely resembled *Pedomicrobium* spp. (Gebers, 1974). This resemblance is enhanced by our findings that they deposit both iron and manganese, a property ascribed to *P. podsolicum* (Aristovskaya, 1963). However, the exact taxonomic position of these and other iron- and manganese- depositing strains awaits clarification of the genus description of *Pedomicrobium*.

Hirsch (1968) reported that iron oxide deposition was initiated at primary active sites on the surfaces of brackish water budding bacteria. In this study, strain SW-809, one of Hirsch's original isolates, as well as strains 868 and 869, normally became encrusted with iron oxide. However, in many instances beaded deposits of iron were observed that could represent primary sites of deposition of the hyphae. Strains 868 and 869 also accumulated manganese oxide particles on their surfaces, indicating that, as suggested by Dow (1974), the active site hypothesis may be applied to the deposition of manganese as well as iron. In any case, further investigation of the mechanisms of deposition of metal oxides by budding bacteria is now possible using the iron- and manganese-depositing strains detected during this work.

ACKNOWLEDGMENT

The senior author was supported by a fellowship from the Alexander von Humboldt Foundation during this work.

REFERENCES

Altmann, H. F. "Bestimmung von in Wasser gelöstem Sauerstoff mit Leucoberbelinblau I. Eine schnelle Winklermethode," *Z. Anal. Chem.* 262:97-99 (1972).

Aristovskaya, T. V. "On the Decomposition of Organic Mineral Compounds in Podzolic Soils," *Potchvoved Akad. Nauk. SSSR.* 1:30-42 (1963).

Aristovskaya, T. V. and G. A. Zavarzin. "Biochemistry of Iron in Soil," in *Soil Biochemistry*, Vol. 2, A. D. McClaren and J. Skujins, Eds. (New York: Marcel Dekker, Inc., 1971), pp. 385-408.

Dow, C. S. "Morphology and Physiology of Morphologically Unusual Bacteria," Ph.D. Dissertation, University of Warwick (1974).

Gebers, R. "Isolierung und Charakterisierung von *Pedomicrobium* spp. aus Boden," Dipl.-Arb. Univ., Kiel (1974).

Glathe, H. and J. C. G. Ottow. "Ökologische und physiologische Aspekte zum Mechanismus der Eisenoxidation und Ockerbildung Eine Übersicht," *Z. Bakt. Parasitk. Infektionskr. Hyg.* 127:749-769 (1972).

Hajj, H. and J. Makemson. "Determination of Growth of *Sphaerotilus discophorus* in the Presence of Manganese," *Appl. Environ. Microbiol.* 32:699-702 (1976).

Herbert, D., P. J. Phipps and R. E. Strange. "Chemical Analysis of Microbial Cells," in *Methods in Microbiology*, Vol. 5B, J. R. Norris and D. W. Ribbons, Eds. (New York: Academic Press, 1971), pp. 209-283.

Hirsch, P. "Biology of Budding Bacteria. IV. Epicellular Deposition of Iron by Aquatic Budding Bacteria," *Arch. Mikrobiol.* 60:201-216 (1968).

Hirsch, P. "Budding Bacteria," *Ann. Rev. Microbiol.* 28:391-444 (1974).

Hirsch, P. and S. F. Conti. "Biology of Budding Bacteria. I. Enrichment, Isolation and Morphology of *Hyphomicrobium* spp," *Arch. Mikrobiol.* 48:339-357 (1964).

Krumbein, W. E. and H. J. Altmann. "A New Method for the Detection and Enumeration of Manganese Oxidizing and Reducing Microorganisms," *Helgolander wiss. Meeresunters*, 25: 347-356 (1973).

MacLeod, R. A., E. Onofrey and E. Norris. "Nutrition and Metabolism of Marine Bacteria. I. Survey of Nutritional Requirements," *J. Bacteriol.* 68:680-686 (1954).

Schweisfurth, R. "Manganoxydierende Mikroorganismen in Trinkwasserversorgungsanlagen," *Gaswasserfach/abwasser* 113:562-572 (1972).

Staley, J. T. *"Prosthecomicrobium* and *Ancalomicrobium:* New Prosthechate Freshwater Bacteria," *J. Bacteriol.* 95:1921-1942 (1968).

Tyler, P. A. "Hyphomicrobia and the Oxidation of Manganese in Aquatic Ecosystems," *Antonie v. Leeuwenhoek* 36:567-578 (1970).

Tyler, P. A. and K. C. Marshall. "Microbial Oxidation of Manganese in Hydroelectric Pipelines," *Antonie v. Leeuwenhoek.* 33:171-183 (1967).

van Ert, M. and J. T. Staley. "Gas Vacuolated Strains of *Microcyclus Aquaticus,"* *J. Bacteriol.* 108:236-240 (1971).

ISOLATION AND INVESTIGATION OF *PEDOMICROBIUM* SPP.,
HEAVY METAL-DEPOSITING BACTERIA FROM SOIL HABITATS

R. GEBERS
P. HIRSCH

Institut für Allgemeine Mikrobiologie
University of Kiel
Federal Republic of Germany

INTRODUCTION

The genus *Pedomicrobium* was thought to play an important
role in the pedogenesis of podzols. First observations were
made by Aristovskaya (1961), who obtained enrichment cultures
from samples of Karelian podzols. The only substrates
successfully employed for enrichment and growth were humic
extracts. These contained fulvic acids complexed with aluminum, iron and manganese sesquioxides. No other media tested
allowed growth of her pedomicrobia.
     Aristovskaya described three species: *P.ferrugineum*
(1961), an iron-depositing culture; *P.manganicum* (1961) with
manganese depositions, and *P.podzolicum* (1963), which accumulated iron and/or manganese. All depositions initiated
by these bacteria consisted mainly of oxidized heavy metal
compounds, *e.g.* hydrated ferric oxides, manganese(III) or
(IV) oxides. Later, Aristovskaya and Zavarzin (1972)
demonstrated iron-oxidizing activity of *P.ferrugineum*.
     It must be assumed that in the aquatic environment
there are further habitats of pedomicrobia. Tyler and Marshall
(1967) isolated a manganese-depositing organism (strain T-37)
from a freshwater pipeline. Morphologically, this strain
resembled *Pedomicrobium* spp. Several other iron-depositing
pedomicrobia were isolated by Hirsch (1968) from sea water
and brackish water, suggesting a wide distribution of these
bacteria. Growth of all aquatic isolates was not dependent
on humic substrates.
     Unfortunately, the original terrestrial *Pedomicrobium*
cultures were lost (Aristovskaya, personal communication,
1975). In order to revive investigation of these interesting

bacteria, new *Pedomicrobium* strains had to be isolated from soils similar to the Karelian podzols. With these new isolates (Gebers, 1974) modern investigation of the taxonomic validity of the genus *Pedomicrobium*, as well as the ecological function of heavy metal deposition, can be carried out.

MATERIALS AND METHODS

Sampling Sites and Soil Analyses

Several parts of Schleswig-Holstein (North Germany) with podzolic soils were investigated. Samples were taken from the "Hennstedter Holz," near Neumünster (sites HH-1 and HH-2,) from the "Reselith-Berg" near Itzehoe (site RB-1) and from soils near Flensburg-Hullerup (FH-1 and FH-2). The soil pH was measured in air-dried samples, suspended for 30 min in 0.1 N KCl. The total water content of the soils and the extracted humic gel was determined gravimetrically after drying at 105° C. Determinations for Fe(II)-, Fe(III)-, and Mn(III; IV) were carried out with $K_3[Fe(CN)_6]$, $K_4[Fe(CN)_6]$, or with benzidine reagent (Fiegl, 1960), respectively.

Media

Humic extracts were prepared from a mixture of A_h, E, B_h and B_{fe} horizons of these soils. Ponomareva's method (1964) of hydrochloric acid extraction (Figure 1) was employed. Media containing 5 g/l (wet wt) of humic gel were solidified with 18 g/l of Bacto Agar (Difco, Detroit, Michigan). Various substrates, such as ferrous salts, sugars, organic acids, amino acids and vitamins, were added to some of these humic gel media. They were either sterilized by filtration or they were autoclaved (121° C, 20 min). The pH was adjusted with NaOH or NCl from 5.0 or up to 9.2. After sterilization the pH was 4.4 or up to 7.2.

In the second set of enrichment experiments artificial media were compared to humic gel media. Agar "151" contained per liter: 1 g D-ribose, 0.5 g Bacto Peptone (Difco), and 20 ml Hutner's basal salts medium (Staley, 1968). Sterile filtered vitamin solution no. 6 (Staley, 1968), final concentration 1% v/v, and actidion (0.75% w/v; Roth, Darmstadt), final concentration 0.015% w/v, were added after autoclaving. All chemicals were "pro analysis" grade (Merck, Darmstadt).

Sampling and Inoculation

Five-gram amounts of mixed samples from the A_h, E and B horizons were thoroughly suspended in 500 ml sterile saline solution. Immediately afterwards, while still at the sampling site, 0.1 ml of this suspension was streaked onto solid media.

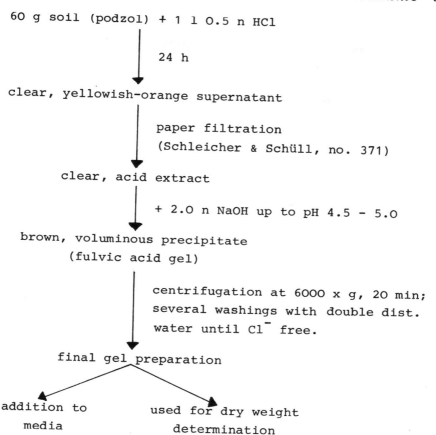

60 g soil (podzol) + 1 1 0.5 n HCl

24 h

clear, yellowish-orange supernatant

paper filtration
(Schleicher & Schüll, no. 371)

clear, acid extract

+ 2.0 n NaOH up to pH 4.5 - 5.0

brown, voluminous precipitate
(fulvic acid gel)

centrifugation at 6000 x g, 20 min;
several washings with double dist.
water until Cl⁻ free.

final gel preparation

addition to   used for dry weight
media   determination

Figure 1.   Preparation of humic gel (fulvic acid iron ses-
quioxide complexes), after Ponomareva (1964).

Growth Conditions

      Various parameters, such as temperature, light and
atmosphere, that could possibly influence the growth of
pedomicrobia and accompanying microorganisms were tested
for selective influence. The variations of atmospheric
conditions were achieved in a desiccator after replacing the
air twice with N_2 fillings. Light influence was tested on
a window sill with an additional 60-W bulb at a distance of
80 cm. Light intensity varied between 80 and 100-ft cd
depending on the intensity of the sunlight.

Microscopy

      For observation of living cells with a Zeiss Phase
Contrast Photomicroscope II, agar-coated, dried glass slides
(2% w/v Bacto Noble Agar; Difco) were used. Preparation of

cell suspensions for transmission electron microscopy
("TEM") was carried out with formvar-(0.75% polyvinylformal-
dyhyde) coated copper grids (200 mesh). For negative staining phosphotungstic acid (1% w/v; pH 6.8) was used. Pt-C
shadowing was done with a Balzers BAE 300 freeze etching
unit. TEM observations were conducted with a Philips EM-300
(Philips, Eindhoven, Netherlands), kindly supported by Dr.
H. Volker, Kiel.

RESULTS

     The first series of enrichment experiments was conducted
during autumn, winter and spring, and at two sampling sites
in the "Hennstedter Holz." Only humic gel agars with or
without supplementary substrates were used. One sample,
taken in November from site HH-1, was positive for pedomicrobia.
At this location the soil had a podzol profile with a 50-cm
B_{fe} horizon. Further characteristics of this soil are given
in Table I. Samples from site HH-2 with a podzolic brown
forest soil were all negative.

Table I
Properties of an Iron Podzol at "Hennsteder Holz,"
Site HH-1 from which *Pedomicrobium* Strains
P-111, Q-112, R-121, S-122 and T-123 were Isolated

Determinations	Total Number of Determinations	Average Value
pH_{KCL}	2	3.1
Fe (II,III)	3	Present
Mn (II, III, IV)	3	Absent
Total Water Content of Soil	3	21.27%
Yield of Humic Gel (wet wt)	5	6.00%
Yield of Humic Gel (dry wt)	3	0.74%
Water Content of Humic Gel	4	91.50%

     Pedomicrobium colonies from the HH-1 sample were kept
aerobic and dark, and at 20° C they developed within 41 days.
These budding bacteria were easily distinguished from other
forms by up to three long, thin hyphae that grew out from the
mother cells (Figure 2). The hyphae were often branched
and produced young buds at their tips (Figures 3 and 4).
Mature buds were flagellated ("swarmers"; Figure 5). After
losing mobility, these produced hyphae and buds. Mother

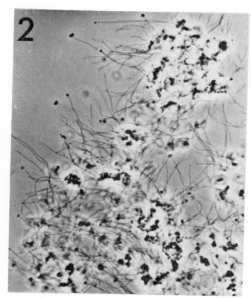

Figure 2. *Pedomicrobium ferrugineum* strain S-122, edge of a colony. Phase contrast; magnification 1200 X.

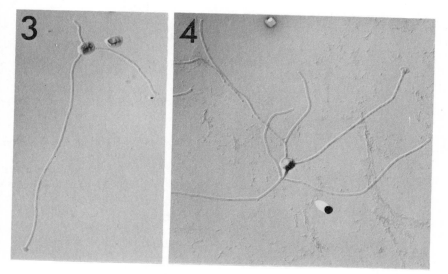

Figures 3 and 4. *Pedomicrobium ferrugineum* S-122 (left), and *P.manganicum* E-211 (right) with several hyphae and young buds at the hyphae tips. TEM; Pt-C shadow; magnification 5300 X.

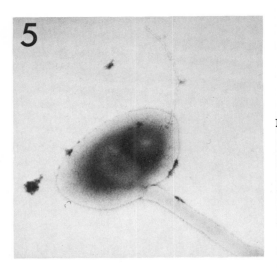

Figure 5. *Pedomicrobium ferrugineum* P-111, mature bud with flagellum. Negative stain with 1 percent phosphotungstic acid. Magnification 38000 X.

cells and swarmers were tetrahedral, up to 1 µm wide and 1.5 µm long. Initially, young buds were spherical and only later changed to an oval shape, with the longitudinal axis rectangular to the hyphae. These cell shapes, as well as the number and insertion of hyphae, were used as morphological markers to distinguish between *Pedomicrobium* and *Hyphomicrobium* spp. (*Bergey's Manual*, 8th ed.).

In the first enrichments, several colonies were strongly cohering and consisted of approximately 30 percent pedomicrobia; it was almost impossible to break up these colonies and to spread them on agar. Several techniques were tested to disperse these cells to a homogenous suspension in saline solution. Adequate distribution of cells was eventually obtained by a 1-min manual treatment with a Potter-Elvehjem glass homogenizer.

For the isolation, *Pedomicrobium* colonies were homogenized in 0.5-1 ml saline solution and streaked onto agar media. Growth occurred at incubation temperatures of 20° or 30° C, But not at 11° C. Light had no influence on growth, but cultures were usually incubated in the dark. In addition to air, reduced pO_2 of 16, or 1 vol% of traces of oxygen, respectively, allowed growth of pedomicrobia. Thirty vol% carbon monoxide did not hinder the development of these budding bacteria. Reduced oxygen pressure and carbon monoxide could be used to increase the selectivity of isolation procedures, since strict aerophiles and CO-sensitive organisms were suppressed. Only a methanol-saturated, aerobic atmosphere seemed to hinder the growth of *Pedomicrobium* spp.

Pedomicrobia grew slowly on all media employed as long as the pH remained above 5.0. Organic compounds added to humic gel agar seemed to support growth of contaminants, but not of pedomicrobia. The highest selectivity was observed

with humic extract as the sole added substrate, and at a pH
of 5 to 6. These conditions reduced the development of many
contaminating bacteria but not of fungi. The selective
stimulation did not depend on the concentration of the humic
gel.

After four to six weeks of incubation, tiny yellowish-
brown colonies of *Pedomicrobium* spp. were seen at 40-fold
magnification. They were often overgrown with molds, actinomycetes or bacteria. Areas containing pedomicrobia were
recognized by the brownish colonies with frayed edges somewhat similar to those of actinomycetes (Figure 6).

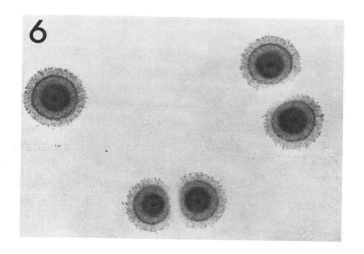

Figure 6. *Pedomicrobium ferrugineum* P-111, growth on humic
gel agar; pH 5.6. Transmission illumination; magnification
30X.

The isolation procedure had to be repeated three times
before pure cultures of *Pedomicrobium* spp. were obtained. But
now the cells had an appearance quite unlike that of cells
in the enrichment cultures. They were irregularly shaped with
short distorted hyphae and they contained large storage
granules. However, the addition to the humic gel medium of
1 vol% vitamin solution no. 6 allowed "normal" growth to
proceed again. Other supplements tested did not overcome
the pleomorphy. Five strains (P-111, Q-112, R-121, S-122,
T-123) were isolated from this sample. They were identified
according to *Bergey's Manual* (8th ed.) as *Pedomicrobium
ferrugineum*.

Additional isolation attempts were carried out at three other sampling sites (RB-1, FH-1, FH-2) during the summer. Pure humic gel media were used and compared to agar 151, with 0.015% (w/v) actidion added to prevent growth of eucaryonts. One additional *Pedomicrobium* strain (F-311) was isolated with the methods described above. For this the sample was taken at site FH-1 from the upper part (40-70 cm depth) of the B_h and B_{fe} horizons of an iron-podzol with well-developed E and B_{fe} horizons. The iron accumulations can best be described as a hardpan ("Ortstein") layer. In this last case, tiny areas of *Pedomicrobium* growth were observed on actidion agar 151 after three months. Many bacteria, but only a few molds resistent to actidion, contaminated the culture. After three subcultures the strain was pure. Identification of this culture is in progress.

A water sample from a quartzite rock soil ("Opferkessel") in the forest of Fontainebleau near Paris, France was kindly provided by Dr. F. Eckhardt, Kiel. This sample was thought to contain *Pedomicrobium* spp. An isolation was carried out on pure humic gel agar as well as on actidion agar 151. This latter strain (E-211) closely resembled *P.manganicum* (*Bergey's Manual*, 8th ed.) except that the cell size was larger (1 to 1.5 μm instead of 0.4 μm) than that described by Aristovskaya (1961).

All seven isolates grew slowly on humic gel agar. A liquid medium (171) allowing faster and better growth was developed. It contained (per liter): 1 g D-ribose, 0.5 g Bacto Peptone (or 0.5 g Bacto Yeast Extract), 10 ml vitamin solution no. 6, and 1 ml trace element solution ("metals 44"; Staley, 1968). The pH was adjusted to 9.0 with NaOH, and the medium was sterilized by membrane filtration. Humic substances were found to be unnecessary for the growth of these *Pedomicrobium* strains.

The investigation of heavy metal deposition of strains S-122 and E-211 revealed that S-122 accumulated oxidized iron compounds but not manganese, whereas E-211 deposited oxidized manganese compounds but no iron. *Pedomicrobium* S-122 showed brown, voluminous depositions of Fe(III) oxides on mother cells and hyphae (Figures 7, 8, 9 and 10) when grown in liquid media with sterile iron sources such as 400 mg paper clips, 400 mg iron powder or 630 mg ferrous sulfide per 50 ml nutrient broth 171. The quantity and activity of a possibly oxidizing ability have not yet been investigated. At pH 4.5 strain S-122 was able to cause oxidation of as much as 10 percent of the ferrous sulfate added at a concentration of 1 μg Fe^{2+}/ml within 6 hr, whereas there was no oxidation in the sterile control. However, at pH 6.0 or 7.0 the bacteria seemed to stabilize the reduced state of iron, while the sterile control was oxidized by air.

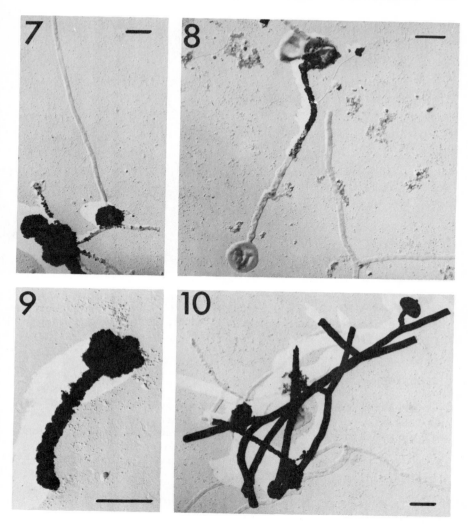

Figures 7, 8, 9 and 10. *Pedomicrobium ferrugineum* S-122, grown in liquid medium 171 with 1.26% (w/v) FeS. Note iron deposition on mother cells and some hyphae. TEM; Pt-C shadow; markers represent 1 µm.

Mother cells of strain E-211 were covered with a thick brown layer consisting of manganese oxides (Figure 11) when grown on solid or liquid media containing 0.75 mg/1 Mn(II). This manganese coat was so rigid that it resisted glass knife cutting as performed for ultrathin sectioning. Manganese depositions were not observed on the hyphae.

Figure 11. *Pedomicrobium manganicum* E-211, growth in liquid
    medium 171 containing 0.075% (w/v) Mn^{2+}. Note manganese
    depositions on spherical cells. TEM; Pt-C shadow; magni-
    fication 31000 X.

DISCUSSION

    The methods described allowed selective enrichment
and isolation of pedomicrobia. Successful enrichment from a
soil suspension depended on (1) long incubation periods, and
(2) on the addition of a vitamin mixture to the isolation
media. Lack of vitamins led to an abnormal, pleomorphic
appearance of our pedomicrobia. This could conceivably prevent their recognition.
    In North German podzols *Pedomicrobium* spp. were less
abundant than in Karelian soils. This could have caused the
paucity of positive enrichment cultures, although various
different media were employed. This assumption is supported
by our pedoscope observations applied to investigate the
natural development and distribution of *Pedomicrobium* spp.
The Russian authors, Aristovskaya and Parinkana (1961),
Aristovskaya and Zavarzin (1972), and Khak-Mun (1967),
had observed large numbers of iron- and manganese-depositing
pedomicrobia in pedoscope capillaries. They were, especially
during the dry seasons, dominant in Russian soils. In our
investigations with pedoscopes, the pedomicrobia were never
abundant, not even in the summer. Environmental parameters
such as temperature, pH, or soil water content, as well as
seasonal influences, cannot be compared since these were
not given in the original publications.

The *Pedomicrobium* strains obtained now for the first time in pure culture probably belong to two different species. Further investigations can now be conducted on their physiology, ecology, geomicrobiological significance, and taxonomical relationship to other budding bacteria. Physiological characterization and a taxonomical comparison with *Hyphomicrobium* spp. is now is progress. Together with a forthcoming description of our strains, neotype cultures will be deposited in culture collections.

REFERENCES

Aristovskaya, T. V. "Accumulation of Iron in Breakdown of Organomineral Humus Complexes by Microorganisms," *Dok. Akad. Nauk SSSR* (Transl.) 136:954-957 (1961).

Aristovskaya, T. V. "Decomposition of Organomineral Compounds in Podzolic Soils," *Pochvovedenie* (Transl.) 1:30-43 (1963).

Aristovskaya, T. V. and O. M. Parinkina. "Neue methodische Beispiele in der Erforschung von Gemeinschaften der Bodenorganismen," *Pochvovedenie* (Transl.) 1:20-28 (1961).

Aristovskaya, T. V. and G. A. Zavarzin. "Biochemistry of Iron in Soil," *Soil Biochem.* 2:385-408 (1972).

Bergey's Manual of Determinative Bacteriology, 8th ed. (Baltimore: Williams andWilkins, 1974), pp. 151-153.

Feigl, F. *Tupfelanalyse* I. (Frankfurt/Main: Akad. Verl.-Ges., 1960).

Gebers, R. "Isolierung und Charakterisierung von *Pedomicrobium* spp. aus Boden," M.S. Thesis, Kiel University (1974).

Hirsch, P. "Biology of Budding Bacteria IV. Epicellular Deposition of Iron by Aquatic Budding Bacteria," *Arch. Mikrobiol.* 60:201-216 (1968).

Khak-Mun, T. "Iron- and Manganese-Oxidizing Microorganisms in Soils of South Sakhalin," *Mikrobiologiya* (Transl.) 36:337-344 (1967).

Ponomareva, W. W. "Theory of Podzolisation," *Acad. Sci. USSR* (Transl.) pp. 41-73 (1964).

Staley, J. T.   *Prosthecomicrobium* and *Ancalomicrobium*,
New Prosthecate Freshwater Bacteria," *J. Bacteriol.*
95:1921–1942 (1968).

Tyler, P. A. and K. C. Marshall.   "Pleomorphy in Stalked,
Budding Bacteria," *J. Bacteriol.* 93:1132–1136 (1967).

CHAPTER 73

MICROBIOLOGY OF THE PRECIPITATION OF MANGANESE

R. SCHWEISFURTH
D. ELEFTHERIADIS
H. GUNDLACH
M. JACOBS
W. JUNG

Fachrichtung Hygiene und Mikrobiologie
Universität des Saarlandes, Medizinische Fakultat
D-6650 Homburg
Saar und Bundesanstalt für Geowissenschaften und Rohstoffe
Postfach 510153, D-3000 Hannover 51
Federal Republic of Germany

INTRODUCTION

Dependent on Eh and pH and a few other factors, Mn(II) is oxidized by free or dissolved oxygen. Below pH 8 and above an Eh value of +200 mV, manganese is oxidized only by microorganisms, under natural conditions. To what extent organic complexes with Mn(II) and Mn(III) shift the specified values is not known to us.

The number of strains at hand as pure cultures in laboratories has increased in the last years. While from the genera and species described up to 1968 (Schweisfurth, 1973a) all except *Sphaerotilus discophorus* (*Leptothrix discophora*; Dondero, 1976), *Pseudomonas manganoxidans* (Schweisfurth, 1973b) and manganese-oxidizing fungi (Schweisfurth, 1971) were no longer available or had ceased to oxidize manganese. (A few such genera as *Metallogenium*, *Kusnezovia*, *Caulosoccus* or *Pedomicrobium* were unavailable at that time. Presently the following bacteria are in culture: *Arthrobacter* (Ehrlich, 1963, 1968), *Arthrobacter* 216 (v. Veen, 1973), *Arthrobacter* (Bromfield, 1974), *Arthrobacter siderocapsulatus* (Dubinina and Zhdanov, 1975), a few cultures out of manganese nodules, by Ottow and Schutte (personal communication), strains of *Pseudomonas putida* and *P. alcaligenes* with the capability of manganese oxidation (Jung and Schweisfurth, 1976) and

Hyphomicrobium manganoxidans (Eleftheriadis, 1976,
Eleftheriadis, Schweisfurth and Wenzel, 1976) as well as
additional fungal species (Timonin, Illman and Hartgerink,
1972).

EXPERIMENTS AND RESULTS

The conditions for the occurrence of manganese-
oxidizing microorganisms in the locations of freshwater, salt
water (Krumbein, 1971), thermal springs, soil and oxidized
manganese deposits have thus far been defined as: pH 5.5 to
8, Eh above +200 mV, temperature of 10° to 44° C, and a lower
limit for O_2 (dissolved) of 3-5 mg/l. *In situ* measurements
of the Eh values in the microzonal region, for example, can
only be accomplished (compare Perfil'ev *et al.*, 1964) when
the platinum electrodes are protected by a membrane against
the entry of manganese oxide; otherwise elevated Eh values
are recorded (Schweisfurth, 1976). Numbers for species and
genera in the designated locations cannot yet be cited. In
oxidized manganese deposits one can demonstrate through culture: *Metallogenium* (Sokolova-Dubinina and Derjugina, 1966)
as well as *Hyphomicrobium* species, *Metallogenium personatum,*
Pseudomonas, Achromobacter, aerobic *Actinomycetes* and manganese-oxidizing fungi (Schweisfurth and Jung, 1975).

It is conceivable that a specific enrichment of elements
occurs, with microbial manganese oxidation; it differs in
quantity or type from those as they appear in a chemical
Mn(II) oxidation. Corresponding laboratory tests, in which
one works with Mn(II) and bacteria on the one hand and with
identical O_2-containing solutions at a pH of 12 on the other,
have shown in primary tests that, from the elements examined,
Co, Cu, Ni, Zn and Fe, Co as well as Cu, Zn and Fe were enriched in the microbially formed manganese oxide. Circumstances permitting, such processes are suitable to clarify the
enrichment of the above-mentioned elements in manganese
nodules, especially since in January 1976 manganese-oxidizing
bacteria were detected in manganese nodules from the Pacific
during the "Valdivia" cruises (Schütte, personal communication).

The first culture of manganese-oxidizing microorganisms
and their further cultivation as pure cultures under preserva-
tion of the manganese-oxidizing capacity requires a great
number of different media. Depending on genus or species,
different optima are shown for Mn(II) concentration and for
type and amount of organic carbon and energy sources. It is
fundamental that the pH value not be lowered too far as a
result of acid production, for example from sugars, and on
the other hand it may not rise above 8, for example by too
high concentrations of fatty acids, whereby either no further
manganese oxidation occurs or *Cloaca cloacae* or *Pseudomonas*
fluorescens with sodium citrate appear as manganese-oxidizing

bacteria (compare with Bromfield, 1974; Schweisfurth, 1976). A buffering of the media can run into difficulties: absence of manganese oxidation by phosphate buffers, inhibition of propagation of bacteria through the buffer, and utilization of buffer substances or insufficient buffering capacity.

Experiments on pure cultures meet difficulties with the recording of growth curves on the basis of protein and DNA determinations (Hajj and Makemson, 1976) because Mn(II) and Mn(IV) disturb the methods. Misunderstandings were caused in this way in experiments on the biological effect of manganese oxidation. Indications of a positive effect of manganese oxidation of protein and DNA production are presently found only by Ehrlich (1975); Eleftheriadis (1976) found a multiplication of *Hyphomicrobium manganoxidans* only in the presence of and by oxidation of Mn(II) by addition of $NaHCO_3$ or organic C_1-compounds. With this organism, in contrast to *Pseudomonas manganoxidans* (ATCC 23483) or *Sphaerotilus discophorus* (Hajj and Makemson, 1976), manganese oxidation begins with the exponential growth phase and not just at the end.

ADDITIONAL RESULTS

Additional results for *Pseudomonas manganoxidans* (Jung and Schweisfurth, 1976), *Hyphomicrobium manganoxidans* (Eleftheriadis, 1976) and *Metallogenium symbioticum* (Zavarzin, 1964; Schweisfurth, 1972; Schweisfurth and v. Hehn, 1972; Jacobs and Schweisfurth, in preparation) of our research team can be summarized as follows.

Pseudomonas manganoxidans

Mn(II) in concentrations of over 5-10 mg/l inhibits manganese oxidation. Ca^{++} promotes manganese oxidation, and ammonium ion inhibits it below 5 mg/l. In flow cultures, although Mn(II) and its oxidation have no positive effect on the multiplication of bacteria, it is an enrichment of bacteria in the manganese oxides that are produced. Cultures of *Pseudomonas manganoxidans* produce an intracellular, manganese-oxidizing protein during the stationary phase of growth. The protein was heat labile, could be inactivated by protease and has a pH optimum for manganese oxidation at pH 7. Mn(II) is oxidized only at concentrations below $3 \cdot 10^{-5}$ M. The occurrence of the protein is not dependent on the presence of Mn(II) but is clearly related to the cessation of growth after the end of the exponential growth phase. Cell extracts contain several species of manganese-oxidizing protein, which show great variations in molecular weight. Oxygen, coenzymes and low-molecular-weight components of the cell extract are not involved in the reaction as electron acceptors. Continued manganese oxidation by manganese-oxidizing protein results in a gradual decrease in activity, which corresponds to the amounts of formed Mn(IV). This behavior suggests a direct, noncatalytic participation of the protein in the reaction.

Hyphomicrobium manganoxidans

This involves a morphologically typical Hyphomicrobium, which multiplies at an optimal temperature of 37° to 44° C only in the presence of Mn(II) and its oxidation. The isolation was successful from Mn(IV)-Fe(III) deposits (Reissacherite) of the thermal springs in Badgastein. *H. manganoxidans* utilizes soil extract, methylamine, formiate, urea, methanol and sodium bicarbonate. Carbon-14 as bicarbonate is incorporated.

Metallogenium symbioticum

Thus far we have succeeded neither in producing a fungus-free culture of *M. symbioticum* according to the instructions of Dubinina (1970) for culture on Mycoplasma media, nor in obtaining a host-free culture with Griseofulvin or Nystatin according to Bolotina *et al.* (1973). Manganese oxidation through fungus-free filtrate occurs. It is dependent on the age of the culture and begins with the utilization of a 30-hr-old fungus mycel. The greatest number of manganese-oxidizing (fungus-free) units is reached after 48 hr. The manganese oxidation using filtrate is additionally dependent on the filtrate amount and the Mn(II) concentration in the solution. The filtrate has protein character.

The positive effect of such gelling substances as gelatine, agar-agar or gum arab on the manganese oxidation and thereby also the production of "arai" is based on a decrease of the Mn(II) concentration in the medium by complexing. In autoradiographical tests it was determined that tritiated Thymidin is not incorporated into the manganese oxide-containing filamentous structures of fungi. Similar experiments with marked amino acids are not yet completed.

ACKNOWLEDGMENTS

All research was supported by grants of the Deutsche Forschungsgemeinschaft.

REFERENCES

Bolotina, I. I., T. G. Mircink and D. I. Nikitin. "Über die Natur und Verbreitung von manganoxidierenden Mikroorganismen, die Begleiter von Pilzen sind," *Pocvevedenie* 9:75-81 (1973).

Bromfield, S. M. "Bacterial Oxidation of Manganous Ions as Affected by Organic Substrate Concentration and Composition," *Soil Biol. Biochem.* 6:383-392 (1974).

Dondero, N. C. "The Sphaerotilus-Leptothrix group," *Ann. Rev. Microbiul.* 29:407-428 (1975).

Dubinina, G. A. "Untersuchungen über die Morphologie von Metallogenium und die Beziehungen zu Mycoplasma," *A. Allg. Mikrobiol.* 10:309-320 (1970).

Dubinina, G. A. and A. V. Zhdanov. "Recognization of the Iron Bacteria *Siderocapsa* as *Arthrobacter* and Description of *Arthrobacter siderocapsulatus,*" *Int. J. System. Bact.* 25:340-350 (1975).

Ehrlich, H. L. "Bacteriology of Manganese Nodules. I. Bacterial Action on Manganese in Nodule Enrichments," *Appl. Microbiol.* 11:15-19 (1963).

Ehrlich, H. L. "Bacteriology of Manganese Nodules. II. Manganese Oxidation by Cell-Free Extract from a Manganese Nodule Bacterium," *Appl. Microbiol.* 16:197-202 (1968).

Ehrlich, H. L. "The Formation of Ores in the Sedimentary Environment of the Deep Sea with Microbial Participation: The Case for Ferromanganese Concretions," *Soil Sci.* 119: 36-41 (1975).

Eleftheriadis, D. "Mangan- und Eisenoxidation in Mineral- und Thermalquellen - Mikrobiologie, Chemie und Geochemie," Dissertation, Universität des Saarlandes, Saarbruecken, BRD (1976).

Eleftheriadis, D., R. Schweisfurth and A. Wenzel. "The Occurrence of Iron and Manganese-Oxidizing Bacteria in Mineral and Thermal Springs of Greece and Austria," *Intern. Congr. Thermal Waters, Geothermal Energy and Vulcanisms of the Mediterranean Area, Athens,* Vol. 2 (1976).

Hajj, H. and J. Makemson. "Determination of Growth of *Sphaerotilus discophorus* in the Presence of Manganese," *Appl. Environ. Microbiol.* 32:699-702 (1976).

Jung, W. K. and R. Schweisfurth. "Manganoxidierende Bakterien. III. Wachstum und Manganoxidation bei Pseudomonas Manganoxidans Schw," *Z. Allg. Mikroboil.* 16:587-597 (1976).

Krumbein, W. E. "Manganese-Oxidizing Fungi and Bacteria in Recent Shelf Sediments of the Bay of Biscay and the North Sea," *Naturwissenschaften* 58:56-57 (1971).

Schweisfurth, R. "Manganoxidierende Pilze. I. Vorkommen, Isolierungen und mikroskopische Untersuchungen," *Z. Allg. Mikrobiol.* 11:415-430 (1971).

Schweisfurth, R. "Manganoxidierende Pilze. II. Untersuchungen an Laboratoriumskulturen," *Z. Allg. Mikrobiol.* 12: 667-671 (1972).

Schweisfurth, R. "Manganoxidierende Bakterien. Literaturübersicht (Bestandsaufnahme beschriebener Arten)," *Zbl. Bakt., I. Ref.* 233:257-270 (1973a).

Schweisfurth, R. "Manganoxidierende Bakterien. I. Isolierung und Bestimmung einiger Stämme von Manganbakterien," *Z. Allg. Mikrobiol.* 13:341-347 (1973b).

Schweisfurth, R. "Manganoxidierende Bakterien. II. Erste Untersuchungen an Reinkulturen der Pseudomonas manganoxidans-Gruppe," *Z. Allg. Mikrobiol.* 16:133-147 (1976).

Schweisfurth, R. and G. v. Hehn. "Licht- und elektronenmikroskopische Untersuchungen sowie Kulturversuche zum Metallogenium-Problem," *Zbl. Bakt. Hyg., I. Abt. Orig. A* 220:357-361 (1972).

Schweisfurth, R. and W. Jung. "Manganoxidierende Mikroorganismen in Manganoxid-Konzentrationen," *Geochemie der Lagerstättenbildung und -proppektion.* Heft 28 d. Schriften der GDMB, Clausthal, BRD (1975).

Schweisfurth, R., W. K. Jung and H. Gundlach. "Manganese-Oxidizing Microorganisms and Their Importance for the Genesis of Manganese Ore Deposits," Intern. Monograph on Geol. and Geochem. of Manganese - *Proceedings of the 2nd International Symposium on Geology and Geochemistry of Manganese, 25 IGC, Australia* (1976).

Sokolova-Dubinina, G. A. and Z. P. Derjugina. "Die Beteiligung von Mikroorganismen an der Bildung oxidierter Erze im Mangan-Lager von Ciatura," *Mikrobiologiya (Moskau)* 35:344-349 (1966).

Timonin, M. I., W. I. Illman and T. Hargerink. "Oxidation of Manganous Salts of Manganese by Soil Fungi," *Can. J. Microbiol.* 18:793-799 (1972).

Veen Van, W. L. "Biological Oxidation of Manganese in Soils," *Ant. v. Leeuwenh.* 39:657-662 (1973).

Zavarzin, G. A. "Metallogenium Symbioticum," *Z. Allg. Mikrobiol.* 4:390-395 (1964).

CHAPTER 74

ANTIMONY-OXIDIZING BACTERIA
AND THEIR GEOCHEMICAL ACTIVITY

N. N. LYALIKOVA

Institute of Microbiology
USSR Academy of Sciences
Moscow, USSR

Microorganisms are marked by extremely high adaptability to the environment. They fill all ecological niches using the oxidation energy of most diverse chemical compounds. Consideration of ore deposits as habitats for microorganisms shows clearly that they form a suitable ecological niche for autotrophs. The almost complete absence of organic substances in igneous rocks and the reduced state of sulfur and other elements are suitable conditions for development of organisms involved in chemosynthesis. In the works of S. M. Vinogradsky, who discovered chemosynthesis in 1887, and then in the works of such scientists as Beijerninck, Waksman *et al.* it was reported that microorganisms can obtain energy from oxidation of protoxidic compounds of nitrogen, sulfur, iron and hydrogen as well as use carbon monoxide.

Consideration of theoretical possibilities for the existence of autotrophs using oxidation energy of other elements resulted in our concentrating on antimony deposits as a suitable ecological niche. Antimony does not belong to dispersed elements; it occurs in nature in shaped shoots and constitutes $4 \cdot 10^{-5}$ of weight percent of the earth crust. In nature both tri- and pentavalent antimony compounds exist. The oxidation of 1 gram-atom of trivalent antimony produces about 30 kcal, *i.e.*, the energy sufficient for forming the macrergic ATP bond. The facts mentioned above preconditioned the search of a new autotrophic microorganism obtaining energy from antimony oxidation.

It is known that *Thiobacillus ferrooxidans* is able to oxidize antimony sulfide – antimonite Sb_2S_3 (Silverman and Ehrlich, 1964; Lyalikova, 1966). But as was shown in our studies (Lyalikova, Shlain, 1969), the effect of this organism on antimonite results in formation of Sb_2O_3 — antimony trioxide, corresponding to senarmontite, a natural mineral, whereas in the oxidation zone of antimony deposits there are such minerals as cervantite Sb_2O_4 and minerals of stibiconite group formed on the basis of antimony pentoxide. Chemical oxidation may hardly account for the presence of pentavalent antimony in oxidation zone of antimony deposits since the noticeable oxidation of antimony trioxide in atmospheric conditions starts at 375° C. There are evidently two stages of biological oxidation of the basic antimony ore in nature, antimonite. In the first stage the antimonite sulfur is oxidized by thiobacilli *Th. ferrooxidans* under acid conditions and by the organism close to *Th. thioparus*, marked by us as Th."y," under neutral conditions. The antimony trioxide produced must be oxidized by an unknown organism for which it is an energy process.

For isolation of this organism the following composition of mineral medium was used   per 1 liter of distilled water: $(NH_4)_2SO_4$, 0.3 g; $Ca(NO_3)_2$, 0.1 g; $MgSO_4 \cdot 7H_2O$, 0.1 g; KCl, 0.05 g; KH_2PO_4, 1 g; $NaHCO_3$, 0.5 g. As the energy source, 300–500 mg of antimony trioxide per 100 ml of the medium were added separately to the solution and the pH was brought to 7.5. This pH was chosen because the mine waters of antimony deposits are usually neutral or slightly alkaline.

The antimony deposit in Zajaca, Yugoslavia, seemed to us most suitable for search of the new organism. The oxidation processes are so intensive in this deposit that in some mine sections up to 90 percent of the ore is represented by oxides.

Alterations were revealed in the medium three to four weeks after contamination of the mineral medium with samples of oxidized ores and waters of Zajaca deposit. The pH of the medium dropped from 7.5 to 4–5, and the lowest pH later observed in cultures was 3.7. The medium became turbid because of numerous colloid particles represented by 0.02–0.5 μm balls rather than because of bacterial cells, the number of which was negligible. Later the turbidity of the medium decreased since the colloids precipitate to the bottom, at which time the powder of antimony trioxide attaches to the flask bottom; after two to three months its color changes from white to cream or light yellow.

After producing the enrichment culture it was necessary to purify it, to show qualitatively antimony oxidation and the ability of the organism under study to fix carbon dioxide on the account of antimony oxidation energy. We succeeded in reducing the number of contaminants by using reagents of specific purity. Pure culture was obtained by the method of negative colonies suggested by S. N. Vinogradsky. The culture was cultivated with dilutions on potato and beef extract agar dishes; two to three days later, when the colonies of the contaminants appeared, the agar pieces without growth were cut out with a sterile lancet and transferred to flasks with mineral medium. The young culture at the age of three to ten days is represented by mobile 0.6-1.8 x 0.5 rods with one flagellum located subterminally. On the 10-14th day, coinciding with a sharp drop of pH, the cells lose their mobility and their shape becomes more irregular; in old cultures mycelial growth is sometimes observed. The cells are positively Gram-stained. Evidently, the culture is close to mycobacteria. The bacteria were called *Stibiobacter* from stibium-antimony senarmontii from senarmontite mineral of the basic oxidized substance.

Antinomy oxidation was studied by means of several methods. Quantitatively the trivalent antimony was determined by bromatometry, qualitatively the pentavalent antimony was detected at the compound forming of antimony chlorostibate with rhodamine B. To prove antimony oxidation and to study new mineralogical formation in cultures, two methods of X-ray structural analysis were used: diffractometry and Debai technique. It was shown by chemical analyses that 500-2000 mg/l of culture are oxidized by bacteria for a month, while in sterile control only 20-40 mg/l are oxidized.

A decrease in senarmontite peak (Sb_2S_3) by 5-7 percent was observed by us in diffractograms of samples taken from young (two to three week) cultures, whereas the peak corresponding to pentavalent antimony compounds had not appeared yet. The diffractograms of five-month new growth (Figure 1) show a decrease in senarmontite peak by 30 percent and the appearance of a small peak of antimony pyrochlore phase in Bragg angle region of 29-31° corresponding to 2.96 interplanar distance. In addition, a small peak of cervantite, antimony tetroxide, appeared. While the amount of senarmontite of cubic modification trioxide decreased by 30 percent the amount of valentinite of rhombic modification trioxide (reflex 121, Figure 1) remained invariable. The preference of antimony cubic modification by bacteria was seen from laboratory experiments with artificial and natural modifications of trioxide (Table I).

As previously mentioned, at bacteria development, mineral new growths of colloid nature appear in the culture. The colloids from a one-month culture were separated by filtration through membrane filters of different density - preliminary filter and filter No I. According to microchemical and spectral analysis the colloids contain, apart from antimony, a rather great amount of sodium, less potassium, negligible amounts of calcium and up to 14.7 percent of water.

The X-ray diffraction picture of a fresh new growth (Table II) shows only some diffused maxima, indicating weak recrystallization of this compound. The broad diffused lines of 2.94 as well as 2.5, 1.8, 1.54 and 1.1 represent the basic reflexes of stibiconite. In the course of time the

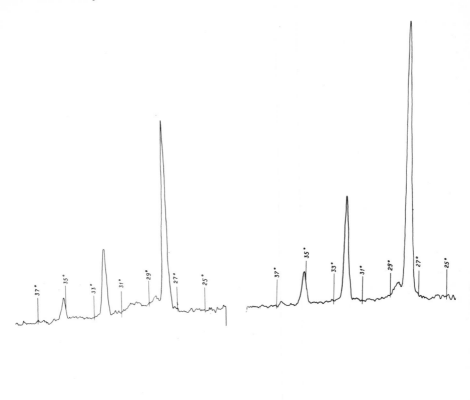

a   *b*

Figure 1. Diffractograms of antimony trioxide: a) with
   Stibiobacter senarmontii; b) without bacteria (control).

crystallization process goes on, the diffraction maxima
become sharper and new ones appear. The ten-month culture
precipitate reveals almost all reflexes characteristic of
stibiconite and its artificial analogue (Vitaliano and
Mason, 1952; Dihlström and Westgren, 1937). The transformation of trivalent antimony into pentavalent was also proved
by using Mёssbauer's effect.
     To prove the autotrophy of the isolated organism it
was necessary to establish its ability to fix carbon dioxide
and its fixation dependence on the amount of antimony oxidized.
For that purpose the experiments with labeled carbon dioxide
were conducted. The experiments were performed in closed
vessels, cell radioactivity was determined after the experiment, and the amount of oxidized antimony was estimated
bromatometrically. The experiments showed that the amount

Table I
Oxidation of Different Crystalline Forms of
Antimony Trioxide (average data) with
Stibiobacter Senarmontii Culture

Experimental Conditions	Initial Amount of Antimony Trioxide	The Amount (mg) at the end of Experiment	Oxidation for 1 month in 1000 ml of the (mg) medium
1. Senarmontite + Bacteria	403.8	307.2	96.6
2. Sterile Senarmontite, Control	403.8	398	5.8
3. Valentite + Bacteria	162.8	130.3	32.5
4. Sterile Valentinite, Control	162.8	159.0	3.8

of fixed carbon dioxide corresponded approximately to the amount of oxidized antimony. The percentage of energy consumption varied from 10 to 20, *i.e.*, it was close to that of other autotrophs.

The performance of biochemical investigations was hampered by complex biomass production; it was particularly difficult to separate the cells from antimony trioxide. To avoid it, the culture was grown in flasks in which antimony trioxide, having 1.6 mg/l solubility in water, was separated from the medium by a semipermeable cellophane membrane.

The experiment on studying the assimilation of labeled bicarbonate in the cells of *Stibiobacter senarmontii* was performed by Warburg vessels containing 1.8 ml of suspension produced by 10-fold condensation of the initial culture and 0.2 ml of $NaH^{14}CO_3$. For 30 minutes the involvement of labeled bicarbonate into acid proof products of biosynthesis is proportional to the incubation time. The mean rate of involvement is 0.02 $\mu M/min/1$ of the medium (Lyalikova, Vedenina, Romanova, 1976). The specific activity of ribuloso-1.5-diphosphate carboxylase (RDPC) is equal to 1 mE/ml of unpurified extract protein (protein content - 1 mg/ml of enzymic mixture). Both the rate of bicarbonate assimilation and the ratio between RDPC and PEPC (phosphoenolpyruvate carbocarboxylase), equalling 5:1, are lower than those usually observed in other autotrophs. This ratio was observed at delayed growth of some cultures and is evidently caused by slow culture growth because of the lack of energy substrate on account of low solubility of antimony trioxide.

Table II
Interspace Distance of New Mineralogical Formation
In Cultures of Different Ages

Time of Growth (1 month)		Time of Growth (10 months)		Stibiconite According to Vitaliano and Mason		$Sb_3O_6(OH)$ According to Dihlstrom and Westgren	
l	d	l	d	l	d	l	d
				90	5.13	-	
10	3.17[a]	7	3.20[a]				
				70	3.09	6	3.096
6[b]	2.94	10	2.93	100	2.96	10	2.998
		2	2.79[a]				
1	2.50	4	2.55	40	2.57	8	2.570
				10	2.36	2	2.357
		1	2.17			2	2.102
0.5	1.988	7	1.970	30	1.98	6	1.981
10	1.815	10	1.817	80	1.81	8	1.819
3	1.680[a]	7	1.677[a]				
		1	1.609[a]				
				20	1.57	4	1.569
6[b]	1.547	10	1.542	60	1.55	8	1.551
		1	1483	30	1.48	6	1.487
		1	1.447	30	1.44	6	1.441
		7	1.388	30	1.34	6	1.34
				20	1.28	6	1.287
		7	1.248[a]				
		5	1.184	40	1.18		
		5	1.138	10	1.13		
		5	1.074	10	1.08		
		4	1.039	20	1.05		

Fe rad.2R-57.3 mm,d-0.6 mm

[a]Lines related to senarmontite.

[b]Wide illegible line.

The study of carbon dioxide fixation products has shown that after five-minute chemosynthesis, the radioactivity is found in phosphoric ethers of sugars, phosphoglyceric acid and aspartic acid. The data indicate the ability of the investigated organism for autotrophic feeding, involving the reduction pentosophosphate Calvin cycle.

Since *Stibiobacter* was isolated from the Yugoslavian deposit, its distribution in antimony deposits of the Soviet Union has been studied. Its presence in Kadamzhaiskoye, Nikitovskoye and Tyrnyauzskoye deposits has been established. In the oxidation zone of Dzhizhikrut antimony deposit, the

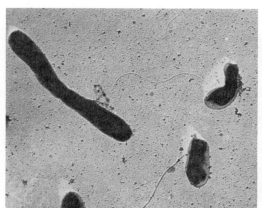
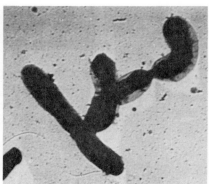

Figure 2. Electron photomicrographs of *Stibiobacter senarmontii*: a) shadowed by chrom, 15000 X; b) *Stibiobacter senarmontii* attached to crystal of senarmontite, 25000 X.

antimony-oxidizing microorganisms were estimated quantitatively.
They made up 10,000 cells per 1 g of ore. The above data
indicate that *Stibiobacter* is widespread in antimony deposits
and ore manifestations and participates in transfer of lower
antimony oxides into the higher ones. The activity of
this organism results in the appearance of minerals of stibiconite type in the deposits, and antimony becomes a new
element involved in the biological cycle.

REFERENCES

Dihlström, K. and A. Westgren. "Über den Bau des sogenannten
   Antimontetroxydes und des damit isomorfen Verbindung
   V_2O_6Ft," *Z. anorgan. allgem. Chem.* 235:153 (1937).

Lyalikova, N. "Oxidation of Sulfides by Culture *Thiobacillus
   ferrooxidans*," (Russian) *Transact. of the Moscow Society
   of Naturalists*, XXIV:211-216 (1966).

Lyalikova, N., I. Vedenina and A. Romanova. "Assimilation
   of Carbon Dioxide by *Stibiobacter senarmontii*," (Russian)
   Mikrobiologiya XLV(N3):552-554 (1976).

Lyalikova, N. and L. Schlain. "Formation of Senarmontit by
   Bacteria," (Russian) *Proceed. Acad. Sci. USSR*, 184(N6):
   1419-1422 (1969).

Silverman, M. and H. Ehrlich. "Microbial Formation and
   Degradation of Minerals," *Adv. Appl. Microbiol. N.Y.* (1964).

Vitaliano, C. and B. Mason. "Stibiconite and Cervantite,"
   Am. Mineral. 37(N11-12):996 (1952).

CHAPTER 75

MICROENVIRONMENTS OF SOME MODERN AND FOSSIL
IRON- AND MANGANESE-OXIDIZING BACTERIA

M. D. MUIR

Department of Geology
Royal School of Mines
Prince Consort Road
London SW7 2BP, England

INTRODUCTION

In the geological literature, there are a number of
descriptions of microfossils, which are presumed to be the
petrified remains of iron- and manganese-oxidizing bacteria
(Barghoorn and Knoll, 1975; Barghoorn and Tyler, 1965;
Bubela et al., 1975; Cloud, 1976; Harder, 1919; Kline, 1975;
Knoll and Barghoorn, 1975; Muir, Hamilton, Grant, and Spicer,
1974a; Muir, Spicer, Grant and Giddens, 1974b; Peat, 1977;
Walter, 1975; Walter, Goode and Hall, 1976). In most cases,
the specimens have been found in petrographic thin sections,
and their morphology and mineralogy have been studied in the
light microscope. Morphologically, nonseptate filaments,
either singly or in colonies, are the most common: the small
radiating colonies of *Metallogenium-* and *Eoastrion-*types
occur fairly frequently. No cells have been reported in the
fossilized sheaths, but Cloud (1976) has pointed out that
"distal swellings on fossil trichomes [may be] similar to the
terminal reproductive cells of *Metallogenium.*"
Chemically, most of the fossilized examples are
mineralized with oxides (mainly haematite) or hydroxides
(mainly goethite) or iron, which are readily identified in
the light microscope, but Muir et al. (1974b), using X-ray
microanalysis in the scanning electron microscope were able
to demonstrate encrustation with manganese dioxide of a number
of morphologies. The microenvironments that the microorganisms
inhabited have not previously been examined in detail, but
Cloud (1976) commented that, although the modern *Metallogenium*

is a freshwater form, it may have been able to tolerate euryhaline conditions in the past. He further postulates that, because the modern organism grows in regions with low O_2 tension, the presence of the fossils in shallow marine to intertidal environments would indicate very low O_2 levels in the atmosphere at that time (about 1.6×10^9 years ago). It should be noted that microfossils that are encrusted or preserved in iron minerals tend to occur in rocks that are rich in iron, whereas manganese-encrusted fossils have so far been found in carbonate rock sequences.

MICROENVIRONMENTS OF MODERN IRON- AND MANGANESE-OXIDIZING BACTERIA

The amount of information on the microenvironments of these organisms is rather sparse, but a number of generally consistent points can be assembled. In both the cases of iron and manganese precipitation, it is important to establish the conditions under which abiotic precipitation will take place. For iron, above pH 5, most precipitation is abiotic (Mulder, 1972; Walsh and Mitchell, 1972b). Below this pH level, bacterial precipitation is much more efficient; for a pH of 4.1, Walsh and Mitchell (1973) quote an abiotic precipitation rate of 1.0 mg/1/day, compared with an optimum 58.0 mg/1/day for an iron-oxidizing *Metallogenium*. For manganese, abiotic precipitation occurs only above pH 9, and chemical precipitation in the presence of certain organic acids can occur at pH 8. In the case of certain microorganisms (*Leptothrix* spp., some soil bacteria and fungi) maximum precipitation occurs at from pH 5 to pH 8 (Mulder, 1972). The iron bacteria tolerate acid conditions from pH 2.5 to pH 6.8, but are most efficient at around pH 4.1 (Walsh and Mitchell, 1972a), whereas the manganese bacteria are effective from pH 5 to pH 8 (Mulder, 1972).

The iron bacteria (*Leptothrix, Gallionella*) live in iron-rich acidic waters in streams, ditches, springs, iron pipes and filter beds. They generally require little or no organic nutrient (Mulder, 1972), but growth of some forms may be inhibited under high iron concentrations unless phthalate is present (Walsh and Mitchell, 1972a). Most of the manganese-oxidizing organisms live in fresh waters, such as running streams, but some live in soils, and some live in marine conditions. They generally require some form of organic substrate and tolerate only low concentrations of manganese, in sharp contrast to some of the iron bacteria that can tolerate high concentrations of iron. Furthermore, manganese oxidation can take place at some distance from organisms, and a protein intermediary plays an important role in this (Mulder, 1972). Empty *Leptothrix* sheaths have a strong manganese-oxidizing effect.

Although most of the references to iron- and manganese-oxidizing bacteria describe occurrences in fresh water or soils, Gebers and Hirsch (1977) have isolated *Pedomicrobium ferrugineum* and *P. manganicum* from podzolic soils of northern Germany, and have been able to culture them in both fresh water and sea water. Thus it is clear that at least some iron-oxidizing bacteria can survive under marine conditions and precipitate ferric iron given suitable conditions. Unfortunately the presumed fossil examples are morphologically more similar to modern freshwater types. The activity of bacteria during the formation of manganese nodules in oceanic environments is generally accepted, and indicates that it is not unreasonable to expect similar organisms to occur in shallower marine waters; see Trimble and Ehrlich (1968) for a description of the activities of some organisms associated with nodule formation. Krumbein (1971) has also described Mn-oxidizing fungi and *Metallogenium symbioticum* from marine environments.

MORPHOLOGY OF MODERN IRON- AND MANGANESE-OXIDIZING BACTERIA COMPARED WITH FOSSIL EXAMPLES

Mulder (1972) describes a number of iron-oxidizing bacteria, two of which are relevant to the fossil record: (1) *Leptothrix* spp. where the bacteria remain within their filamentous sheaths for only a very short time, before leaving to form new sheaths. Ferric iron is deposited both within the sheaths and in the surrounding mucilagenous material. The cells may be capable of oxidizing ferrous iron, but most of the deposition of the iron is a function of some property of the sheath and *postdates* the exit of the cells. Thus the macroscopically visible ochreous masses of *Leptothrix* are frequently composed only of empty sheaths. (2) *Gallionella* is a fibrillar mass (which may or may not contain viable material) that arises from a cellular base.

Both *Leptothrix* and *Gallionella* can oxidize either ferrous or manganous ions. *Metallogenium*, with its characteristic trichocysts, mostly oxidizes manganous ions, but Walsh and Mitchell (1972a) have described an iron-oxidizing *Metallogenium*. *Hyphomicrobium* (Mn^{2+}) is a very fine filamentous structure with small cells attached to hyphae.

From the fossil record, forms resembling both iron- and manganese-encrusted trichocysts occur in several continents and at several stratigraphic horizons from Lower Proterozoic times onwards. Iron encrustation is common and the iron minerals can usually be identified using the light microscope. Occasionally, organic-walled microfossils of morphologies characteristic of other groups are secondarily replaced by iron minerals such as haematite or pyrite, but these are excluded from the present discussion. Manganese encrustation has to be confirmed using X-ray microanalysis techniques (see Muir *et al.*, 1974 a and b for a discussion of the methods), although other examples in the literature, associated with an opaque mineral may probably also be encrusted with manganese dioxide (Kline, 1975). With one exception (Peat, 1977), all the fossil forms are found in fine-grained cherts. These are siliceous rocks found in association with fine-grained carbonate sequences, and also with iron formations, and they are believed to be formed early in diagenesis, thus preserving in three dimensions any microorganisms that have been buried with the sediment. In adiition to trichocysts, both iron- and manganese-encrusted filaments have been reported, usually between 1 and 5 microns in diameter and of varying lengths. Examples of manganese-encrusted bacteria are shown in Figures 1 to 3. For examples of iron-encrusted bacteria, readers are referred to illustrations in Barghoorn and Tyler (1965), Cloud (1976), and Walter *et al.* (1976) for photomicrographs of *Eoastrion*.

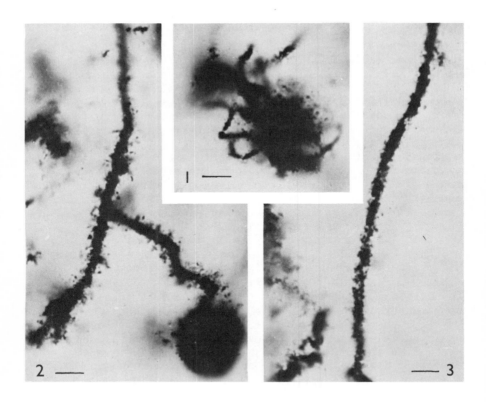

Figures 1, 2 and 3. Manganese-encrusted bacteria from the 1600-yr-old Cooley Dolonite (McArthur Group), Northern Territory, Australia. Filaments (Figures 2 and 3) and tri-chocyst (Figure 1) are encrusted with manganese dioxide. The scale bar on each photomicrograph is 5 microns long.

ASSESSMENT AND DISCUSSION OF ENVIRONMENTAL PARAMETERS FOR
FOSSIL IRON- AND MANGANESE-OXIDIZING BACTERIA

The fossils are found in cherts, which by their litho-
logical associations must have been deposited in two distinct
types of environment. The manganese-oxidizing bacteria are
preserved in cherts associated with shallow water carbonate
sediments. These are deposited, usually at low latitudes,
under high pH conditions, around pH 8. There is therefore
no reason why the fossil manganese-oxidizing bacteria should
not be indigenous to that environment. The sediments are
also usually rich in the remains of blue-green algae, which
may have provided a source of organic matter for the bacterial
metabolism.

The iron-oxidizing bacteria are usually found in association with banded iron formations, a term given to the deposits
of alternating laminae of silica and iron oxides that are
assumed to have been chemically deposited under marine conditions. These would also be precipitated at high pH levels,
which would tend to favor the abiotic precipitation of iron.
Some iron-precipitating bacteria can tolerate marine conditions, but these are not morphologically so closely comparable
with most of the fossils, and most modern iron-precipitating
bacteria favor low pH conditions and fresh water.

Thus a number of questions arise:

(1) Were the fossil organisms, although morphologically
and chemically similar, *not* related to the modern ones?
Perhaps we have here a case of morphological and chemical convergence of two unrelated forms that required
entirely different conditions for their growth.

(2) If the fossil and modern forms *are* indeed related,
perhaps they had different kinds of growth requirements
Is it possible that adaptation to fresh water conditions may have arisen through the course of time in
an originally marine stock?

(3) If the fossil and modern forms are related and if they
had the same growth and environmental requirements,
could the fossils have been washed from their fresh
water habitats into the marine basins of the banded
iron formations? Many of the banded iron formations
contain abundant detrital material derived from
weathering and transport (presumably by fresh water
streams and rivers) of preexisting materials. It
could be asked if the depositional basins of the
banded iron formations were all invariably marine
The distribution of assemblages of *Eoastrion* could perhaps
be reexamined with this prospect in mind. If the
fossils should prove to have been washed in, then we
can begin to learn something about conditions in
Precambrian streams and soils.

(4) Most of the modern forms are attached or stalked bacteria (Hirsch, 1975), but they can attach themselves to almost any kind of interface (oil/water, solid/water, even air/water; Marshall and Cruickshank, 1973). If the fossils were related, and had the same ability, then they could have lived at the surface of the waters, under environmental conditions which, because of stratification effects (Degens and Stouffer, 1976), could have been entirely different from those at the sediment/water interface.

(5) With very ancient sediments, considerable amounts of diagenetic and phreatic alterations are certain to have occurred. It is easily conceivable that these subsequent alterations have so changed the character of the rocks that it is not possible to deduce the conditions prevailing at the time they were deposited. If this is so, then we can make no estimation of the conditions required for the fossil microorganisms.

At the present time is is difficult to determine which of the above represents an accurate answer to the problem. It seems reasonable to accept a strong degree of similarity between the fossil and modern organisms, although interpretation of the microenvironments of the iron-oxidizing bacteria, in particular, is far from unequivocal.

ACKNOWLEDGMENTS

Thanks are due to the organizers of the ISEB for their financial help and in particular to Professor W. E. Krumbein for the invitation to attend the Wolfenbuttel meeting. The Natural Environmental Research Council and RTZ (Services) Ltd. have supported the research, and I am grateful to both these bodies.

REFERENCES

Barghoorn, E. S. and A. H. Knoll. "*Eoastrion* and the *Metallo-genium* Problem," *Chemical Evolution of the Precambrian* (abstract), 2nd College Park Colloquium on Chemical Evolution, University of Maryland, p. 24 (1975).

Barghoorn, E. S. and S. A. Tyler. "Microorganisms from the Gunflint Chert," *Science* 147:563-577 (1965).

Bubela, B. V., B. Cumming, H. E. Jones, D. Z. Oehler, J. H. Oehler, G. W. Skyring and P. A. Trudinger. "Micropalaeontology and Chemical Palaeontology of Australian Precambrian Seminents," *C.S.I.R.O. Minerals Research Laboratories (Australia), Annual Report* 20-21 (1974-1975).

Cloud, P. E. Jr.   "Beginnings of Biospheric Evolution and Their Biogeochemical Consequences," *Paleobiology* 2(4): 351-387 (1976).

Degens, E. T. and P. Stouffer.   "Stratified Waters as a Key to the Past," *Nature* 263:22-27 (1976).

Gebers, R. and P. Hirsch.   "Isolation and Investigation of *Pedomicrobium* spp., Iron-Depositing Budding Bacteria from Soil," *3rd ISEB, Wolfenbuttel*, March 1977, abstracts, W. E. Krumbein, Ed. (1977).

Harder, E. B.   "Iron-Depositing Bacteria and Their Geologic Relations," *U.S.G.S. Prof. Paper* 43:1-89 (1919).

Hirsch, P.   "The Budding Bacteria," *Ann Review Microbiol.* 28:391-444 (1975).

Kline, G.   "*Metallogenium*-like Microorganisms from the Paradise Creek Formation, Australia," *Geol. Soc. Am., Abstracts with Programs* 75(3):336 (1975).

Knoll, A. H. and E. S. Barghoorn.   "A Gunflint-type Flora from the Duck Creek Dolomite, Western Australia," *Chemical Evolution of the Precambrian* (abstract), 2nd College Park Colloquium on Chemical Evolution, University of Maryland, p. 61 (1975).

Krumbein, W. E.   "Manganese Oxidizing Fungi and Bacteria in Recent Shelf Sediments of the Bay of Biscay and the North Sea," *Naturwisseurhoffen* 58:56-57 (1971).

Marshall, K. C. and R. H. Cruickshank.   "Cell Surface Hydrophobicity and the Orientation of Certain Bacteria at Interfaces," *Arch. Mikrobiol.* 91:29-40 (1973).

Muir, M. D., L. H. Hamilton, P. R. Grant and R. A. Spicer.   "A Comparative Study of Modern and Fossil Microbes, Using X-Ray Microanalysis and Cathodoluminescence," in *Microprobe Analysis as Applied to Cells and Tissues*, T. Hall. P. Echlin and R. Kaufmann, Eds. (London and New York: Academic Press, 1974a), pp. 33-58.

Muir, M. D., R. A. Spicer, P. R. Grant and R. Giddens.   "X-Ray Microanalysis in the SEM for the Determination of Elements in Modern and Fossil Microorganisms," *Proc. VIII International Congress on Electron Microscopy*, Canberra II:104-105 (1974b).

Mulder, E. G.   "Le cycle biologique, tellurique et aquatique du fer et du manganese," *Rev. Ecol. Biol. Soc.* IX(3):321-348 (1972).

Peat, C. J. "Microfossils from the Roper Group (Proterozoic), Northern Territory, Australia," Thesis, University of London (1977).

Trimble, R. B. and H. L. Ehrlich. "Bacteriology of Manganese Nodules. III. Reduction of MnO_2 by Two Strains of Nodule Bacteria," *Appl. Microbiol.* 16:695-702 (1968).

Walsh, F. and R. Mitchell. "An Acid-Tolerant Iron-Oxidizing *Metallogenium*," *J. Gen. Microbiol.* 72:369-376 (1972a).

Walsh, F. and R. Mitchell. "A pH-Dependent Succession of Iron Bacteria," *Environ. Sci. Technol.* 6:810-812 (1972b).

Walsh, F. and R. Mitchell. "Differentiation Between *Gallionella* and *Metallogenium*," *Arch. Mikrobiol.* 90: 19-25 (1973).

Walter, M. R. "The Biostratigraphic Significance and Biological Affinities of Microfossils from a Newly Discovered Precambrian Stromatolitic Iron Formation in Weatern Australia," *Internat. Geol. Correlation Programme Symposium, 'Correlation of the Precambrian,'* Moscow, Abstracts, pp. 41-42 (1975).

Walter, M. R., A. D. T. Goode and W. D. M. Hall. "Microfossils from a Newly Discovered Precambrian Stromatolitic Iron Formation in Western Australia," *Nature* 261:221-223 (1976).

SECTION IV

BIOGEOCHEMISTRY OF MAN'S FINGERPRINTS
IN NATURE (METAL-ORGANIC RELATIONS)

CHAPTER 76

METAL-ORGANIC INTERACTION AT THE REDOXCLINE

ROLF HALLBERG

Department of Geology
University of Stockholm
Box 6801
S-113 86 Stockholm, Sweden

INTRODUCTION

Many recent investigations of trace metal distributions in modern anaerobic sedimentary environments have indicated that the relative and absolute concentrations of several trace metals in interstitial waters are inconsistent with a mechanism involving direct precipitation of metal sulfides. Generally, complexing of the metals by dissolved organic compounds or inorganic ions is considered to be responsible for maintaining high concentrations of metals in the pore waters. This chapter emphasizes the idea that the metals are complexed or chelated before they reach the sulfide zone. Because of that they are transported as dissolved species upwards and can thus be enriched in the uppermost oxidized layer of the sediment, thereby offsetting the relative concentrations in the lower sulfidized layers.

DISCUSSION

Howell (1957) is one of many who has defined the term "diagenesis," He defines it as, "the chemical and physical changes that sediments undergo during and after their accumulation, but before consolidation takes place." The environmental biogeochemist should place emphasis on the early stage of that process, usually referred to as "early diagenesis."
    With few exceptions, a sediment is composed of relatively porous clay aggregates and randomly distributed coarser grains (Figure 1). The arrangement of the aggregates takes place, to a great extent, before deposition. Within these aggregates

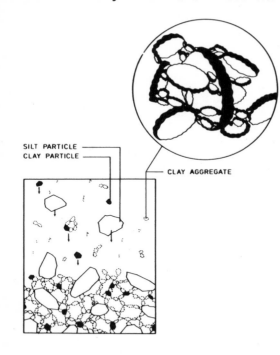

SILT PARTICLE
CLAY PARTICLE

CLAY AGGREGATE

Figure 1. Hypothetical particle arrangement in a sediment and a clay aggregate.

forces are set up between atoms, molecules and ions. For the most part, these forces are dependent on the ionic strength of the electrolyte. The arrangement of the particles will thus be different in freshwater and marine environments. The particle arrangements within the clay aggregates are of the "corner/plane cardhouse" type suggested by Lambe (1958) and Tan (1957). From microstructural investigations of these "cardhouse" aggregates (Pusch, 1970), it can be concluded that during the compaction process the links break down to "domains" and the aggregates approach each other and find new positions of equilibrium (Figure 2).

Thus the initial state of compaction results in a collapse of the more unstable original structures and rearrangement of the particles so that a closer packing is obtained. An increased packing will give a decreased porosity, thereby expelling the interstitial water from the sediment. For the upper part of the sediment, where the sea/sediment interaction is most predominant, steady-state diagenesis is an acceptable assumption as porosity and accordingly compaction undergo linear changes during burial (see Figure 3). Compaction will thus give rise to a transport of ions from the sediment to the overlying water.

Another transport parameter is the diffusion. As defined by Crank (1956), "diffusion is the process by which matter is transported from one part of a system to another as a result of random molecular motions," In a sediment, however, an ion cannot generally be transported along all

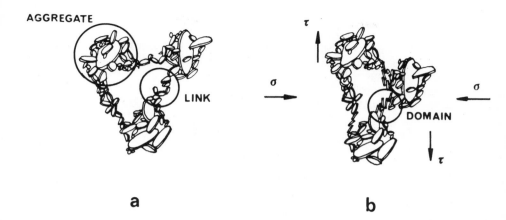

Figure 2. Schematic picture of the failure process. (a) Natural microstructural pattern; (b) breakdown of particle links resulting in domain formation (σ represents consolidation pressure and τ shear stress). (From Pusch, 1970).

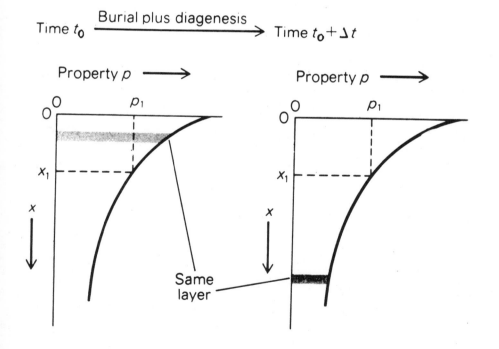

Figure 3. Diagrammatic representation of steady-state diagenesis. Note that at a given *depth* x_1, the sediment property $p = p_1$ does not change with time but that p for a given *layer* changes as it is buried. (From Berner, 1971).

randomly chosen lines between two points but is hindered by the particles.

The chemical transformation in a sediment during early diagenesis is dependent on the reactivity and concentration of the components taking part in the reaction. When transformation occurs, the original concentration of these components is depleted, thereby setting up a gradient in the interstitial water. This gradient will be the driving force for the diffusion that frequently is the process to replenish the reactant. The diffusional transport and the kinetics of the transformation reaction will together determine the net effectiveness of the chemical reaction.

As sediments accumulate, the oxidized sedimentary top layer is buried and will gradually become more deficient in oxygen because of the oxygen consumption by the endofauna and the limited contribution of oxygen to the sediment by diffusion. Consequently, the reducing reactions will become predominant in the subsurface part of the sediment where H_2S is produced by the sulfate-reducing bacteria. This results in a gradual sulfidation of the oxidized layer. During this sulfidation, some compounds (*e.g.*, hydroxides, oxihydroxides and various carbonates), because of physicochemical reasons, have not the same stability in the sulfide as in the oxide zone and therefore are redissolved.

In sediments the microbiological decomposition processes of organic matter are nonsynchronized and result in an increase of intermediate compounds, which may act as metal chelates. Therefore, there will be a competition for the heavy metals between the chelating agents and the hydrogen sulfide.

At the beginning we can expect most of the H_2S to be precipitated as metal sulfides and, therefore, the chelating agents will be left to meet the new metals that have been buried later in the sediment. If a metal chelating compound has an upward transport rate in the sediment that is greater than that of the H_2S, the chelated metal can be expected to be withdrawn from the H_2S zone. This leads to a mineral cycle above the redoxcline where the chelated metals are transported upwards, also enhanced by compaction of the sediment (Figure 4).

The inflection point of the redox gradient at around +200 mV is the most predominant in sediments and constitutes the boundary between the oxidizing and reducing environments. Mortimer (1942) settled that value to +200 mV, but because of natural variations, a range of +200 mV ±50 mV would probably be more correct. This boundary is named redoxcline, defined by Hallberg (1972, p. 195), and put on par with often recognizable natural boundaries, *e.g.*, halocline.

As the sediments accumulate, the metals can thus cling with them. They become concentrated in the uppermost layers, and escape from being trapped and fixed as stationary sulfides

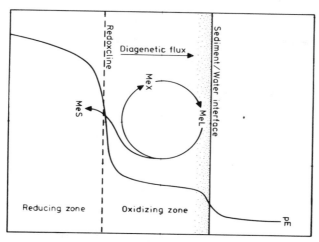

Figure 4. The cycle of chelated heavy metals above the redoxcline.

(see also Elderfield and Hepworth, 1975). Metals differ in their ability to chelate. The more easily they chelate, the more they tend to become enriched in the uppermost layer. In contrast to Gardner (1974) and Emerson (1976) I assume a dynamic system that is more relevant for natural processes. In this dynamic system the metals are chelated or complexed *before* they meet the sulfide environment. Thus even if the chelators are not very competitive for heavy metals in the presence of significant amounts of sulfide, they can play a major role under relatively more oxidizing conditions.

In a simulated sedimentary system Hallberg, Bubela and Ferguson have obtained experimental evidence for the involvement of organic matter in the distribution of trace metals in sediments by examining the mechanisms of incorporation of Cu and Zn at the redoxcline of a sulfide-rich sediment. The presence of sulfide in the absence of organic compounds created a common precipitation mechanism for Cu and Zn, presumably as CuS and ZnS. Thus, when a sulfide-bearing brine comes in contact with a solution of heavy metals, they are precipitated and fixed in a common sedimentary layer (Figure 5).

When organic compounds are present and especially when they are used as a nutrient by sulfate-reducing bacteria to create H_2S, the precipitation and fixation mechanism for metals is more complex. Such a system provides good evidence that under such conditions Cu and Zn are separated and fixed in different sedimentary layers (Figure 5).

Hallberg (1972) studied the Cu/Zn ratio theoretically. He showed it to be a valid indicator of the environment at the time of deposition. The same paper gives good experimental evidence of this theory. Modern Baltic sediments were

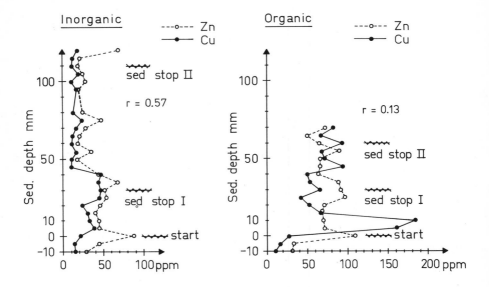

Figure 5. Precipitation of Cu and Zn in two experimental
systems with continuous sedimentation. In the *inorganic*
system sulfide was contributed as a sulfide solution in
the absence of organic matter. In the *organic* system,
sulfide was produced by sulphate reducing bacteria during
their degradation of added organic matter. Note the
common precipitation for the inorganic system (r = 0.57)
opposite to the organic system (r = 0.13). (From Hallberg,
Bubela and Ferguson, in preparation).

investigated *in situ* and conditions in a closed system were
controlled. The Cu/Zn ratio in the sediment decreased when
conditions were transformed from oxidizing to reducing ones
because Cu escaped into the free water phase above the sediment. The ratio of certain heavy metals could also be used
to trace anoxic and oxic environments in both recent and
fossil sediments. The ratio (Cu + Mn)/Zn was used (Hallberg,
1974) with confidence to indicate paleoredox conditions in
one of the Baltic basins during the last 400 years.

In none of these cases, however, was it possible to
identify specific metal-organic complexes, and the possibility
that inorganic ions or phases were involved in the equilibria
cannot be discounted.

REFERENCES

Berner, R. A. *Principles of Chemical Sedimentology* (New York: McGraw-Hill, Inc., 1971).

Crank, J. *The Mathematics of Diffusion* (Oxford: Clarendon Press, 1956).

Elderfield, H. and A. Hepworth. "Diagenesis, Metals and Pollution in Estuaries," *Marine Poll. Bull.* 6(6):85-87 (1975).

Emerson, S. "Early Diagenesis in Anaerobic Lake Sediments: Chemical Equilibria in Inserstitial Waters," *Geochim. Cosmochim. Acta* 40:925-934 (1976).

Gardner, L. R. "Organic Versus Inorganic Trace Metal Complexes in Sulfidic Marine Waters — Some Speculative Calculations Based on Available Stability Constants," *Geochim. Cosmochim. Acta* 38:1297-1302 (1974).

Hallberg, R. O. "Sedimentary Sulfide Mineral Formation: An Energy Circuit System Approach," *Mineral Deposita* 7:189-211 (1972).

Hallberg, R. O. "Paleoredox Conditions in the Eastern Gotland Basin During the Recent Centuries," *Havsforskningsinst. Skr. Helsinki* 238:3-16 (1974).

Howell, J. V. *Glossary of Geology and Related Sciences* (Washington, D. C.: American Geology Institution, under NAS-NRC, 1957).

Lambe, T. W. "The Structure of Compacted Clay," *J. Soil Mech. a. Found. Div., Proc. ASCE, SM2*, 84:1, paper 1654 (1958).

Mortimer, C. H. "The Exchange of Dissolved Substances Between Mud and Water in Lakes. III and IV," *J. Ecol.* 30:147-201 (1942).

Pusch, R. "Clay Microstructure," *Document D 8:1970 National Swedish Building Research* (1970).

Tan, T-K. "Discussion on: Soil Properties and Their Measurement," *Proc. 4. Int. Soil Mech. Found. Eng.* 3:87-89 (1957).

CHAPTER 77

THE UNIONID MUSSEL AS A BIOGEOCHEMICAL INDICATOR OF METAL POLLUTION

MARGARET MERLINI
GRAZIELLA CADARIO
B. OREGIONI

Biology Group, Ispra
G. D. Research, Science and Education, C.E.C.
Euratom J.R.C.
21020 Ispra, Italy

INTRODUCTION

The Unionidae are excellent index organisms for metals discharged by industry into land waters. First, they have an affinity for heavy metals, (Korringa, 1952; Schulz-Baldes, 1974) and second, as sedentary animals they reflect their immediate environment of water and sediment in which they are partially imbedded. This capacity to integrate those elements in water as well as in sediment makes them ideal biogeochemical indicators of pollution.

The purpose of this study was to evaluate the pollution of a river by an electroplating industry before and after the installation of a water purifier by determining the concentration of five metals - Mn, Cu, Fe, Zn, Cr - in different segments of the molluscan soft tissues.

MATERIALS AND METHODS

The bivalve *Unio mancus* variation *elongatulus* (Pfeiffer) was always collected from the same site in the River Bardello (which empties into Lake Maggiore, North Italy) two meters south of the water discharged from a galvanizing industry. They were found partially buried in the sediment close to clumps of growing macrophytes.

The polluted industrial water was kept in 100-liter tanks before being released at the rate of 15 m^3 per hour. It contained various zinc and manganese complexes, iron as chloride, chromium as an acid and an oxide, traces of copper sulfate, ammonium chloride, sulfur and aldehydes. After the first collection of clams in January, a water purifier was installed to remove the heavy metals and the other chemicals before the water tank was filled (Table I).

In the laboratory the animals were weighed, measured, and dissected into the following parts: gills, gill-base, pericardium (auricle, ventricle, plus kidney), mantle, adductor muscles, labial palps, visceral sac and foot (Figure 1). Each part was weighed, dried at 105° C, reweighed, ashed at 450° C and weighed again (Table II). The metals were determined using a Perkin-Elmer atomic absorption spectrometer.

RESULTS

It can be seen from Figure 2 that about 3 weeks after installation of the water purifier (April collection), the concentration of the metals in the soft tissues decreased with respect to the first collection, except for iron and copper. It should be pointed out, however, that this collection was made immediately after the water was discharged from the holding tank. Six months later the metal content (ppm dry weight) had increased above the levels found in January before the water purifier began to function.

When the organs and tissues are examined individually (Figures 3, 4, 5 and 6) it becomes apparent that (1) the gill-base was the tissue with the highest concentration of the five metals, followed by the gills, mantle and pericardium, (2) manganese predominated in all the organs, then Fe and Zn to a lesser degree, and (3) significantly less Cu and Cr were found in all the parts. Since it was not possible to detect accurately less than 0.1 ppm of Cr, the palps contained this amount or less.

DISCUSSION

From analyses of water and sediment taken from different areas in Lake Maggiore by Gommes and Muntau (1975) it was evident that the quantity of heavy metals was highest in the water and sediment at points where there were industrial discharges, such as at Monvallina and Bardello. Also, the installation of a water purifier by the galvanizing factory on the River Bardello reduced the metal content in the water as well as in the soft tissues of the bivalve (April collection). However, the results obtained in September showed an increase in metal levels in *Unio* over and above those of the first collection in January (Figure 1), verifying that the purifier had always functioned.

Table I

Pertinent Information Concerning the Collections of the Bivalves
Unio Mancus from the River Bardello (mean ± standard error)

Month Collected	Water Temperature	Length	Width	Remarks
Jan. 14, 1968	4.0 ± 0.5°C	6.25 ± 0.27	3.46 ± 0.10	Before installation of water purifier
April 7, 1968	9.0 ± 0.5°C	6.41 ± 0.19	3.41 ± 0.19	Three weeks after water purifier was installed
Sept. 1, 1968	20 ± 1.0°C	6.76 ± 0.15	3.61 ± 0.17	Six months after installation of water purifier

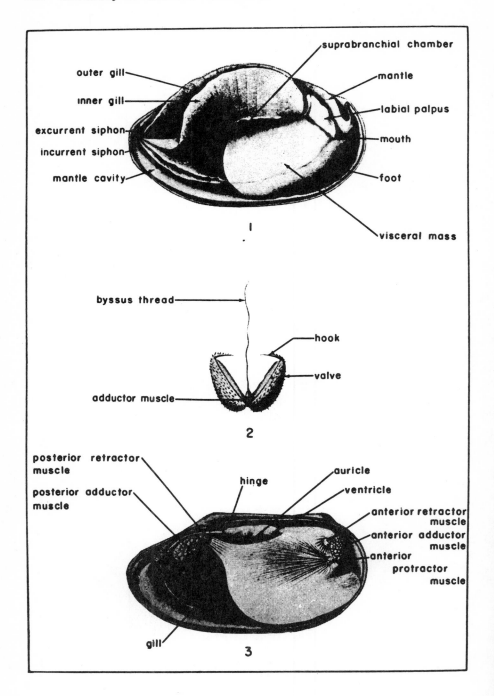

Figure 1. The soft tissues of *Unio mancus* as seen from a photograph taken from *Handbook of Unionid Mussels*.

Table II
Different Segments of the Soft Tissues of *Unio*.
The dry and ash contents of each part are expressed as
percentages of the fresh weight (mean ± S.D.)

Part	Dry matter (105°C) (as % fresh weight)	Ash (450°C) (as % fresh weight)
Gills	14.3 ± 0.66	7.0 ± 0.60
Base of Gills	26.8 ± 1.34	15,5 ± 1.00
Pericardium	13.1 ± 0.55	4.0 ± 0.05
Mantle	15.3 ± 0.92	5.4 ± 0.09
Muscles (adductor)	15.6 ± 1.05	2.1 ± 0.20
Palps	11.9 ± 0.55	1.3 ± 0.20
Visceral Sac	19.7 ± 0.95	2.9 ± 0.01
Foot	15.3 ± 2.30	1.3 ± 0.03
Soft Tissues	17.3 ± 1.01	4.92 ± 0.11

The most probable explanation for the increase in the metal content of the soft tissues in September is that the sediment had accumulated the metals over the years before installation of the purifier. Since the bivalves live in the water-sediment interface, it is likely that the purifier changed the water quality, which, with time, changed the physico-chemical state of the elements, rendering them more available to *Unio*. In April the purifier had been in function a short time and the collection was made after the stored water had been released. It is likely, then, that any released metals were carried downstream by the water before the clams had the opportunity to concentrate them.

It is interesting that the classification of the metal abundance made by Gommes and Muntau (1975) for the sediment has the same rank order as that in the clam. For the sediment it was: Mn, Zn, Cr, Cu, Ni (Fe was not determined); for *Unio* : Mn, Fe, Zn. Cr, Cu.

The avidity with which *Unio* picks up and retains Mn has long been known (Merlini *et al.*, 1965; Merlini, 1966) and it is clear that the sediment plays an important role in returning metals to the hydrosphere. Apparently, defined treatment processes can remove oxidized manganese but not

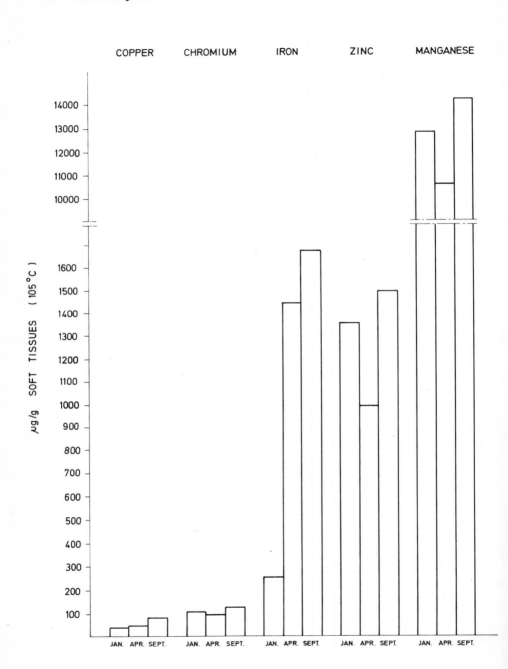

Figure 2.   The concentration of Mn, Zn, Fe, Cr and Cu in the soft tissues of *Unio mancus* (µg/g dry wt) collected at different times in the River Bardello.

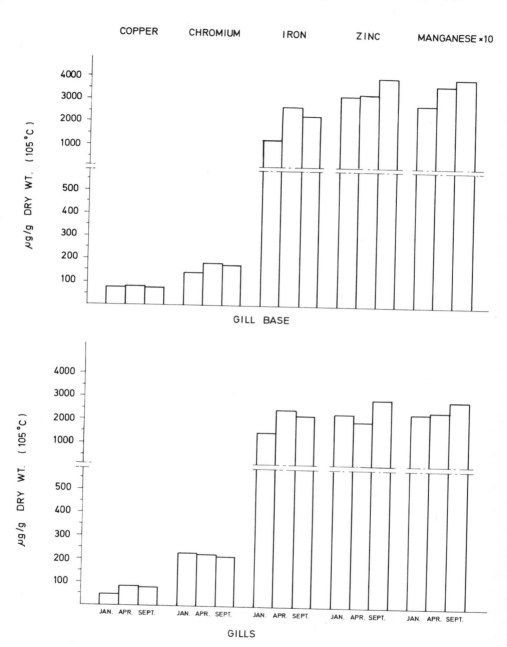

Figure 3. The repartition of the six metals in soft tissues of *Unio mancus* from the River Bardello.

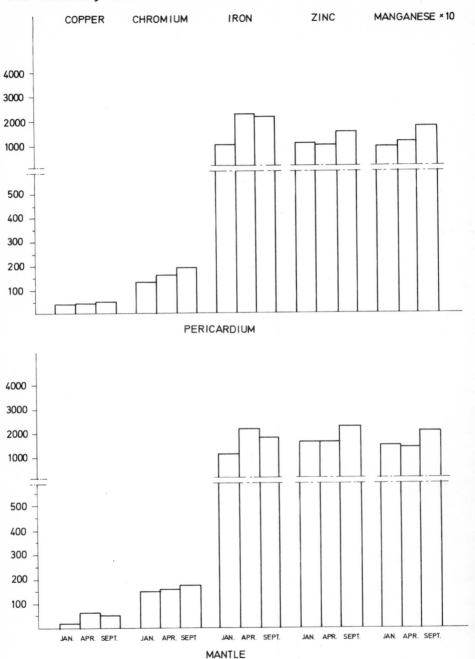

Figure 4. The repartition of the six metals in soft tissues
of *Unio mancus* from the River Bardello.

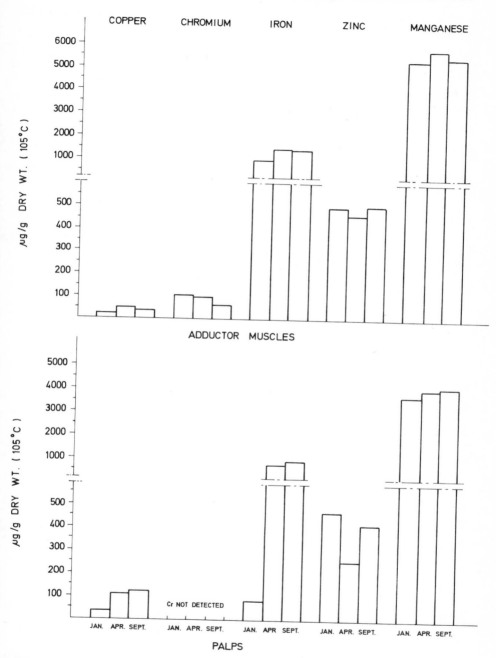

Figure 5. The repartition of the six metals in soft tissues of *Unio mancus* from the River Bardello.

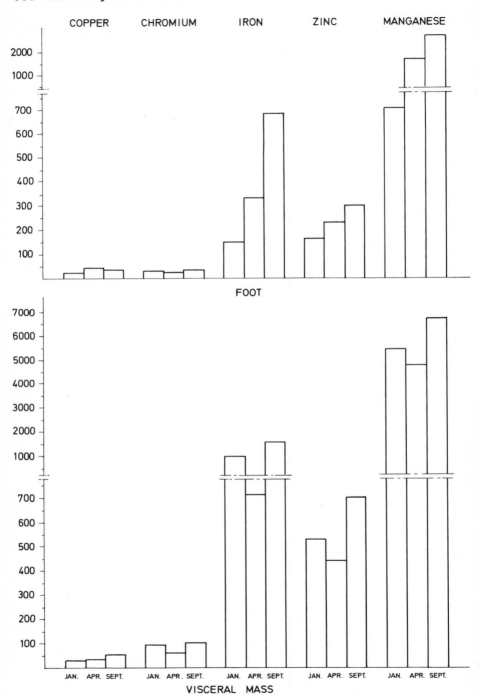

Figure 6.   The repartition of the six metals in soft tissues
of *Unio mancus* from the River Bardello.

soluble Mn^{++} (Water Quality Criteria, 1972), which is a form available to the biota. In addition, it was stated (Water Quality Criteria, 1972) that iron-containing effluents discharged into waters where bottom organisms are present should be avoided; *Unio* is a good example of a bottom organism that accumulates Fe to a great extent.

In conclusion, it should be recalled that metals are nondestructive and often end up in the sediment. It is the sediment, then, that refurnishes the water with metals. Therefore, the installation of a water purifier by an industry that discharges metals into water (rivers, lakes, oceans) does not necessarily eliminate them completely but rather, with a change in water quality, the purifier may actually enhance the uptake and accumulation by aquatic organisms.

REFERENCES

Gommes, R. and H. Muntau. "La distribution de quelques metaux lourds (Mn, Cu, Cr, Ni, Mn, Co) dans la zone littorale des bassins sud et de Pallanza du Lac Majeur," *Mem. Inst. Ital. Idrobiol.* 32:1-15 (1975).

Korringa, P. "Recent Advances in Oyster Biology," *Quart Rev. Biol.* 27:266-308 (1952).

Merlini, M., F. Girardi, P. Pietra and A. Brazzelli. "The Stable Manganese Content of Molluscs from Lake Maggiore Determined by Activation Analysis," *Limnol. Oceanog.* 10:371-378 (1965).

Merlini, Margaret. "The Freshwater Clam as a Biological Indicator of Radiomanganese," in *Radioecological Concentradion Processes* (Oxford and New York: Pergamon Press, 1966), pp. 977-982.

Schulz-Baldes, M. "Lead Uptake and Loss in *Mytilus*," *Mar. Biol.* 25:177-193 (1974).

Water Quality Criteria. EPA. R3.73.033 March 1973 (Washington, D. C.: The Environmental Protection Agency, 1972).

CHAPTER 78

TRACE ELEMENT COMPOSITION OF FIVE CYANOBACTERIA

GALEN E. JONES*
LINDSAY MURRAY**
NOEL G. CARR

Department of Oceanography and Department of Biochemistry
The University of Liverpool
Liverpool, England

INTRODUCTION

The recognition over the last 20 years that blue-green algae were prokaryotic (Stanier and van Niel, 1962; Echlin and Morris, 1965) led to dissatisfaction with the use of the term "algae" and the introduction of a variety of names that emphasize the bacterial nature of this large group of microorganisms. We use the name cyanobacteria, which has connotations of the typical accessory pigments, phycobili-proteins, and recognizes their prokaryotic structure.

Although considerable attention has been directed to understanding the inorganic nutrition of cyanobacteria with respect to phosphate, nitrate and major cations, little information is available regarding trace element content. An advantage of cyanobacteria for trace element analysis is their growth in the absence or near absence of organic molecules that create diverse organometallic interactions prior to and during heterotrophic culture (Jones, Royle and Murray, 1976).

*Present address: Department of Microbiology and The Jackson Estuarine Laboratory, The University of New Hampshire, Durham, New Hampshire 03824, USA.

**Present address: Ministry of Agriculture, Fisheries and Food, Fisheries Laboratory, Burnham-on-Crouch, Essex, England.

MATERIALS AND METHODS

Organisms

The cyanobacteria were assembled and grown in the
laboratory of Dr. N. G. Carr. They consisted of: *Anabaena
cylindrica* (No. 1403/29, The Culture Collection of Algae and
Protozoa, Botany School, Downing Street, Cambridge), *Anabaena
variabilis* (strain of Professor J. Myers, Department of
Zoology, University of Texas, Austin, Texas), *Anacysti
nidulans* (UTEX 625, The Collection of Algae at the University
of Texas, Austin, Texas), *Chlorogloea fritschii* (No. 1411/1,
Cambridge), and *Nostoc muscorum* (Professor J. Myers).

Culture Medium

The growth medium was blue-green algae Medium C.
The composition was as follows on a mg/l basis:
Na citrate·$2H_2O$, 165; $Fe_2(SO_4)_3$·$6H_2O$, 4; $Ca(NO_3)_2$·$4H_2O$, 25;
$MgSO_4$·$7H_2O$, 250; KNO_3, 1000; K_2HPO_4, 1000; $NaHCO_3$, 1000;
micronutrient solution, 1 ml; and distilled water, 1000 ml.
The micronutrient solution was composed of the following
constituents on a liter basis in mg: H_3BO_3, 2860; $MnCl_2$·$4H_2O$,
1810; $ZnSO_4$·$7H_2O$, 222; MoO_3 (85%), 17.7; $CuSO_4$·$5H_2O$, 79;
and distilled water, 1000 ml. Medium C and the micronutrient
solution were sterilized by autoclaving at 121° C for 15 min.

Cultural Conditions

The cyanobacteria were inoculated from fresh cultures
as 1 ml into 500 ml of sterile medium C in one-liter bottles.
The cells were grown to late-logarithmic growth for 72-96
hr at 34° C in static culture using light energy.

Harvesting the Cells

The cells were centrifuged from the medium at 6500 g
at 4° C and dried immediately at 105-110° C. The cells were
not washed, and the dry weight varied from 400 to 750 mg.

Trace Element Analyses

Cells were analyzed as described by Jones, Royle
and Murray (1976).

RESULTS

The Zn, Fe, Cu, Pb, Ni, Mn and Cd content of the five
cultures of cyanobacteria are presented in Table I. The
concentrations of trace elements by the cyanobacteria after
growth in Medium C varied from an average of 3.6 ppm Cd to

Table I

Weight as ppm and Concentration Factors of Trace Metals in Five Cyanobacterial Cultures

Cyanobacterial Culture	Zn		Fe		Cu		Pb		Ni		Mn		Cd	
	Cells[a]	C.F.[b]	Cells[a]	C.F.[b]	Cells[a]	C.F.[b]	Cells[a]	C.F.[b]	Cells[a]	C.F.[b]	Cells[a]	C.F.[b]	Cells[a]	C.F.[b]
Anabaena cylindrica	33	1257	6287	6287	38	633	14	700	7.2	720	137	228	1.5	75
Anabaena variablis	48	649	659	659	53	883	9	450	5.1	510	51	85	2.3	115
Anacystis nidulans	81	1095	1062	1062	76	1266	13	650	2.1	210	76	126	2.3	115
Chloroglea fritschii	109	1473	1846	1846	61	1017	10	500	6.3	630	123	205	2.9	145
Nostoc muscorum	479	6473	8279	8279	159	2650	20	1000	9.4	940	1183	1972	9.1	455
Average Me in Cells	162		3626		77		13		6.0		97[c]		3.6	
Average C.F. in Cells		2189		3626		1290		660		602		161[c]		181
Me Content in Medium (calculated) μg/liter	74		1000		60		20		10		600		20	

[a] Weight as ppm of metals in dried cells grown in Medium C at 34°C.

[b] C.F. (Concentration factor) indicates the increase of metals in cells compared to medium.

[c] The figure for *N. muscorum* not included.

an average of 3626 ppm Fe. There were considerable variations
in trace metal assimilation by cyanobacteria from species to
species. *A. variabilis* accumulated the least Zn, Fe, Pb and
Mn of all the cultures tested, namely 48, 659, 9 and 51,
respectively. *N. muscorum* accumulated the highest levels of
all the elements, namely, 479 ppm Zn, 8279 ppm Fe, 159 ppm
Cu, 20 ppm Pb, 9.4 ppm Ni, 1183 ppm Mn, and 9.1 ppm Cd. The
mucilaginous nature of *N. muscorum* may account for the retention of many of these high amounts of trace metal ions,
particularly since the cells were not washed. Based on the
concentration factors from the growth medium, the metals
were concentrated from the medium in the following order
Fe > Zn > Cu > Pb > Ni > Cd > Mn. Nevertheless, the Mn
concentrated by the cyanobacteria were over an order of
magnitude greater than the Mn content of heterotrophic
bacterial cells (unpublished data).

The outstanding difference between the trace element
content of the cyanobacteria and those of heterotrophic bacteria was in their Fe and Mn contents. Fe concentrations
were from 3 to 20 times higher than in the bacteria, and Mn
concentrations from 20 to 400 times higher. The concentration
of other trace metals was more similar to those found in the
bacterial cells, averaging generally somewhat higher than in
heterotrophic bacterial cells in all media. Comparisons of
this type are made with extreme caution as the bacterial cells
in previous investigations on the trace metal content of
bacteria grown in different culture media indicated that
trace element uptake was regulated by several factors
including the concentration of the element in solution and
the concentration of complexing agents in the media (Jones,
Royle and Murray, 1976). The cyanobacteria in this study
were not washed and may have retained some trace elements
compared to those removed in the other bacterial studies.
The cyanobacteria tended to retain metals in the cells in
much the same order of decreasing concentration as the bacteria except for Mn.

DISCUSSION

When one considers the concentrations in several
different types of organisms, some interesting parallels
can be made (Table II). Zinc is highly concentrated, to an
average of 2600 ppm dry weight in phytoplankton, but runs
very similar in cyanobacteria (162 ppm), bacteria (134 ppm),
brown algae (150 ppm), bryophytes (50 ppm), fungi (150 ppm)
and mollusca (200 ppm). Iron is concentrated most by cyanobacteria (3626 ppm) followed closely by phytoplankton
(3500 ppm), bryophytes (1200 ppm), brown algae (690 ppm);
the value for bacteria, fungi and mollusca is quite close
to 200 ppm. Copper is concentrated most by phytoplankton

Table II

Trace Metal Composition of Types of Organisms

Element	Phytoplankton[a]	Brown algae[b]	Bryophytes[b]	Mollusca[b]	Fungi[b]	Bacteria[c]	Bacteria[d]	Cyanobacteria[d]
Zn	2600	150	50	200	150		134	162
Fe	3500	690	1200	200	130	250	262	3626
Cu	200	11	7	20	15	42	25	77
Pb	5	8.4	3.3	0.7	50		19	13
Ni	36	3	2.5	4	1.5		2.7	6
Mn	75	53	293	10	25	30	2.5	97
Cd	0.4	0.4	0.1	3	4		3.7	3.6

[a] Data from Vinogradova and Kobalsky (1962).

[b] Data from Bowen (1966).

[c] Data from Porter (1946).

[d] Data from Table I and unpublished analysis of 23 heterotrophic bacteria.

(200 ppm), next by cyanobacteria (77 ppm), and rather similarly
in other organisms to bacteria, about 25 ppm. Lead is concentrated most by fungi (50 ppm), followed by bacteria (19 ppm)
and cyanobacteria (13 ppm), with most of the organisms containing from 1 to 10 ppm Pb. Nickel is concentrated most by
phytoplankton (36 ppm) followed by cyanobacteria, mollusca,
brown algae, bacteria, bryophytes and fungi, all in the range
of 1.5 to 6 ppm. Manganese is highly concentrated by bryophytes (293 ppm) followed by cyanobacteria (97 ppm), phytoplankton (75 ppm), brown algae (53 ppm), fungi (25 ppm),
mollusca (10 ppm) and bacteria (2.5 ppm). Cadmium is concentrated most by the fungi, bacteria and cyanobacteria
namely 4, 3.7 and 3.6 ppm Cd, respectively. Mollusca contain
3 ppm Cd, and the plant material contains less than 0.4 ppm
Cd.

The comparison between cyanobacteria and other bacteria
indicates their close taxonomic relation as reflected by
trace element content. Nevertheless, it must be emphasized
that trace element concentrations in microorganisms cultured
in the laboratory may not be similar to those of the same
species in nature. There is still a considerable need for
qualitative and quantitative analyses of naturally occurring
microorganisms, together with the data on the water from
which they are isolated in order to provide baseline data for
reliable concentration factors and accurate information on
the elemental composition of microorganisms.

ACKNOWLEDGMENTS

The authors wish to thank Professor J. P. Riley of
the Department of Oceanography, The University of Liverpool,
England, for advice and laboratory space.

This investigation was supported, in part, by the
Oceanography Section of the National Science Foundation,
Washington, D. C., under grant GA-34101.

REFERENCES

Bowen, H. J. M. *Trace Elements in Biochemistry*, (London:
   Academic Press, 1966).

Echlin, P. and I. Morris. "The Relationship Between Blue-
   Green Algae and Bacteria," *Biol. Rev.* 40:143-187 (1965).

Jones, G. E., L. G. Royle and L. Murray. "The Assimilation
   of Trace Metal Ions by the Marine Bacteria,"*Arthrobacter
   marinus* and *Pseudomonas cuprodurans*," in *Proc. Third
   Internat. Biodegrad. Symposium*, J. M. Sharpley and A. M.
   Kaplan, Eds. (London: Applied Science Publishers Ltd.,
   1976), pp. 889-898.

Porter, J. R. *Bacterial Chemistry and Physiology* (New York: J. Wiley and Sons, 1946).

Riley, J. P. and I. Roth. "The Distribution of Trace Elements in some Species of Phytoplankton Grown in Culture," *J. Mar. Biol. Assoc., U.K.* 51:63-72 (1971).

Stanier, R. Y. and C. B. van Niel. "The Concept of Bacterium," *Arch. Mikrobiol.* 42:17-35 (1962).

Vinogradova, Z. A. and V. V. Kobalsky. "Elemental Composition of the Black Sea Plankton," *Dokl. Akad. Nauk SSSR* 147:1458-1460 (1962).

CHAPTER 79

THE INTERACTION OF METALS IN AQUEOUS SOLUTION WITH BACTERIAL CELL WALLS FROM *BACILLUS SUBTILIS*

T. J. BEVERIDGE

Department of Bacteriology and Immunology
University of Western Ontario
London, Ontario, Canada

INTRODUCTION

Some rich sedimentary ore horizons contain a high organic content and, conversely, deposits of organic fossil fuels are rich in metals encompassing much of the periodic table (Davis, 1967). In fact, the high concentration elements include many that are not normally considered to be "trace elements" necessary for life (*e.g.*, V) (Williams, 1971). It is apparent that sediments rich in constituents of biological origin are involved but the mechanisms leading to these accumulations of metals are unknown. Metabolic mechanisms and the metalloenzymes are insufficient for explanation. Cells of all kinds are negatively charged. Most microbes have a highly organized enveloping structure, the cell wall, which is in contact with the aqueous environment first. For bacteria, these walls consist of diverse anionic polymers and heteropolymers, which should act as traps for cations (Beveridge and Murray, 1976). These are the most durable of the cellular materials and are not easily degraded in nature; in fact, they are identifiable and persistent in many environments including sedimentary horizons of considerable age.

Many of the major inland water systems of the world are suffering from heavy-metal anthropogenic loading (Kemp *et al.*, 1976 is representative), resulting in unusually high concentrations of potentially toxic metals and/or their organic complexes in the bottom sediments. The motility and concentrating mechanisms for these metals in natural aqueous systems have been thought of primarily in geochemical terms,

even though most of the sediments contain high concentrations
of organic matter, presumably of biological origin.

Studies, using isolated and purified cell walls from
the ubiquitous Gram-positive bacterium *Bacillus subtilis*
as a model system, have demonstrated that the constituent
wall polymers can interact selectively with discrete metals
in solution, and large (often nonstoichiometric) amounts of
metal may accumulate (Beveridge and Murray, 1976). This
chapter extends these preliminary observations and reports
on initial experiments in which metal-loaded walls have been
geologically aged artificially.

METHODS

A detailed methodology can be found in Beveridge
and Murray (1976).

Preparation of Bacterial Cell Walls

The walls were isolated and purified from exponentially
growing cells.

pH Titrations

Titrations were carried out in 50 ml (1 mg dry wt/ml)
of continuously stirred, deoxygenated, deionized water under
a continuous stream of nitrogen gas. Increments of 5 µmol
of acid (HCl) or base (NH$_4$OH) were added during the titration,
and the results were volume adjusted before plotting on
paper.

Analytical Procedures

For metal uptake studies 1 ml of a 10-mM metal solution
was mixed with one ml (1 mg dry wt) of a wall suspension for
10 min at 22°C. The walls were trapped by a Millipore filter
and washed well with 80 ml deionized distilled water. Both
the filter (which contained the walls) and the filtrate
were then analyzed by suitable means for metal. Both atomic
absorption (in either the flame or graphite furnace modes)
and X-ray fluorescence were used for these analyses. The
crystalline order of the bound metal was determined by X-ray
analysis. Nitric acid-leached plastic ware was used throughout.

Electron Microscopic Analyses

Metal uptakes were accomplished as outlined in
"Analytical Procedures." After the walls had been well
washed, they were fixed for 60 min at 22° C with 4% aqueous
glutaraldehyde, dehydrated and embedded in Epon 812. Thin

sections were cut on a Reichert OMU2 ultramicrotome, mounted on Formvar, carbon-coated copper grids and examined in a Phillips EM300 microscope operating at 60 kV. No stain other than the *in situ* metal of the uptake reaction was used on these electron microscopic images. In a few instances (*i.e.*, reactions with low Z elements) ferritin conjugated to concanavalin A was used as a specific stain for the wall surface.

Wall thicknesses were determined from at least 30 separate and random measurements taken from micrographs (magnification between 200,000 and 300,000X) of cross sections (both transverse and longitudinal cuts) of walls treated with each of the metal salts. From this data a mean thickness (μ), a standard deviation (α_s) and a standard error (st. er.) was calculated.

Geological Aging of Metal-Loaded Walls

Five ml of wall suspension (1 mg dry wt/ml) was mixed with 5 ml of a 10-mM $ZrOCl_2 \cdot 8H_2O$ solution and incubated for 10 min at 22°C. After being washed well with 300 ml deionized distilled water, the cells were mixed with amorphous silicate (wall: SiO_4 on a dry wt basis was 1:2) and packed in a 2 x 20-mm hollow gold cylinder; the cylinder was sealed. It was then sealed in a thick-walled, 1.5 x 20-cm glass tube containing oxalic acid (to produce a low redox potential) and the whole unit was then heated to 220° C for 20 days. This heat treatment liberated excess CO_2 from the aqueous oxalic acid solution and created a positive pressure during the incubation. After this period the unit was carefully opened, the SiO_4-wall matrix scraped from the gold cylinder, and the specimen processed for electron microscopy (*i.e.*, for thin sectioning).

RESULTS

The Gram-positive cell wall has been compared to a low-density ion exchange resin that can freely exchange ions with the aqueous environment (Carstensen and Marquis, 1975; Marquis *et al.*, 1976; Ou and Marquis, 1970, 1972). In the case of cell walls of *Bacillus megaterium, Micrococcus lysodeikticus, Staphylococcus aureus, Streptococcus faecalis,* and *S. mutans*, the ion exchange capacity appears to be correlated with a relatively open system (Marquis *et al.*, 1976), whereas with walls of *B. subtilis*, a more condensed version occurs (Beveridge and Murray, 1976). Cell walls of *B. subtilis* (Marburg strain) are negatively charged and react to aqueous cations by binding them. Small cations (such as the hydronium ion) interact with these negatively charged sites and progressively penetrate the intermolecular spaces

of the wall as the sites are neutralized. Therefore pH
titration of the walls is possible, giving an electrochemical
response that is measurable (Figure 1). These titrations
demonstrate that these bacterial fragments provide strong

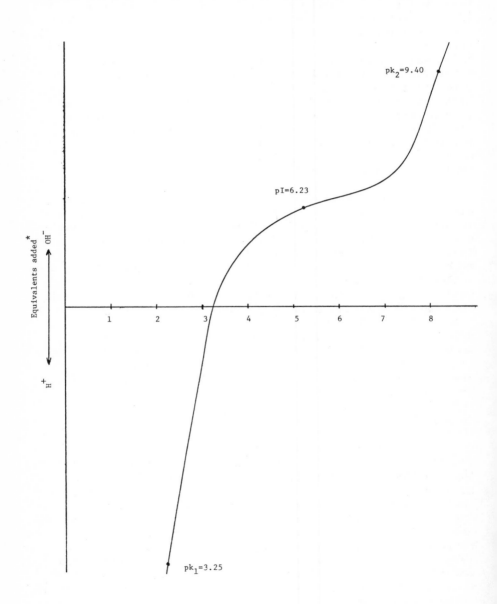

Figure 1. pH titration of *Bacillus subtilis* cell walls. As
5 µmol H^+ or OH^- increments to 50 mg of wall fragments.
Adjusted for volume increases during titration.

buffering action at $4.2 \geqslant pH \geqslant 8.2$ and have $pk_1 = 3.25$, $pI = 6.23$ and $pk_2 = 9.40$, respectively. It is distinctive that strong buffering action occurs at pH levels deleterious for growth of this organism, and it may be possible that the walls serve as a protective device against localized pH extremes in the environment

Aqueous metal ions and their various hydrated complexes act as Lewis acids in solution and, accordingly, also interact with these wall fragments. Previous to the work reported we have demonstrated, using 18 distinct metals, that the wall's uptake and tenacity of binding can be specific (Beveridge and Murray, 1976). The uptake analyses have now been expanded to 40 metals, which include members of the alkali metals, alkaline earth metals, transition elements I, II and III, and group III, IV and V elements. In general, electron microscopy of thin sections of metal-reacted cell walls demonstrated four distinct types of electron scattering profiles: (1) an amorphous staining response (see Figure 5, which is representative), (2) walls with electron dense aggregates (Figure 3A is representative), (3) walls with electron dense "crystalloids" (*i.e.*, some "ordering or lattice network can be seen; Figure 2 is representative), and (4) walls with definite electron dense crystals (Figure 4A is representative). Those walls exhibiting the responses typified in processes (2) to (4) usually contain larger amounts of bound metal than those exhibiting process (1) Table I.

These processes can be studied on a time sequence basis and from these experiments at least two events could be followed by electron microscopy: (1) the first **event** in time is the initial uptake of stoichiometric amounts of metal which (2) act as nucleation sites for the inorganic deposition of either elemental metal (*e.g.*, Au III, Figure 4A and 4B) or hydrated metal (*e.g.*, Fe III, Figure 2; and Pd II, Figure 3A and 3B). Gold was the only metal we have studied that demonstrated a crystallization to the elemental form, but many others have shown a tendency to form hydrous aggregates actively within the wall fabric (*e.g.*, La, Ce, Pr, Sm, Er, Fe, Ru and Pd).

Dimensional analyses of the sectioned walls after incubation with the various metals showed that the wall fabric can expand or contract under the influence of a specific metal. For example, the wall thickness after treatment with indium III was 28.46 ± 2.87 nm, whereas after yttrium III it was 16.33 ± 2.98 nm. In fact, time and concentration of metal can be factors in both the uptake and dimensional responses of the walls (Table II). In general, the longer the incubation time, the more contracted the wall thickness becomes and the greater the metal deposition. In the case of metals that do not show a precipitation or

Figure 2. A: Thin section of a *Bacillus subtilis* cell wall
that has been exposed to Fe III. The arrow points the
"crystalloids" of the oxide hydrate, which are closely
associated with the wall substance. In this and other
micrographs no stain other than the *in situ* metal has
been used on the walls, and the bar denotes 100 nm.
B: Typical "crystalloid" with lattice structure.

Figure 3. A: A wall after exposure to Pd II. B: X-Ray
diffractogram of the walls after exposure to Pd II. Only
a faint band is seen (arrow) indicating the low crystal-
linity of the metal aggregate.

Figure 4. A: A wall after exposure to Au III. B: X-Ray
diffractogram of these walls, showing many distinct bands
and therefore high crystalline order.

Figure 5. A wall after exposure to 5 mM uranyl acetate
for 10 min at 22° C.

Figure 6. A wall after exposure to 1% uranyl acetate for
10 min at 22° C.

Figure 7. Same as Figure 6 but after 60 min of incubation.

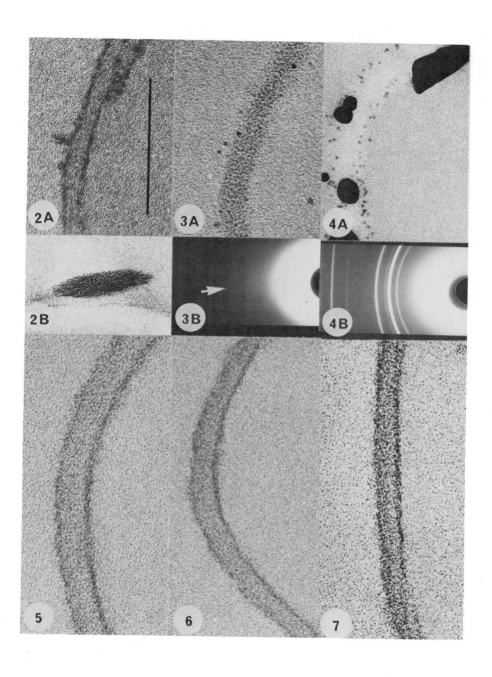

Table I

Representative Metal Uptakes by the Walls of
Bacillus subtilis and Their
Corresponding Staining Responses

Metal	Uptake (μmol/mg dry wt wall)	Staining Response
Rb	0.014	Diffuse
Ca	0.399	Diffuse
La	1.760	Aggregates
Mn	0.810	Diffuse
Fe III	3.581	Aggregates
Pd	0.190	Aggregates
Au	0.363	Crystals

Table II

Effect of the Concentration and Incubation Time of
Uranyl Acetate on the Quantity of Metal Uptake and the
Thickness of the *Bacillus subtilis* Wall

Concentration of Uranyl Acetate	Incubation Time (min)	Uptake (μmol/mg dry wt wall)	Thickness (nm)
5 mM	10	5.462	26.77
5 mM	60	9.700	24.92
1%	10	10.400	22.81
1%	60	10.400	20.76

crystallization process (e.*g.*, U IV), the walls rapidly
become saturated with metal at high concentration although
longer incubation can still affect wall dimensions (compare
the 1% uranyl acetate incubations of 10 and 60 min, Table
II). Under these conditions the contraction of the wall
becomes quite apparent as does the increase in electron
scattering power (compare Figures 5, 6 and 7). The situation
is more complex if a precipitation or crystallization process
occurs since aggregates (or crystals) may continue to grow
under these conditions (Beveridge and Murray, 1976).

Since we had shown that metals can interact strongly
with the *B. subtilis* wall it was of interest to determine
this response under geochemical conditions. For this reason

we attempted to apply geological conditions (*i.e.*, heat, pressure and low redox potential) to zirconium-loaded walls in the laboratory (see Methods). Under these conditions the morphological attributes of the walls were profoundly altered (*e.g.*, the laminations found in the organic component of the sample had a spacing of 15.92 ± 2.52 nm compared to the original zirconium wall thickness of 27.28 ± 3.21 nm – compare Figures 8 and 9), but they had retained the zirconium (Figure 9), aptly demonstrating the tenacity of the metal binding.

DISCUSSION

Cell walls of *Bacillus subtilis* may contain as much as 70 percent of their dry weight as teichoic acid (Ellwood and Tempest, 1969), which is an anionic polymer of α-D-glucopyranosyl glycerol (or ribitol) phosphate and is covalently linked to the peptidoglycan, the remaining (major) wall component (Hughes, 1970; Warth and Strominger, 1971). This peptidoglycan consists of an alternating polymer of β-(1,4)-linked N-acetylglucosamine and N-acetylmuramic residues, the latter unit bearing a short peptide side chain (L-Ala-D-Glu-(L)-meso-Dpm-D-Ala) of which approximately 35 percent are cross-linked through D-alanyl-(D)-meso-diaminopimelyl bonds to adjacent glycopeptide strands (Hughes, 1970; Warth and Strominger, 1971). Therefore, these walls consist of sugar, phosphate and amino acid residues and are an appropriate model system for studying the interaction of metals with biological polymers.

This chapter has demonstrated that these walls strongly interact with metals in solution, and may initiate an inorganic precipitation process that allows the immobilization of substantial quantities of the soluble form. A mechanism such as this could have strong implications on the mobilization and concentration of metal in aqueous environments. One can imagine that waters engender a constant but light rain of complex anionic polymers of biological origin, forming a variable proportion of the total sediment that accumulates at the bottom. Since the absorption of metal can be specific (at least in the case of *B. subtilis* walls; see Beveridge and Murray, 1976), it would be possible to establish high yields of discrete metal in the sediment by these durable cell fragments, and they eventually would be exposed to geochemical processes. Our results suggest that even under these strongly reducing conditions this organic component retards metal leaching of this particular metal and probably all the tightly bound metals.

Traces of microbes have been found in sediments from ancient geological horizons, *e.g.*, the isoprenoid hydrocarbons from the Precambrian Nonesuch formation (Eglinton *et al.*, 1964),

Figure 8.   Thin-section of a wall fragment of *Bacillus subtilis*, which has been loaded with zirconium (*i.e.*, suspended in a 5-m*M* zirconium solution for 10 min at 22° C).   The zirconium has imparted electron scattering power to the wall fabric.   The arrows point to granules of ferritin-concanavalin A, which are acting as surface markers.   Bar = 100 nm.

Figure 9.   Thin-section of the "remains" of wall fragments such as in Figure 2 after 20-day incubation with a hydrated amorphous silica matrix under reducing conditions—positive pressure and high temperature (220° C).   Very little is recognizable as bacterial wall except for faint linear striations of compacted nature in the organic matrix (large arrows).   These wall remains have retained high electron scattering power, an indication that substantial zirconium is still present.   Bar = 100 nm.

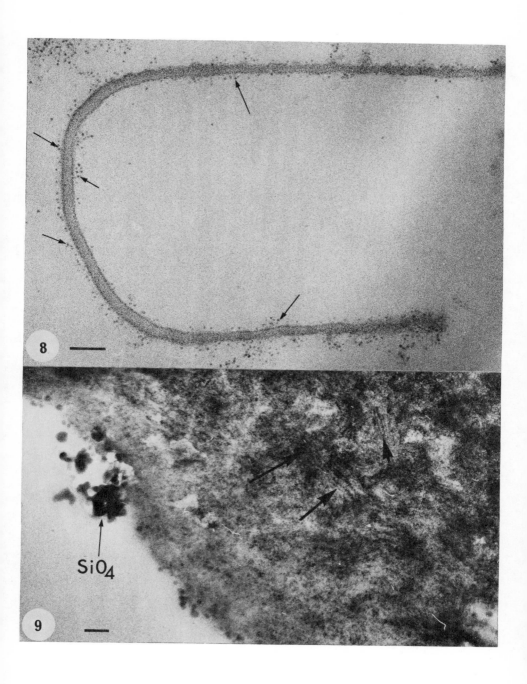

SiO$_4$

the mineralized remains of microorganisms from the Precambrian Gunflint chert of northern Lake Superior (Barghoorn and Tyler, 1965), and possible microfossils from Precambrian iron formations found in the United States, Canada, Australia and South Africa (La Berge, 1967). These are usually closely associated with metal deposits, often of large proportions. The exact manner of deposition of these metals is open to debate, and the associated microbial remnants lead one to speculate as to the possibility of their biological origin.

ACKNOWLEDGMENTS

The author is indebted for the interest and advice of R. G. E. Murray, W. Fyfe and J. Zajic (Department of Microbiology and Immunology, Geology and Bioengineering of the University of Western Ontario, Canada) and for the technical assistance of F. Williams. This work was supported in part by a Richard Ivey Foundation Grant (London, Canada) and a National Research Council of Canada Co-op grant. The electron microscopic facilities are maintained by an operating grant from the Medical Research Council of Canada, whereas the atomic absorption, X-ray fluorescence and X-ray diffraction units are maintained by an operating grant from the National Research Council of Canada.

REFERENCES

Barghoorn, E. S. and S. A. Tyler. "Microorganisms from the Gunflint Chert," *Science* 147:563–577 (1965).

Beveridge, T. J. and R. G. E. Murray. "Uptake and Retention of Metals by Cell Walls of *Bacillus subtilis*," *J. Bacteriol.* 127:1502–1518 (1976).

Carstensen, E. L. and R. E. Marquis. "Dielectric and Electrochemical Properties of Bacterial Cells," *Spores VI, A.S.M. Publication* pp. 563–571 (1975).

Davis, J. B. *Petroleum Microbiology* (Amsterdam: Elsevier Publishing Co., 1967).

Eglinton, G., P. M. Scott, T. Belsky, A. L. Burlingame and M. Calvin. "Hydrocarbons of Biological Origin from a One-Billion-Year-Old Sediment," *Science* 145:263–264 (1964).

Ellwood, D. C. and D. W. Tempest. "Control of Teichoic Acid and Teichuronic Acid Biosynthesis in Chemostat Cultures of *Bacillus subtilis* var. niger," *Biochem. J.* 111:1–5 (1969).

Hughes, R. C. "Autolysis of Isolated Cells Walls of *Bacillus licheniformis* N.C.T.C. 6346 and *Bacillus subtilis* Marburg strain 168. Separation of the Products and Characterization of the Mucopeptide Fragments," *Biochem. J.* 119:849-860 (1970).

Kemp, A. L. W., R. L. Thomas, C. I. Dell and J. -M. Jaquet. "Cultural Impact on the Geochemistry of Sediments in Lake Erie," *J. Fish. Res. Board Can.* 33:440-462 (1976).

La Berge, G. L. "Microfossils and Precambrian Iron-Formations," *Geol. Soc. Am. Bull.* 78:331-342 (1967).

Marquis, R. E., K. Mayzel and E. L. Carstensen. "Cation Exchange in Cell Walls of Gram-Positive Bacteria," *Can. J. Microbiol.* 22:975-982 (1976).

Ou, L-T.,and R. E. Marquis. "Electromechanical Interactions in Cell Walls of Gram-Positive Cocci," *J. Bacteriol.* 101:92-101 (1970).

Ou, L-T. and R. E. Marquis. "Coccal Cell Wall Compactness and the Swelling Action of Denaturants," *Can. J. Microbiol.* 18:623-629 (1972).

Warth, A. D. and J. L. Strominger. "Structure of the Peptidoglycan from Vegetative Cell Walls of *Bacillus subtilis*," *Biochemistry* 10:4349-4358 (1971).

Williams, D. R. *Metals of Life* (New York: Van Nostrand Reinhold Co., 1971).

CHAPTER 80

EFFECTS OF LEAD ON PROPERTIES OF LEAD-SENSITIVE
AND LEAD-TOLERANT CELLS

P. DOELMAN

Research Institute for Nature Management
Arnhem, The Netherlands

INTRODUCTION

Previous studies discussed the effects of lead added
to soil on respiration of the aerobic microflora, the decomposition of defined organic substrates and the composition of
the bacterial flora (Doelman, 1977 a, b, c). The sensitivity
of soil bacteria towards lead is highly variable. This
difference in sensitivity may be caused by differences in
external and internal physical and chemical properties of
the bacteria. To trace these differences, a comparative
study was made of the effect of lead on various properties
of lead-sensitive and lead-tolerant bacterial strains.
Bacteria were considered lead-sensitive when no growth
occurred at a lead concentration of 4 ppm in a defined
nutrient medium. They were considered lead-tolerant when
normal growth occurred at a lead concentration of 30 ppm in
the nutrient medium.

MATERIAL AND METHODS

The following bacterial strains (except for *Escherichia
coli* which included all representatives of the soil microflora)
were used in this study: *Arthrobacter globiformis* strains
A 17, A 18, Ac 1, Ac 34 and Ac 403, *Escherichia coli* strain
Ml 308-225, *Bacillus subtilis* strains B 28 and W 23, a
Pseudomonas fluorescens strain P 8, and some unidentified
Gram-negative rods, numbered 4-1, 4-40, 4-50, 4-107 and
4-143. The lead-sensitive strains were A 17, A 18, Ac 1,
Ac 34, Ac 403, P 8, 4-1, 4-40, 4-50 and 4-59. The lead toler-
ant strains were B 28, W 23, Ml 308-225, 4-107 and 4-143.

Determination of the Potential Electrostatic Charge

The electrophoretic mobility (EPM) of the Gram-negative rods 4-1, 4-40, 4-59, 4-107 and 4-143 was measured with a Zeta potential meter of the Riddick type (Riddick, 1961). The EPM was used as a measure for the charge, as was done by Marshall (1969) and Kiremidjian (1973). All the bacterial strains under study had the same shape and size and were Gram-negative rods. Their EPM was measured by timing their movement over a distance of 20 or 40 μ in a 4.8-V/cm field gradient (48-V potential across a 10-cm electrophoretic cell).

The bacteria were cultured in media A, B or C at pH 6.6. Medium A contained per 1 liter: 1 g yeast extract, 1 g glucose. Medium B contained per liter: 0.1 g yeast extract, 1 g glucose, 50 ml soil extract, 2 g NH_4NO_3. Medium C contained per liter: 0.1 g yeast extract, 1 g glucose, 50 ml soil extract, 1 g NH_4NO_3, 1 g $CaCl_2$, 1 g $MgCl_2$. Cultures were harvested at the end of their logarithmic phase. As the chemical environment of the growth medium may affect the composition of the outer membrane and the charge of the cell envelope (Bier, 1955), the EPM was measured after washing three times in demineralized water and resuspending 0.1 ml of the bacterial cells in 15 ml of salt solutions of defined ionic strength (I.S.).

At every measuring point the EPM of 20 cells was determined in the defined medium. The standard error of the mean never exceeded 3.5 percent. The reliability of the instrument was verified by calibration against standard EPM values of defined clay minerals (Kiremidjian, 1973).

Preparation and Activity Measurements of Bacterial Membrane Vesicles

Cultures were grown in 300-ml conical flasks containing 50 ml medium. The flasks were placed in a rotary shaker (350 rpm). Membrane vesicles of A 17 *Arthrobacter globiformis,* W 23 *Bacillus subtilis* and ML 308-225 *Escherichia coli,* cultured in a yeast extract glucose solution (yeast extract 1 g/l, glucose 1 g/l, pH 6.6) were prepared according to the Kaback (1970) method, with two modifications. First, to obtain a more vigorous activity of lysozyme, extra $MgCl_2$ was added, which resulted in a better vesicle formation of A 17. Second, the vesicles were not stored in phosphate buffer but in imidazol buffer to avoid problems with precipitation of lead phosphate.

NADH, L-malate, succinate and D-lactate were used to determine the oxygen consumption of the membrane vesicles. These measurements were carried out in a biological oxygen monitor (BOM) as described by Matin and Konings (1973). The composition and the final concentration of the medium as applied in the BOM were: imidazol 0.05 M, $MgCl_2$ 0.01 M, pH 6.6. The final lead concentrations were 0, 5, 50, 100 and 200 ppm. Determination of the effect of lead on the transport of a ^{14}C-amino acid mixture, with phenazine methosulphate (pms) and ascorbate as electron donor, was carried out as described by Matin and Konings (1973). Uniformly ^{14}C-labeled amino acid mixture and ^{210}Pb were obtained from the Radiochemical Center (Amersham). The measurements of ^{210}Pb transport through the vesicles were similar to the ^{14}C-amino acid transport measurements. Radioactivity of ^{210}Pb was measured with a spectrophotometer. The amount of ^{210}Pb added lead was 34,000 in counts per five minutes.

Determination of the Maximal Specific Growth Rate

The maximal specific growth rate (μmax) was determined in a liquid medium containing yeast extract 0.7 g/l and glucose 1 g/l, pH 6.6 at 25° C. Growth conditions were similar to those specified above. At the end of the logarithmic growth phase, the bacterial strains were transferred to fresh medium. After 2-4 hr they were again subcultured in a medium of the same composition to which was added 0, 1, 2, 5, 10, 15 and 25 ppm $PbCl_2$; μ was calculated from optical density (O.D.) measurements made hourly at 420 nm.

RESULTS AND DISCUSSION

The Electrophoretic Mobility of Lead-Sensitive and Lead-Tolerant Bacteria

The EPM of any bacterial strain cultured in medium A, B or C, though often initially different, was the same after three washings in demineralized water. Figure 1 shows the influence of pH on the EPM of the typically lead-sensitive strain 4-40, and the lead-tolerant strain 4-107. Strain 4-40 had the same lead sensitivity as A 17. The isoelectric point (I.P.) was located at approximately pH 3; between pH 5 and 8.5 EPM values from 1.75 to 2.0 were found. The shape of these pH-EPM curves is in agreement with earlier findings (Bier, 1955). Lead-sensitive and lead-tolerant bacteria showed no difference in charge sensitivity towards H^+ ions.

Figure 2 shows the influence of cations on the EPM of the strains 4-40 (lead-sensitive) and 4-107 (lead-tolerant). In the presence of lead ions the EPM of both strains increases with increasing Pb ions, but with the lead-sensitive strains ten times as many cations (I.S. = $3 \cdot 10^{-3}$) were required for the EPM to become zero than with the lead-tolerant strains (I.S. = $3 \cdot 10^{-4}$). The influence of Na^+ ions on the EPM of

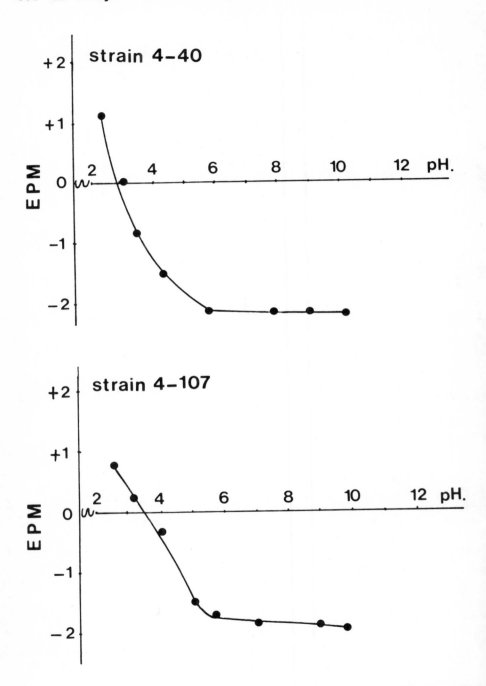

Figure 1.   The influence of pH on the electrophoretic mobility (EPM) of the lead-sensitive strain 4-40 and the lead-tolerant strain 4-107.

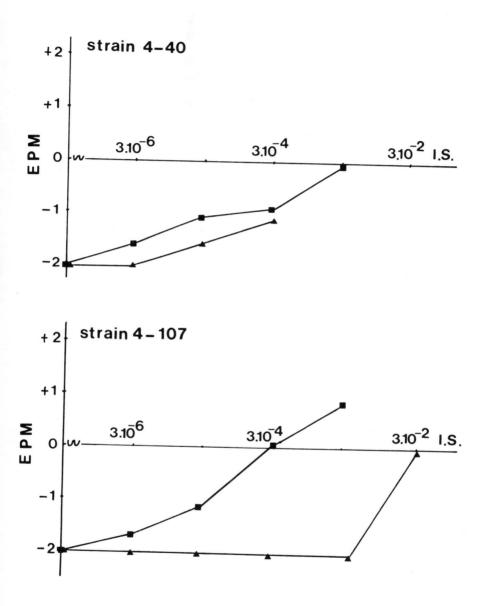

Figure 2. The influence of the cation concentration (= ionic strength = I.S.) on the electrophoretic mobility (EPM) of the lead-sensitive strain 4-40 and of the lead-tolerant strain 4-107. ■—■ Pb2+, ▲—▲ Na+.

lead-tolerant strains was hardly visible up to I.S. = $3 \cdot 10^{-3}$. At a higher I.S. the EPM reached zero rapidly (at I.S. = $3 \cdot 10^{-2}$.

The influence of Na^+ ions on lead-sensitive strains was more gradual. The influence of H^+, Na^+ or Pb^{2+} on the various bacteria indicates the disposition of the charge-determining components. For example, when lead-tolerant strains have more divalent cations adsorbed than lead-sensitive strains to their cell envelope, monovalent cations cannot influence the EPM at low I.S. This might be the reason why lead-tolerant strains need less Pb^{2+} ions (I.S. = $3 \cdot 10^{-4}$) than lead-sensitive strains to reach the I.P. Since the lead-sensitive strains more easily adsorb divalent cations such as Pb^{2+}, ten times as many ($3 \cdot 10^{-3}$) cations are necessary to reach the I.P. The diagram given by Costerton (1974) illustrates the various adsorption and interaction sites of cations with the envelope layers.

The cell envelope may accumulate heavy metal ions and thus detoxify the cell's environment (Friedman and Dugan, 1968). Tonomura (1968) explains the resistance of microorganisms to mercury pesticides by their fixation of mercury to the cell surface, which would prevent mercury from reaching the inner parts of the cell. Cadmium-accommodated *Escherichia coli* strains were able to bind 56 percent more Cd to their cell wall than the nonaccommodated strains, 2 percent (Mitra, 1975).

Activity of the Cytoplasmic Membrane Vesicles

Oxygen Consumption

The membrane vesicles of the lead-sensitive *Arthrobacter globiformis*, A 17, and of the lead-tolerant *Bacillus subtilis*, W 23, showed no endogenous oxidation. Strain A 17 was able to use NADH and L-malate as electron donors but succinate and D-lactate could not be used. Strain W 23 could use NADH as an electron donor. Addition of lead to actively oxidizing systems did not cause an inhibition of the oxidation rate. Even at a concentration of 200 ppm lead no inhibition was found. This means the cytochrome system was not affected by lead. It is surprising that even the electron transport system of the most sensitive bacteria such as A 17 was not affected by lead. Overneli (1975) observed an inhibitory effect of lead on photosynthesis of freshwater algae.

Amino Acid Transport

Figure 3 shows the effect of lead on ^{14}C-amino acid transport by membrane vesicles of A 17 and W 23. Preincubation of the A 17 vesicles with lead for 90 min did not give different results. The effect of lead appeared to be independent of the length of the period in which vesicles were equilibrated in a lead-containing solution, before adding amino acids. The amino acid transport of the A 17 vesicles was clearly affected by the presence of lead. At lead concentrations of 5 ppm and 50 ppm the steady-state levels were approximately 30 percent and 20 percent lower, respectively, as compared to the control without lead. This is an inversion effect. The lower steady-state level in the presence of 5 ppm Pb suggests a greater efflux of amino acids.

By adding lead to an actively transporting system, the steady-state level was immediately reduced (Figure 4). The efflux that occurs when lead is added to red blood cells (Passow, 1964) is probably due to a reduction of the mobility of phospholipids of the membranes that caused the leaking.

Lead Binding Properties of Membrane Vesicles

Figure 5 shows the transport of ^{210}Pb through the membrane vesicles of the lead-sensitive *Arthrobacter globiformic*, A 17, and the lead-tolerant *Escherichia coli*, ML 308-225. The bindings of ^{210}Pb by the vesicles of A 17 was expressed counts per 5 min, 2600 - 1000 = 1600 = 4.7 percent of the total amount (34000 c.p./5 m) of added lead. The fixation by ML 308-225 vesicles was 2200 - 1000 = 1200 c.p./5 m = 3.5 percent. In the presence of an energy source, such as ascorbate-pms, these percentages were 3 and 3, respectively. The fact that ascorbate-pms did not increase lead fixation shows that either no active transport of lead occurred, or that ascorbate-pms was the wrong energy source for lead transport. Working with *Micrococcus luteus Azotobacter vinelandii*, Tornabene and Edwards (1972) found 93 percent and 99 percent, respectively, of the added amount of lead associated with the cell envelope.

Maximal Specific Growth Rate

Figure 6 shows the effect of lead on the maximal specific growth rate (μmax) of the lead-sensitive strains A 17 and 4-50 and of the lead-tolerant strain B 28. One ppm Pb caused an inhibition of 95 percent and 25 ppm caused an inhibition of 75 percent for strain A 17. A higher lead concentration caused a smaller inhibition effect than a lower concentration (inversion effect). With the strain B 28, 1 ppm Pb hardly caused growth inhibition and 25 ppm caused an inhibition of

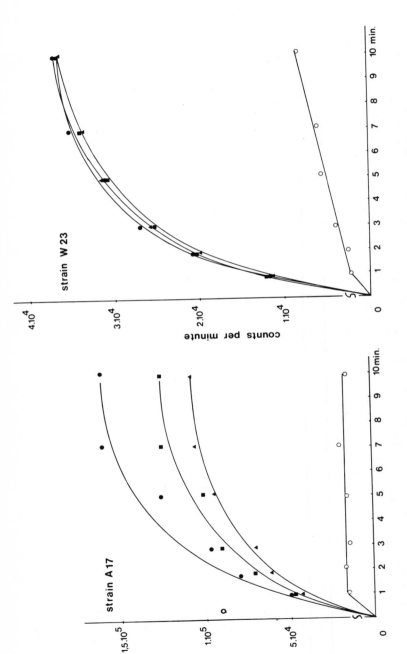

Figure 3. The effect of lead on the transport of a ^{14}C-amino acid mixture through the cytoplasmic membrane vesicles of the lead-sensitive *Arthrobacter globiformis*, A 17 and of the lead-tolerant *Bacillus subtilis*, W 23. The amount of ^{14}C-amino acid mixture transported is expressed in counts per minute. O—O no energy source added, ●—● ascorbate (10 mM)-pms (100 μM). ◀—◀ ascorbate-pms and Pb^{2+} (5 ppm), ■—■ ascorbate-pms and Pb^{2+} (50 ppm).

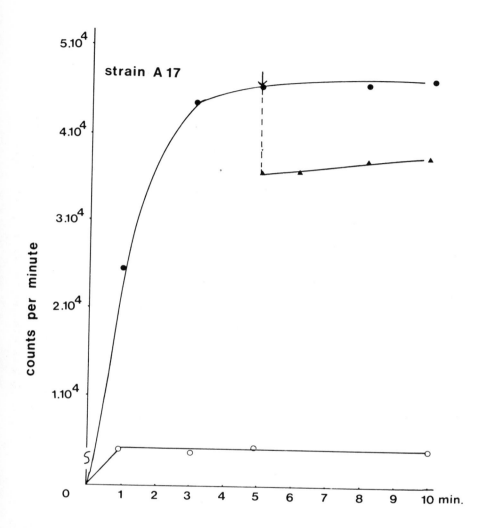

Figure 4. A greater ^{14}C-amino acid efflux, induced by lead, of the lead-sensitive *Arthrobacter globiformis*, A 17. Lead (final concentration 5 ppm) was added as indicated (⬇)——— 5 min after the start of the experiment. O—O no energy source, ●—● ascorbate (10 mM) – pms (100 μM), ▲—▲ ascorbate pms and Pb^{2+} (5 ppm).

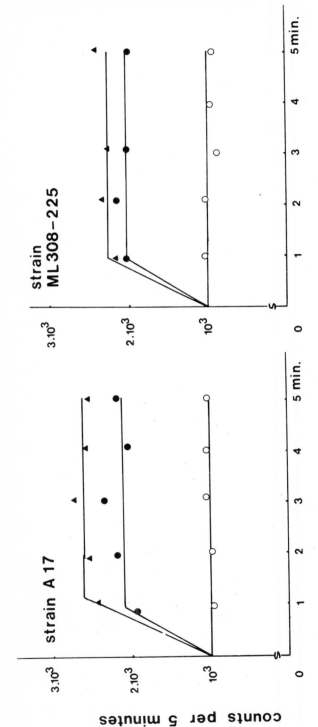

Figure 5. Binding of ^{210}Pb by the cytoplasmic membranes of the lead-sensitive *Arthrobacter globiformis*, A 17, and lead-tolerant *Escherichia coli*, ML 308-225. The binding of ^{210}Pb is expressed in counts per 5 min (γ – spectrophotometer). O—O membrane filter, ▲—▲ membrane filter, vesicles, no energy, ●—● membrane filter, vesicles, ascorbate (10 mM)-pms (100 μM).

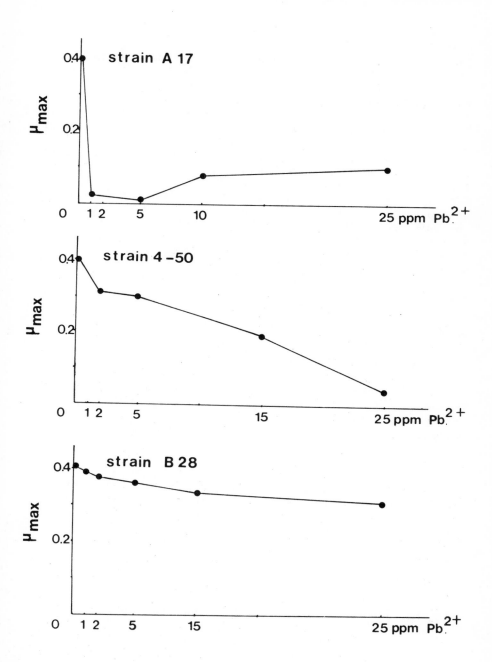

Figure 6. The influence of lead (Pb^{2+}) on the maximal specific growth rate (μmax.) of the lead-sensitive bacteria *Arthrobacter globiformis* A 17, strain 4-50 and of the lead-tolerant strain *Bacillus subtilis* B 28.

approximately 20 percent and 25 ppm of approximately 80 percent for the 4-50 strain. The dose response curves of B 28
and 4-50 were regular (a higher lead concentration increased
inhibition), while A 17 showed an inverse response.

All *Arthrobacter globiformis* strains (A 18, Ac 1, Ac 34
and Ac 403) showed response curves identical to strain A 17.
A similar inversion effect has been observed by Kaars
Sypesteyn and Janssen (1959) who observed that the inhibitory
effect of dithiocarbamates on fungal growth is influenced
by the state of the equilibrium $Cu^{2+} + 1$ e $\quad Cu^+$, divalent
copper being more toxic than monovalent copper. Likewise
lead can occur in two valencies: $Pb^{2+} - 2$ e $\quad Pb^{4+}$
$(PbCl_2^{2-} - 2$ e $\quad PbCl_2)$. Since the inversion effect does
not appear in all cases, while all the strains were tested in
the same media, this effect must be related to a specific
activity of particular bacterial strains. Without exception
this effect was observed on the *Arthrobacter globiformis*
strains and not on Gram-negative rods.

Gray and Ventilla (1973) used the retardation of the
specific growth of marine-living Protozoa by heavy metals as
a measure for the toxicity of those metals.

CONCLUSIONS

Differences between lead-sensitive and lead-tolerant
strains are manifested at various cell envelope levels
(microenvironment). Lead-sensitive strains attract more lead
to their cell envelope than lead-tolerant strains. This may
be the reason that lead can affect the cytoplasmic membrane
of lead-sensitive strains and not that of lead-tolerant strains.

ACKNOWLEDGMENTS

Experiments on EPM were carried out in the Department
of Microbiology of the New York University, and experiments
on membrane transport in the Department of Microbiology of
the University of Groningen. I am indebted to Professor
G. Stotzky and Dr. W. N. Konings for their help with these
experiments.

REFERENCES

Bier, M. *Electrophoresis* (New York: Academic Press, 1959).

Costerton, J. W., J. M. Ingram and K. J. Cheng. "Structure
and Function of the Cell Envelope of Gram-Negative
Bacteria," *Bacteriol. Rev.* 38(1):87-110 (1974).

Doelman, P.   (a) Effects of lead on soil respiration. (b) Effects of lead on decomposition of defined organic substrates. (c) Effects of lead on the composition of the bacteria flora.   To be published in: *Soil Biology and Biochemistry* (1977).

Friedman, B. A. and P. R. Dugan.   "Concentration and Accumulation of Metallic Ions by Bacterium *Zoogloea*," *Devel. Ind. Microbiol.* 9:381-388 (1968).

Gray, J. S. and R. J. Ventilla.   "Growth Rates of Sediment-Living Marine Protozoen as a Toxicity Indicator for Heavy Metals," *Ambio* 2(4):118-121 (1973).

Kaars Sypesteyn, A. and M. J. Janssen.   "On the Mode of Action of Dialkyldithio Carbamates on Moulds and Bacteria," *A. van Leeuwenhoek* 25:422-438 (1959).

Kaback, H. R.   "Preparation and Characterization of Bacterial Membranes," in: *Methods in Enzymology*, vol. 22, W. B. Jakoby, Ed. (New York: Academic Press, 1970).

Kiremidjian, L. and G. Stotzky.   "Effects of Natural Microbial Preparations on the Electrokinetic Potential of Bacterial Cells and Clay Minerals," *Appl. Microbiol.* 25(6):964-971 (1973).

Marshall, K. C.   "Studies by Microelectrophoretic and Microscopic Techniques of the Sorption of Illite and Montmorillonite to Rhizobia," *J. Gen. Microbiol.* 56(301) (1969).

Matin, A. and W. N. Konings.   "Transport of Lactate and Succinate by Membrane Vesikels of *Escherichia coli*, *Bacillus subtilis* and a *Pseudomonas* species," *Eur. J. Biochem.* 34:58-67 (1973).

Mitra, R. S., R. H. Gray, B. Chin and I. A. Bernstein.   "Molecular Mechanisms of Accommodation in *Escherichia coli* to Toxic Levels of Cd^{2+}," *J. Bacteriol.* 121(3):1180-1188 (1975).

Overneli, J.   "The Effect of Some Heavy Metal Ions on Photosynthesis in a Freshwater Algae," *Pesticide Biochem. Physiol.* 5:19-26 (1975).

Passow, H.   In: *The Red Blood Cell*, C. Bishop and D. M. Surgenor, Eds. (New York: Academic Press, 1964).

Riddick, T. M.   "New Tool for Water Treatment," *Chem. Eng.* June 26, July 10 (1961).

Rothstein, A. "Cell Membrane as Site of Action of Heavy Metals," *Fed. Proc.* 18:1026-1035 (1959).

Tonomura, K. K. Maeda and F. Futai. "Studies on the Action of Mercury-Resistant Microorganism on Mercurials," *J. Ferment Technol.* 46(9):685-692 (1968).

Tornabene, T. G. and H. W. Edwards. "Microbial Uptake of Lead," *Science* 176:1334-1335 (1972).

CHAPTER 81

MICROBIOLOGICAL TRANSFORMATIONS OF SULFUR COMPOUNDS IN INDUSTRIAL WASTE MATERIALS

SEPPO K. SIVELÄ
OLLI H. TUOVINEN

Department of General Microbiology
University of Helsinki
Malminkatu 20
SF-00100 Helsinki 10, Finland

INTRODUCTION

Sulfur compounds in industrial effluents and waste materials may originate from impurities in raw materials or they may be formed as by-products during processing. In Finland the total production of sulfur-containing waste materials amounted to about $7 \cdot 10^6$ tons in 1976. The bulk of these materials is in a solid state and cannot be discarded into sewers or volatilized into the atmosphere. A brief list of the main industrial sources of sulfur indicates that by far the greatest contributor is the mining industry, whereas smaller amounts of sulfur, but in a more toxic form, are emitted into the atmosphere or released into water by other industries (Table I). This chapter outlines some trends that are currently envisaged for the microbiological treatment of these sulfur-containing waste materials in Finland.

SULFUR DIOXIDE

The annual consumption of crude oil in Finland is around $1.2 \cdot 10^7$ ton, with an average sulfur content of 1.7 percent. During oil refinery, about $2 \cdot 10^4$ ton/yr is separated and purified; $8 \cdot 10^3$ ton/yr is retained in the bituminous extract of crude oil. The rest (over $1.8 \cdot 10^5$ ton/yr) is released into the atmosphere. The total emission of sulfur dioxide from the combustion of fuels (oil and coal) amounts to

Table I
Sulfur Compounds in Industrial Wastes in Finland

Compound	Main Industrial Source	Production (t/yr)	Environmental Effects	Microbiological Treatment
SO_2	Fuels (Coal, oil)	500,000	corrosion, acidic rainwater, damage to vegetation	Oxidation to sulfur and sulfates ("biofiltration")
H_2S Methyl Sulfides	Pulp industry (sulfate cellulose)	10,000	maladorous, highly toxic	
Ferrous sulfate	TiO_2 production (from $FeTiO_3$)	200,000	acidity, toxicity	Oxidation to ferric sulfate for use in sewage purification and hydrometallurgy
Mining Waste Materials	Mining	5,500,000	heavy metals, acidity, ground water contamination	Microbiological leaching for the recovery of metals
Gypsum	Fertilizer industry	750,000	acidity	

$5 \cdot 10^5$ ton/yr. Owing to the relatively noncentralized industry and distribution of population in Finland, there has not been any noticeable large-scale environmental pollution caused by acidic rain. Some local corrosion phenomena have been attributed to the presence of sulfur dioxide in the atmosphere and also some changes in the vegetation have been recorded in large municipal and industrial centers.

VOLATILE SULFIDES

Toxic effects caused by sulfur compounds in the air are due mainly to hydrogen sulfide and organic sulfides (methyl mercaptan, dimethyl sulfide, dimethyl disulfide) produced by oil refineries and sulfate cellulose mills at a rate of $1 \cdot 10^4$ ton/yr. These volatile sulfides are extremely malodorous, with a low odor threshold of 0.0001 ppm in the air. The main effects caused by these compounds are local air pollution, corrosion of building materials and toxicity to biological systems.

Volatile sulfur compounds in effluents and waste gases produced by cellulose mills may be removed by the use of layers of pine bark, which contains microorganisms oxidizing these sulfides to sulfates and elemental sulfur. An industrial scale operation has included 3 x 500 m³ units, which have been studied in detail. The operation is clearly dependent on temperature, pH, nutrients and aerobiosis. A fully efficient operation is preceded by a lag period that probably represents the establishment of a microbial population suited to the selective conditions. In full operation, 90-95 percent of the volatile sulfides may be removed from effluents and waste gases by this method with a loading of 2 m³ effluent/m³/day.

It has also been established that the bark material contains thiobacilli, which have developed a high tolerance to hydrogen sulfide and methyl sulfides. Preliminary studies indicate that some isolates of thiobacilli are able to oxidize these sulfides as a source of energy. It remains to be seen whether the same bacteria are also able to metabolize the organic carbon in methyl sulfides.

FERROUS SULFATE

Ferrous sulfate ($2 \cdot 10^5$ ton/yr) is formed as a by-product in titanium dioxide production from ilmenite. Ferrous sulfate is acidic and toxic, and its oxidation to ferric iron both chemically and microbiologically results in oxygen consumption in aquatic environments. It can be oxidized to ferric iron by iron-oxidizing bacteria (*Thiobacillus ferroxidans*) in continuous-flow systems, and possibilities for the industrial use of this product have been explored. The microbiological oxidation process *per se* is feasible and economical

on an industrial scale but its application is limited by
other factors, such as the need for a concentrated product
for transportation from the plant.

GYPSUM

Gypsum, which is a major by-product ($ca.$ $7.5 \cdot 10^5$
ton/yr) from the fertilizer industry, does not have any
further industrial use. It is an acidic waste and, owing to
its partial solubility, it may cause environmental pollution.
The microbiological reduction of gypsum as well as that of
ferrous sulfate to a more insoluble form as sulfide would
require massive amounts of organic material for electron
donor, which is currently not a feasible proposition. For
example, the sludge from the municipal sewage purification
plants in Finland would not be a sufficient amount of organic
material for the microbiological reduction of gypsum. However,
gypsum is amenable to microbiological reduction, and such a
process could be developed to produce sulfur by the microbiological oxidation of sulfide to elemental sulfur.

MINING WASTE MATERIALS

The microbiological leaching of mining wastes and
low-grade ores has been summarized recently in a number of
reports. Problems associated with mining waste materials
in Finland include the possible contamination of ground
water in spite of the precautions adopted by the mining
industry. Refractory slags are a potential source of metals
that may be recovered by the microbiological leaching. These
slags contain sufficient amounts of sulfides to support the
development of sulfur-oxidizing bacteria in these environments. The dissolution of metals from slags is a relatively
slow process, but by appropriate construction and technical
design the recovery of metals would reduce the long-term
pollution effects, such as the ground water contamination.

CONCLUSIONS

Industrial effluents cannot normally be purified in
municipal sewage plants because the microorganisms active
in the activated sludge process are relatively sensitive to
the toxic effects caused by reduced sulfur and other compounds
(Table II). In general, the microbiological pretreatment of
industrial effluents involves the development of populations
of highly specific microorganisms that are resistant to the
toxic chemicals and able to metabolize industrial waste compounds at high rates. Industrial waste materials may be
converted by microbiological treatments to less toxic forms,
which may render the effluents more suitable to conventional

Table II
Toxic Levels of Various Chemicals to
Microbial Metabolism in Activated Sludge[a]

Compound	Toxic Level (ppm)
Arsenate, Arsenite	0.7
Cyanide	1.0
Ferrous Iron	100
Nickel	6
Hydrogen Sulfide and Organic Sulfides	5-25

[a]The levels present values recommended by the Water Protection Board of the Municipal Council of the City of Helsinki.

purification processes involving activated sludge. Small-scale microbiological operations for treating sulfur-containing wastes have already been established. Such plants have given useful information on the applicability of microbiological methods for exploiting and eliminating industrial waste materials, although the current knowledge and experience on an industrial scale remain to be explored and tested in more detail.

CHAPTER 82

THE EFFECT OF COMPLEXING LIGANDS ON TRACE METAL ADSORPTION AT THE SEDIMENT/WATER INTERFACE

JAMES A. DAVIS, III
JAMES O. LECKIE

Environmental Engineering and Science
Department of Civil Engineering
Stanford University
Palo Alto, California   94305   USA

INTRODUCTION

The environmental biogeochemist must be familiar with many physical, chemical and biological processes to understand and predict the distribution of trace metals in natural waters. These processes include hydrolysis, precipitation, complexation, ligand- or ion-exchange reactions, adsorption-desorption phenomena, coprecipitation, redox reactions, and biological accumulation or transformation. For many trace metals, however, accumulation in the unique microenvironment of the sediment/water interface may be one of the most important transport mechanisms in natural aquatic systems. Equilibrium solubility models are useful in establishing simple boundary conditions for the purpose of discussion, but consideration of the interactions at the sediment/water interface region is necessary to account for many of the observed phenomena in natural systems (Leckie and James, 1975).

Natural waters are highly complex, heterogeneous electrolyte systems containing both organic and inorganic matter. The electrolyte composition of natural waters varies widely; transported solids vary from macroscopic to colloidal dimensions. Most experimental work on the adsorptive behavior of trace metals, however, has been conducted in simple electrolyte systems without complexing ligands. These experiments have been extremely useful in determining the important solution parameters controlling adsorption phenomena and in generating fundamental data requisite to the development of phenomenological models describing interactions in the solid/solution interphase (James and Healy, 1972; Hohl and Stumm, 1976; Schindler *et al.*, 1976).

A variety of natural and synthetic organic compounds are present in natural waters. This includes the degradation products of plant and animal tissue (*e.g.*, amino acids, humic acids). The effect of this organic matter and complexing ligands in general on trace metal adsorption is largely unknown. MacNaughton and James (1974) and Vuceta (1976) show that complexing ligands (*e.g.*, chloride, EDTA, citric acid) alter trace metal adsorption by complexing the trace metal. While previous studies concerned effects of nonadsorbing ligands, we have studied the adsorption of several inorganic and organic complexing ligands as part of an investigation of the adsorption of silver and copper on amorphous iron oxide and α-quartz in the presence and absence of complexing ligands. Although the experimental systems are simple in comparison with natural systems, it is now possible to identify and model some of the effects of organics and complexing ligands on trace metal adsorption.

METHODS

Amorphous iron oxide is precipitated from acidified ferric nitrate solution by slow addition of sodium hydroxide. The material is aged for 4 hr at neutral pH before adsorption experiments are begun. Potentiometric titration and salt titration indicate a PZC (point of zero charge) of 7.9 in 0.1 M NaNO$_3$. Surface area measurements by BET nitrogen adsorption on freeze-dried material and negative adsorption of sodium at pH 4.5 are 182 and 300 m^2/g, respectively. The actual surface area in solution is believed to be higher due to porous structure not detected by either surface area measurement technique. Yates (1975) finds a surface area of 260 m^2/g for a similar amorphous iorn oxide by BET adsorption. The iron oxide is X-ray amorphous in agreement with the study of preparation techniques of Avotins (1975).

The preparation of α-quartz for adsorption experiments is described elsewhere (MacNaughton, 1973). A BET surface area of 3.3 m^2/g was determined for the material used in this study. The PZC is approximately 2.5 (MacNaughton and James, 1974).

Adsorption experiments are conducted by adding a known amount of copper, silver and/or ligand to a stirred suspension of either amorphous iron oxide or α-quartz in 0.1 M NaNO$_3$ or NaClO$_4$ under an N$_2$ atmosphere at 25° C. A reaction period of four hours in silver systems and two hours in copper systems is allowed for equilibration. Solid/liquid phase separation is accomplished by centrifugation and the concentration of metal and/or ligands remaining in solution is measured.

Silver analyses are performed by crystal-scintillation counting of Ag-110 m, added with the stock silver as a tracer. Copper is analyzed by flameless atomic absorption spectrometry with an HGA carbon furnace. Ligand analyses are made by liquid scintillation counting or ultraviolet absorbance techniques. Details of all experimental techniques are published elsewhere (Davis, 1977).

RESULTS AND DISCUSSION

Ligand Adsorption on Hydrous Oxides

The adsorption of several inorganic and organic ligands on amorphous iron oxide and α-quartz as a function of pH and total ligand concentration has been studied. The bulk of these data are presented elsewhere (Davis, 1977; Davis and Leckie, 1977a). Figure 1 shows adsorption curves for glutamic acid on amorphous iron oxide as a function of pH. Similar adsorption curves are observed for sulfate and salicylic acid. The data indicate little specific adsorption for these ligands (adsorption approaches zero near the PZC, pH 7.9); coulombic attractive forces appear to dominate the adsorption behavior of these ligands. High surface coverage may be approached at a total ligand concentration of 10^{-3} M. Hydrogen bonding may contribute to the overall bond energy for several ligands (*e.g.*, glutamic acid, picolinic acid, salicylic acid). The hydrogen-bonding contribution and coulombic attraction for acid anions increases as the oxide surface becomes more positively charged (*i.e.*, decrease in pH).

The adsorptive behaviors of thiosulfate, syringic acid, picolinic acid, and 2,3-pyrazinedicarboxylic acid are similar. Coulombic forces control the adsorption and little specific interaction is observed. The magnitude and shape of the adsorption curves vary somewhat among the ligands. In general, the correlation of Hingston *et al.* (1967) between the pK_a of acid anions and inflections in the adsorption curves is observed (Davis and Leckie, 1977a).

Comparisons of the adsorption behavior of various ligands provides indirect evidence for the orientation of adsorbed ligands. For example, adsorption of glutamic acid (Figure 1) probably involves an interaction of the terminal carboxyl group with the surface. This can be inferred from the results of glycine-adsorption experiments, which suggest an extremely low affinity of the zwitterion for the oxide surface, either chemically or coulombically. Thus, the zwitterion functional group of an adsorbed glutamic acid molecule may be available for complexation of trace metals (Davis and Leckie, 1977a). An understanding of the adsorptive behavior and surface bonding mechanisms of complexing ligands is necessary to interpret effects of ligands on trace-metal adsorption in natural aquatic environments.

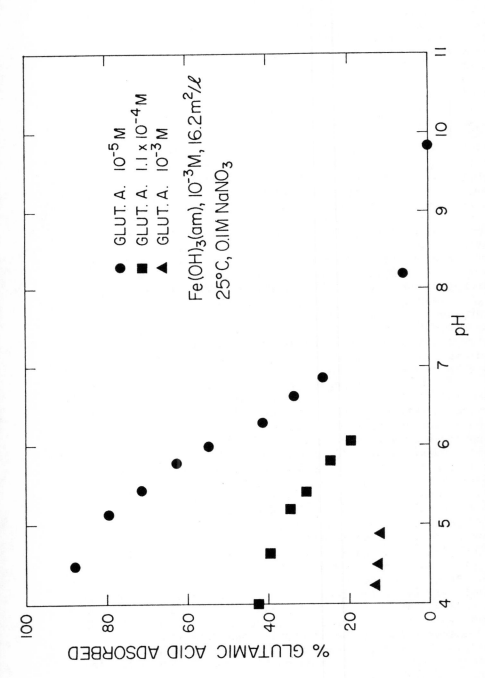

Figure 1.   Adsorption of glutamic acid on amorphous iron oxide
as a function of pH and total glutamic acid concentration.

Effect of Complexing Ligands on Trace Metal Adsorption

Figure 2 shows the adsorption of silver on amorphous iron oxide as a function of pH and various chloride concentrations. Silver chloride precipitation should not occur at these solution conditions. Moderate concentrations of chloride have little effect on the adsorption behavior of silver. At a chloride concentration of 9.4×10^{-2} M, the predominant silver solution species is $AgCl_2^-$. Silver does not adsorb significantly for pH < 9 with this chloride concentration. The hydrolysis products of silver become significant only at pH > 11. Since the increase in adsorption continues until pH 12 in 9.4×10^{-2} M chloride, a hydrolysis product of silver (AgOH) may be involved in the surface reaction in alkaline solutions. It is unlikely that $AgCl^\circ$ is an adsorbing species. Several trace metals are desorbed by high chloride concentrations (MacNaughton and James, 1974).

Cyanide ion at trace concentrations (8×10^{-7} M total) effectively prevents silver adsorption (4×10^{-7} M total) at any pH. The effects of cyanide and chloride can be explained by simple competition between the ligand and the oxide surface for coordination of silver ions. These effects have been described adequately by previous research (MacNaughton, 1973; MacNaughton and James, 1974; Vuceta, 1975). Complexing, nonadsorbing ligands can only decrease trace-metal adsorption. The magnitude of the effect depends on the relative intensities of the metal-ligand and metal-surface bonds. A weakly complexing, nonadsorbing ligand will have a negligible effect on trace-metal adsorption.

Silver forms strong complexes with thiosulfate ($\log \beta_1 = 8.9$; $\log \beta_2 = 13.2$) and other ligands containing sulfur donor groups (Davis and Leckie, 1977b). In solutions containing 4×10^{-7} M total silver concentration and an equal total thiosulfate concentration, approximately 90 percent of each is complexed as $AgS_2O_3^-$. The adsorption of silver as a function of pH and thiosulfate concentration is shown in Figure 3. Adsorption of silver is dramatically increased in the pH region 4-6.5 and decreased for pH > 7 in the presence of thiosulfate. Moreover, an increase in thiosulfate concentration magnifies the observed effects. Nearly quantitative removal of silver occurs at pH 4 for a total thiosulfate concentration of 4×10^{-6} M. The adsorption of silver for 4 < pH < 6.5 closely parallels the adsorption of thiosulfate. Clearly the increased adsorption of silver is related to the adsorption of thiosulfate.

The results of adsorption experiments containing equimolar total silver and thiosulfate (4×10^{-7} M) are displayed in Figure 4. Adsorption of silver and thiosulfate were determined simultaneously and the amount of silver adsorbed equals thiosulfate adsorption in the pH region 4.5-6.5.

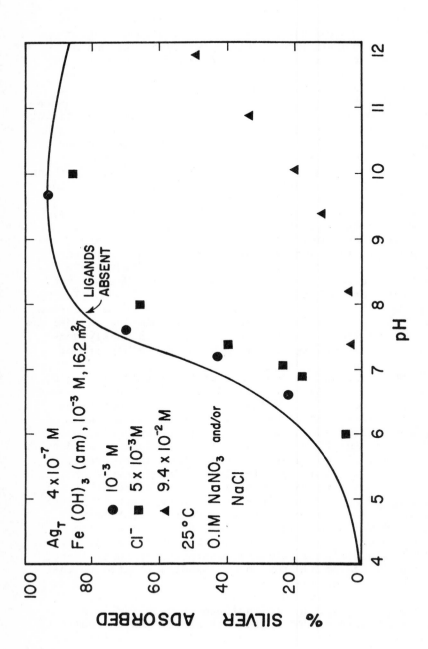

Figure 2.   Silver adsorption on amorphous iron oxide as a
function of pH and chloride concentrations.

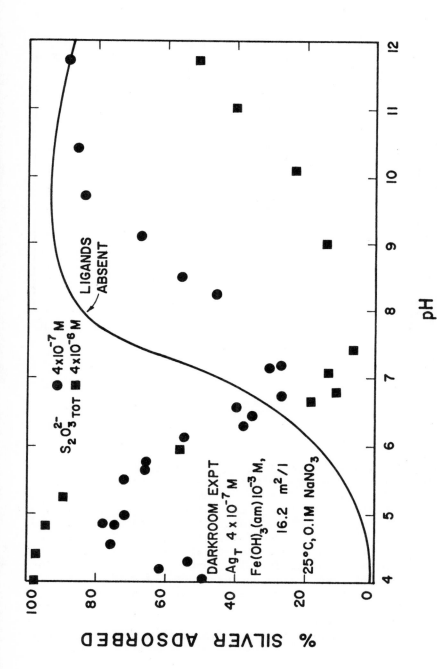

Figure 3. Effect of trace concentrations of thiosulfate on silver adsorption on amorphous iron oxide.

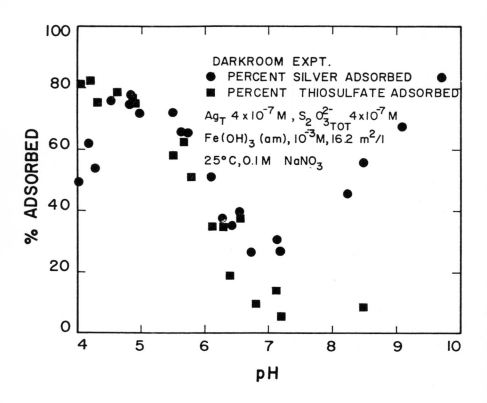

Figure 4. Adsorption of silver and thiosulfate on amorphous
  iron oxide as a function of pH. Total silver and thiosulfate concentrations are 4 x 10⁻⁷ *M*.

Thiosulfate adsorption is slightly greater than in the absence
of silver. Since the predominant solution species for silver
and thiosulfate is $AgS_2O_3^-$, the best explanation for the
observed behavior is the adsorption of the silver-thiosulfate
complex. The strength of the interaction is roughly equal to
the coulombic term for thiosulfate. Adsorption of the silver-
thiosulfate complex occurs by the attraction of the negatively
charged complex to the positively charged surface. As pH increases, the positive charge decreases on the surface and
adsorption of silver thiosulfate decreases to zero near pH 7.5.
At pH 6.5 silver adsorption begins to increase again (Figure 4).
However, thiosulfate adsorption continues to decrease. The increase in silver adsorption at pH 6.5 is thus due to the surface
reaction that occurs in the absence of thiosulfate. At pH 7.5
thiosulfate adsorption is near zero. For pH > 7.5 thiosulfate
functions as a simple complexing agent in solution. Thiosulfate
and the iron oxide surface compete for the coordination of silver.

The proposed reaction scheme is consistent with the results at higher thiosulfate concentration. Since the surface concentration of thiosulfate is now increased, more silver-thiosulfate complex can be adsorbed. Thus, silver adsorption is greater at low pH. At higher pH where thiosulfate is not adsorbed the decrease in silver adsorption is much greater. The case of thiosulfate provides strong evidence that transition metal complexes can adsorb or that transition metals *can be* complexed by adsorbed ligands. The effect of thiosulfate on silver adsorption is of particular interest to natural systems since silver is usually released as a thiosulfate complex from photographic wastes and thiosulfate is a known reaction product of iron monosulfides in low chloride waters (Nelson, 1977).

Figure 5 shows the adsorption of silver on α-quartz in the presence of ethylenediamine. Ethylenediamine adsorption results are not yet available and the hypotheses for this system are tentative. Silver adsorption on α-quartz is apparently increased in the pH region 8-10 by the presence of ethylenediamine. Ethylenediamine is positively charged over most of the pH range of interest according to the following reactions:

$$\underset{NH_3^+-CH_2-CH_2-NH_3^+}{\overset{pH = 7.2}{\longleftrightarrow}} \underset{NH_3^+-CH_2-CH_2-NH_2}{\overset{pH = 10.0}{\longleftrightarrow}} NH_2-CH_2-CH_2-NH_2$$

Silver forms complexes of moderate strength with an uncharged amino group.

α-Quartz is negatively charged only slightly between pH 4 and 6, but the increase in surface charge with pH is rapid above pH 7. Thus, the positively charged ethylenediamine species should be weakly adsorbed by coulombic attraction at pH > 7. For pH > 7.2 the predominant ethylenediamine species has only one positively charged amino group. The uncharged amino group is available for silver complexation. Thus, silver adsorption is probably increased in the pH region 8-10 by adsorption of the ethylenediamine complex. As the pH increases, the ethylenediamine speciation changes again to the uncharged ligand. Complexation of silver in solution then becomes more important and silver adsorption decreases.

The effect of salicylic acid, protocatechuic acid (PCCA), and sulfate on copper adsorption on amorphous iron oxide is illustrated in Figure 6. None of the ligands has a significant effect despite the fact that the two form moderate to strong complexes with copper. However, only a portion of the complexing ligands remains in solution since the copper adsorption edge overlaps the pH region where the ligands are coulombically adsorbed. Protocatechuic acid (PCCA) is significantly adsorbed over the entire pH range and the surface bonding must involve a strong specific chemical interaction (Davis and Leckie, 1977a).

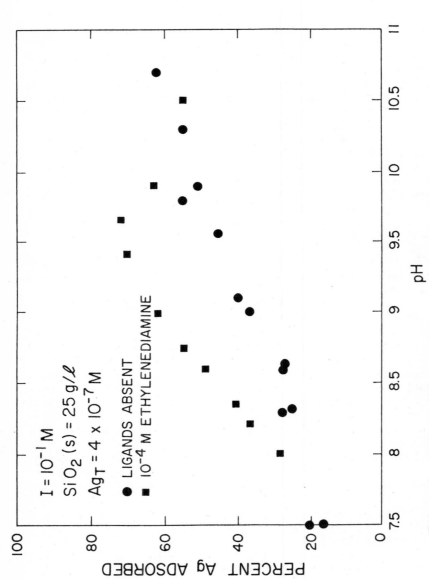

Figure 5. Silver adsorption on α-quartz as a function of pH in the presence and absence of 10^{-4} M ethylenediamine.

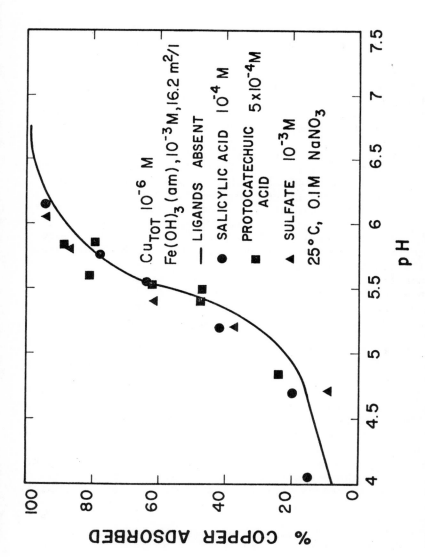

Figure 6. Copper adsorption on amorphous iron oxide in 0.1 *M* NaNO$_3$. Data are shown for systems containing no complexing ligands, salicylic acid, protocatechuic acid and sulfate.

Apparently the sorptive behavior of these complexing ligands has little effect on copper adsorption. In the case of calicylic acid and protocatechuic acid this is expected since the coordinating functional groups used in complexation of metals are the same groups likely to be involved in adsorption reactions. This also suggests that the complexes do not form and adsorb with copper adjacent to the surface. To test this hypothesis experiments were conducted with PCCA where (1) copper was added to the iron oxide suspension and equilibrated before PCCA addition, and (2) copper and PCCA were added to the iron oxide suspension simultaneously. These results were compared with the normal procedure of PCCA addition and equilibrium before copper addition. There are no detectable differences in copper or PCCA adsorption among the three methods.

Figure 7 presents the results for copper adsorption experiments containing glutamic acid, 2,3-pyrazinedicarboxylic acid (2,3-PDCA), or picolinic acid. Copper adsorption is significantly enhanced by the presence of 10^{-4} M glutamic acid. Copper forms complexes of moderate strength with the zwitterion functional group. This functional group is still available for complexation of copper if the glutamic adsorption occurs via the terminal carboxyl group as has been proposed (Davis and Leckie, 1977a). Thus, copper may adsorb by interaction with an oxide surface site or by complexing with an adsorbed glutamic acid molecule. An alternate reaction scheme is plausible: copper-glutamate complexes form in solution and then adsorb. The two hypotheses are thermodynamically indistinguishable.

The effects of picolinic acid and 2,3-PDCA on copper adsorption make an interesting comparison. Both ligands are strong complexers of copper ions and have similar adsorption behavior on amorphous iron oxide (Davis and Leckie, 1977a). Apparently, adsorbed picolinic acid molecules cannot complex copper ions. This is consistent with a surface-bonding scheme that involves electrons from the carboxyl and nitrogen heteroatom. As a result, copper adsorption is dramatically decreased by complexation with excess picolinate in solution.

However, the presence of 2,3-PDCA at a similar total concentration increases copper adsorption. The stereochemistry of the adsorbed 2,3-PDCA is not known absolutely but there is some evidence that the carboxylic groups face the surface (Davis and Leckie, 1977a). The nitrogen heteroatoms must increase the stability of copper-surface bonds at adsorption sites adjacent to the adsorbed ligand.

The varied behavior of the several organic solutes examined in this study indicates that we cannot easily predict the direction and extent of the effect natural organics will have on the adsorptive behavior of trace metals. The organics selected for this study represent plausible organic molecules

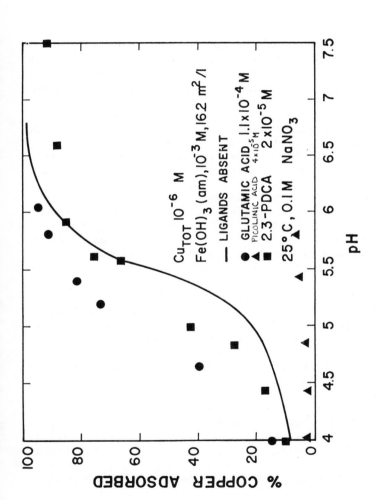

Figure 7. Copper adsorption on amorphous iron oxide in the presence and absence of glutamic acid, picolinic acid, and 2,3-pyrazinedicarboxylic acid (2,3-PDCA).

and moieties to be expected in both aerobic and anaerobic sedimentary environments. Thus, we must gain more insight into the range of types and relative abundance of organic and inorganic chelating agents and ligands in natural systems before we can predict effects on the adsorptive behavior of trace metals.

CONCLUSIONS

Results of these experiments indicate that complexing ligands can be a major factor in determining trace metal adsorption behavior on hydrous oxides in natural systems. The presence of strongly complexing, nonadsorbing ligands at appropriate concentrations can dramatically reduce adsorption by complexing the metal ion in solution. On the other hand, trace metal adsorption can be enhanced when a ligand is adsorbed with a strongly complexing functional group directed outward toward solution. Thus, the adsorptive behavior of ligands and ligand-metal complexes is an important considera- tion in the transport of trace metals via the solid/solution interface.

The role of naturally occurring organic material in promoting or inhibiting trace metal adsorption by suspended and bed sediments in natural waters is largely unknown (Nissenbaum and Swaine, 1976). There have been many observa- tions of association of natural organic material with the sediment phase in natural waters (Neihof and Loeb, 1972; Prashnowsky *et al.*, 1971). Hydrous oxide and silicate particles are likely to be coated with an adsorbed film of organic material Adsorption "sites" for trace metals will be dominated by the functional groups (carboxylic, phenolic, amino, sulfhydryl) of adsorbed organic molecules. Hydrophobic and high-molecular-weight organic compounds will concentrate at interfaces. Thus, the microenvironment of the solid/solu- tion interface will differ substantially in natural systems from that observed in simple electrolyte systems.

Humic and fulvic acids constitute a significant frac- tion of the organic matter in natural waters. Although these materials have not been fully characterized and vary in composition from one environment to another, it is known that they have numerous carboxylic, phenolic and nitrogen functional groups. Laboratory experiments have shown that these materials are strong trace metal complexing agents (Schnitzer and Skinner, 1966). Little is known about the adsorptive behavior of humic substances, but the large size and low solubility of some of these compounds suggest an affinity for the solid/solution interface. Adsorbing humic and fulvic acids would simultaneously transport associated trace elements to the solid/solution interface in natural systems. Additional trace elements subsequently might be complexed by the adsorbed organic material.

Natural organic material is undoubtedly an important contributing factor to the observed association of trace metals with suspended sediment materials. Existing phenomenological models, however, do not account satisfactorily for the effects of adsorbing, complexing natural organic material. Although Davis and Leckie (1977a, 1977c) present an adsorption model that accounts for the effects of complexing ligands in these experiments, more information about the adsorptive behavior of natural organics is needed to predict the distribution of trace elements in their presence. It is necessary to understand the adsorptive behavior of all solution species if an accurate prediction is to be made of the importance of natural solid/solution interfaces in controlling the distribuiton of trace elements in natural waters.

REFERENCES

Avotins, P. V. "Adsorption and Coprecipitation Studies of Mercury on Hydrous Iron Oxides," Ph.D. Thesis, Stanford University (1975).

Davis, J. A. "Adsorption of Trace Metals and Complexing Ligands by Hydrous Oxides," Ph.D. Thesis, Stanford University (1975).

Davis, J. A. and J. O. Leckie. "Adsorption from Aqueous Solution by Hydrous Oxides. III. Adsorption of Anions and Complexing Ligands," in preparation (1977a).

Davis, J. A. and J. O. Leckie. "Aqueous Environmental Chemistry of Silver," in preparation (1977b).

Davis, J. A. and J. O. Leckie. "Adsorption from Aqueous Solution by Hydroux Oxides. I. The Electrical Double Layer and a Site-Binding Adsorption Model," in preparation (1977c).

Hingston, F. J., R. J. Atkinson, *et al.* "Specific Adsorption of Anions," *Nature* 215:1459 (1967).

Hohl, H. and W. Stumm. "Interaction of Pb^{+2} with Hydrous $\gamma-Al_2O_3$," *J. Coll. Int. Sci.* 55:281 (1976).

James, R. O. and T. W. Healy. "Adsorption of Hydrolyzable Metal Ions at the Oxide/Water Interface. III. A Thermodynamic Model of Adsorption," *J. Coll. Int. Sci.* 40:65 (1972).

Leckie, J. O. and R. O. James. "Control Mechanisms for
Trace Metals in Natural Waters," in *Aqueous-Environmental
Chemistry of Metals*, A. J. Rubin, Ed. (Ann Arbor,
Michigan: Ann Arbor Science Publishers, 1975), Chapter 1.

MacNaughton, M. G. "Adsorption of Mercury at the Solid/Water
Interface," Ph.D. Thesis, Stanford University (1973).

MacNaughton, M. G. and R. O. James. "Adsorption of Aqueous
Hg(II) Complexes at Oxide/Water Interface," *J. Coll. Int.
Sci.* 47:431 1974).

Neihof, R. A. and G. I. Loeb. "The Surface Charge of
Particulate Matter in Sea Water," *Limnol. Oceanog.*
17:7 (1972).

Nelson, M. B. "Oxidative Dissolution of Ferrous Monosulfides,"
Ph.D. Thesis, Stanford University (1977).

Nissenbaum, A. and D. J. Swaine. "Organic Matter–Metal
Interactions in Recent Sediments: The Role of Humic
Substances," *Geochim. Cosmochim. Acta* 40:810 (1976).

Prashnowsky, A. A., G. Ebhardt and M. Hobler. "Organic
Compounds in the Water and Suspended Matter of the Main
River (Southern Germany) and in Some Ground Waters,"
Advances in Organic Geochemistry, Gaertner and Wehner, Eds.
(New York: Pergamon Press, 1971), p. 403.

CHAPTER 83

INDUSTRIAL AND NATURAL INPUTS, LEVELS, BEHAVIOR, AND DYNAMICS OF BIOLOGICALLY TOXIC HEAVY METALS IN THE SAGUENAY FJORD, GULF OF ST. LAWRENCE, CANADA

D. H. LORING

Department of Fisheries and the Environment
Fisheries and Marine Service
Marine Ecology Laboratory
Bedford Institute of Oceanography
Dartmouth, Nova Scotia, B2Y 4A2 Canada

INTRODUCTION

Biologically toxic heavy metals in the environment have received considerable attention in Canada, as elsewhere. Initially, high levels of mercury were found in fish in the Great Lakes and, more recently, in the Saguenay river and fjord, which joins the estuary of the St. Lawrence River and the Gulf of St. Lawrence. As a result, most commercial fishing was banned. Some of the mercury is natural, but most is believed to come from industrial sources (Blight, 1970; Fimreite, 1970). As in other countries, the chlor-alkali industry was identified as the major source of industrial mercury in the environment and government regulations were put into effect in 1971 to limit industrial discharge of mercury to the environment.

Investigations have now been made on the levels, behavior and dynamics of Hg and other toxic metals - Zn, Cu, Pb, Co, Ni, Cr and V - in the surface and subsurface sediments, particulate matter (Hg) and water (Hg) in the Saguenay system (Loring, 1975; 1976a,b; Loring and Bewers, 1976). This chapter summarizes these investigations and with new information presents a geochemical mass balance for mercury.

The Saguenay fjord joins the St. Lawrence estuary about 182 km below Quebec city. It is about 93 km long and 1-6 km wide (Figure 1). The submarine morphology is characterized by elongated, deep (200-274 m) basins and by shallow

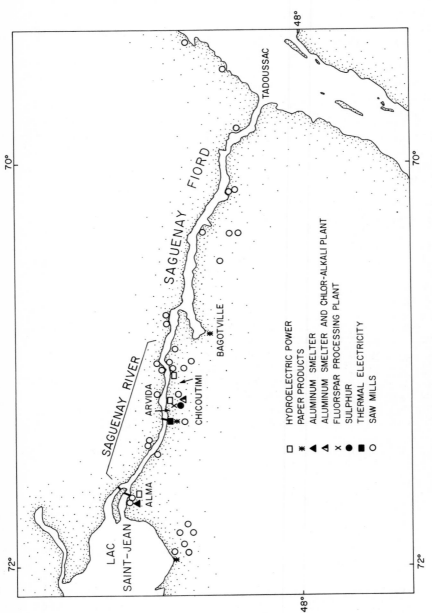

Figure 1.   Industries on the Saguenay Fjord and River.

(20-100 m) sills along its entire length. Surface circulation is marine estuarine in character with the deep water inside the fjord being subject to intrusions of saline water from the St. Lawrence estuary. The waters are well mixed and oxygenated. Salinities in the surface waters (depths less than 3 m) increase seaward from 0.5 ‰ to 28 ‰ whereas the deeper waters have salinities up to 30 ‰. The highest SPM concentrations (20 mgl^{-1}) occur in the waters and decrease seaward with depth to near bottom (less than 20 m) where they sometimes increase.

Black anoxic sandy (5-10 percent) muds occur in the upper arms of the fjord (Figure 2). These grade seaward into dark greenish grey muds that occupy the deep inner basin. Downstream the sediments become coarser grained with the very sandy (> 30 percent) muds occurring in the basins and muddy (5-30 percent) sands covering the broad sills between them. Sand and gravel cover the basin at the mouth of the fjord adjacent to the St. Lawrence estuary.

Most of the freshwater runoff (∿ 90 percent) enters the north arm of the fjord from the Saguenay River, and smaller amounts are supplied from the sides by numerous small rivers. The Saguenay River is about 63 km long and drains Lac St. Jean. It has a drainage area of about 78,000 km^2 and a flow rate of 1100-2200 m^{3}s^{-1}, which is regulated by a series of hydroelectric dams.

Two aluminum smelters, an aluminum plant, a fluorspar processing plant, and pulp and paper mills are situated along the Saguenay River (Figure 1). The largest of these is the aluminum refining complex located at Arvida, about 24 km above the head of the fjord. This plant processes approximately 7100 tonnes per day of bauxite for the production of aluminum by the Bayer process. It has been in operation for about 25 years. A chlor-alkali plant attached to the aluminum plant provides caustic soda for this process as well as 3540 tonnes of chlorine (Cl$_2$) per month. The pulp and paper mills along the Saguenay River as well as the sawmills situated along the adjacent fjord are responsible for the large quantities of wood fibers found in the sediments (Marlowe, 1970; Loring and Nota, 1973). In addition, municipal wastes are derived from the city of Chicoutimi about 10 km above the head of the fjord.

SAMPLING AND ANALYTICAL METHODS

Sediment samples were obtained by a Van Veen grab at 32 locations in the fjord. Nine sediment cores up to 0.9 m long were obtained by gravity corer (50 mm diameter) and piston corer (44 mm diameter) at 3 to 12 km apart along the length of the fjord. The samples were frozen and returned

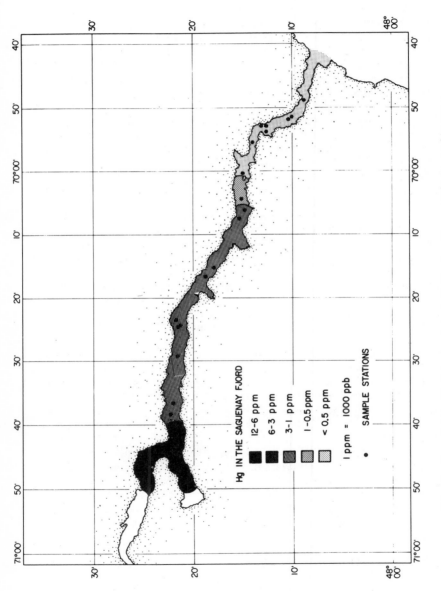

Figure 2.   Distribution of total Hg in the surface sediments.

to the laboratory, where the cores were sampled at 1-cm intervals. Mercury was determined in duplicate in each sample using a cold vapor atomic absorption technique similar to that described by Hatch and Ott (1968) and reported by Loring (1975). Grain size distributions were determined by conventional sieve analyses.

The major inorganic constituents and Zn, Cu, Pb, Co, Ni, Cr and V were determined by the atomic absorption techniques described by Rantala and Loring (1975). Acetic acid (25% v/v) was used for the chemical partition of the total elemental concentrations into their nondetrital (acid-soluble) and detrital fractions. Readily oxidizable organic matter was determined for all samples using the wet oxidation method described by Walkley (1947). Lignin contents and C/N ratios of selected samples were determined and reported by Pocklington (1975). Suspended particulate matter was collected at various depths and locations in the fjord on nuclepore filters. These were analyzed for Hg using the method of Hatch and Ott (1968). Correlation matrices and r-mode factor analyses were used to clarify the relationships between the abundance and distribution of the heavy metals, and the textural and chemical characteristics of the sediments. Pertinent data from government and industrial sources has also been used to construct the Hg budget for the system.

RESULTS AND DISCUSSION

Abundance, Distribution and Partition of the Heavy Metals

Total dry weight mercury concentrations in bottom samples taken along the length of the fjord vary from 0.16 mg kg^{-1} to 12 mg kg^{-1} (average 2.98 mg kg^{-1}) with the highest concentrations occurring in the fine-grained sediments at the head of the fjord. The concentrations are very much higher than those reported from the mercury-contaminated sediments of Lake Ontario (Thomas, 1972) and from other parts of the St. Lawrence estuary and open Gulf of St. Lawrence (Loring, 1975), where background levels are about 0.25 mg kg^{-1}. The concentrations of the other heavy metals are: Zn 43-145 mg kg^{-1}; Pb 14-66 mg kg^{-1}; Cu 16-33 mg kg^{-1}; Co 5-20 mg kg^{-1}; Ni 7-36 mg kg^{-1}; Cr 38-93 mg kg^{-1}; V 67-147 mg kg^{-1}.

The highest concentrations occur in the fine-grained sediments. The concentrations of Zn and Pb in these sediments are much higher than those found in the estuary and open Gulf, whereas those of the other elements are at or near the natural levels found elsewhere.

The surface distribution patterns show that Hg concentrations decrease seaward from the mouth of the Saguenay River (Figure 2). This pattern suggests that there has been a major input of Hg from a local source above the head of the fjord. Total concentrations of Zn, Cu, Pb, Co, Ni, Cr and V also decrease seaward from the head of the fjord.

Chemical partition of the total element concentrations into soluble and insoluble phases were made to determine the components with which the heavy metals are associated within the sediments. The results indicate that 70-90 percent of the total Hg is associated with the organic fraction. This is confirmed by the significant relationship (R = 0.98, P < 0.001) between the Hg concentrations and organic content of the fjord sediments (Figure 3).

Total Hg concentrations also increase with increasing C/N ratios, with the highest concentrations occurring in the sediments at the head of the fjord. This indicates that the amount of Hg in the sediment depends not only on the quantity but also the type of organic material. This is confirmed by the work of Pocklington and MacGregor (1973) who show that the sediments of high C/N ratio contain high concentrations of terrestrial organic material (lignin). Total Hg also varies directly (r = 0.95, P < 0.001) with the amount of lignin in the sediments. From this relationship it is deduced that Hg-rich organic matter comes from terrestrial sources and is most likely represented by the wood fibers observed in the sediments. The wood fibers are apparently derived from the discharges of wood wastes from the many pulp and paper mills situated in the Saguenay drainage area.

Chemical partition of the other metals shows that 9 to 29 percent of the total elemental concentrations are nondetrital and may easily be available to the biota of the fjord. Correlation matrices and r-mode factor analyses of 35 variables for each sediment (depth, sand, mud, major and trace elements) sample indicate the elemental sites and factors that control the abundance and distribution of these elements. They show that nondetrital Zn, Pb and Cu are weakly attached to the organic matter, and their (Zn and Pb) abundance and distribution are controlled by the seaward dispersal pattern of the Hg-rich terrestrial organic matter. Nondetrital Co, Ni, Cr and V, however, are mainly present in ion exchange positions of the ferromagnesium minerals and Fe-Mg oxide grain coatings. Analyses of the detrital fraction that makes up to 71 to 92 percent of the total elemental concentrations indicate that sulfide minerals are the main hosts for Zn, Pb and Cu and minor hosts of Co and Ni, and that the ferromagnesium and oxide minerals (magnetite, chromite) are the most likely host minerals for detrital Co, Ni, Cr and V in the sediments.

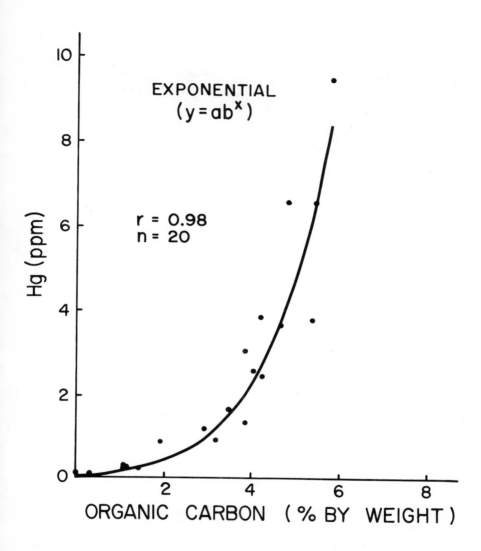

Figure 3. Relationship between total Hg and organic carbon
matter in the surface sediments.

Subsurface Sediments

The extent of the subsurface Hg contamination is
revealed by detailed analyses (1-cm intervals) of a series
of cores taken along the length of the fjord (Figure 4).
These data show that a Hg-rich layer (0.25 mg kg^{-1} to 10 mg
kg^{-1}) is present, decreasing in thickness seaward, from
> 50 cm to < 6 cm over a distance of 65 km or ∿80 km below

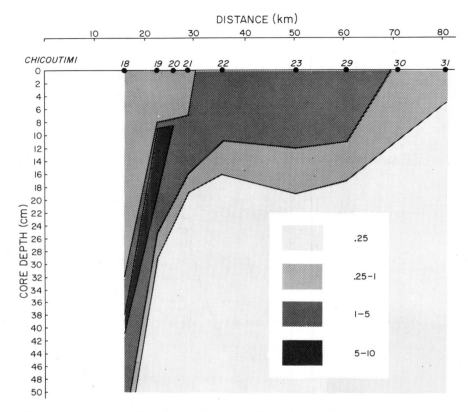

Figure 4.   Distribution of Hg in the subsurface sediments
(units mg kg^{-1}).

Chicoutimi. This layer has distinct variations in Hg concentrations, which indicate that a gradual accumulation of
Hg above a natural level of 0.25 mg kg^{-1} to about 10 mg kg^{-1}
occurred for a sufficient time to deposit the Hg and disperse
the Hg-rich material seaward. This was followed by a decline
in the Hg flux to the sediments. The levels and behavior of
the other metals in the subsurface sediments are comparable
to those noted for the surface sediments.

In the cores, Hg concentrations covary directly ($r =$
$0.70 - 0.95$ P < 0.001) with organic matter, with the decline
in Hg concentrations near the surface being accompanied by a
corresponding decline in organic matter contents. This con-
firms that the flux of Hg as well as nondetrital Zn and Pb
is controlled by the flux of organic matter to the sediments;
it implies that organic matter scavenges Hg from the water
and transfers it to the sediment. Reimer *et al.* (1973) and
Ui (1973) indicate that a decrease in organic material in the
water from industrial wastes results in a higher concentration
of Hg being available for biological accumulation even with
low Hg inputs. This occurs because insufficient organic

matter is available to scavenge all the Hg from the water and transfer it to the sediments.

River Sediments

Analyses of river sediments by Beak (1970) in the vicinity of the chlor-alkali plant at Arvida on the Saguenay River (Figure 1) indicate that this is the main point source of Hg in the system. The results show Hg concentrations in the sediments adjacent to the outfall vary from 20 to 218 mg kg^{-1} (dry weight) Hg to a depth of at least 60 cm. This Hg-rich zone is concentrated along the south of the river at least 1000 m downstream from the outfall. Sediment samples from above the outfall contain < 0.1 mg kg^{-1} Hg.

Suspended Particulate Matter (SPM)

SPM samples obtained at various locations and depths in the fjord were found to contain 1 to 50 mg kg^{-1} (Hg).

Water Samples

Sixteen water samples were collected throughout the water column and analyzed by Dr. Gubeli (University of Laval, Quebec City, P.Q.) in 1973. These were found to contain 0.07 to 0.38 µg l^{-1} (mean 0.16 µg l^{-1}) Hg, with the highest values occurring near the head of the fjord.

Industrial Hg in the Sediments

The amount of industrial Hg in sediments can be estimated from the core data and assumptions of the continuity of Hg concentrations between cores and sediment density. The results of these calculations are summarized in Table I, which also includes an estimate of the industrial Hg that has escaped the fjord and been deposited in the adjacent St. Lawrence estuary, where Hg concentrations vary from 0.25 mg kg^{-1} to 1 mg kg^{-1}. Table I indicates that a total of 117.2 tonnes of industrial Hg resides in the sediments of the Saguenay system.

Industrial Hg Discharges to the System (Pre-1971)

Prior to 1971, 62 percent of the Hg consumed by chlor-alkali plants in Canada was discharged in water effluents, with an average overall loss of 0.22 kg Hg per tonne of Cl$_2$ produced. From this information the Cl$_2$ production (25 years) of the suspected plant, the levels of Hg associated with various by-products, and the approximate plant budget shown in Table I have been estimated. The significant feature is that, in the 25 years before 1971, a minimum of 145 tonnes

Table I

Mercury in the Saguenay

Mercury in the System

Hg in SPM in Fjord
1.1 tonnes
(Natural 0.01 tonnes)

Mercury Dissolved in Fjord Water
8.5 tonnes
(Natural < 3.9 tonnes)

Mercury in River and Fjord Sediments
113.5 tonnes
(Natural 8.3 tonnes)

Pre-1971 Mass Balance

% of Industrial Losses Found in Sediments

Water Effluent	Total
80%	50%

Estimated Loss of Industrial Hg to System over 25 years (tonnes)

Water Effluent	Other	Total
144.5	89.5	234

Industrial Hg in Sediments (tonnes)

River	Fjord Estuary	Total
105.2	12	117.2

Post-1971 Mass Balance

Balance of Hg Flux Unaccounted for
4831 kg/yr

Known Industrial Inputs
1369 kg/yr

Natural Inputs
1417 kg/yr

1973 Flux
7617 kg/yr

Possible Sources of Unaccounted Hg Flux

Additional Chlor-alkali Plant Losses
Based on Actual Plant Inventory
6949 kg/yr

Sediment Transport
?

Methylation
560 kg/yr

of Hg may have been discharged in liquid effluent to the waters of the Saguenay system. This estimate is, therefore, comparable to the 117 tonnes of Hg found in the sediments, as it accounts for 81 percent of the effluent discharges and 50 percent of the estimated total losses of 234 tonnes Hg (9.4 tonnes Hg yr^{-1}). It is possible that other industries in the drainage basin have contributed significant amounts of Hg but have remained undetected because of the dominant role, apparently, played by the chlor-alkali plant.

1973 Mercury Flux

Analyses of Hg in the water, SPM, and certain species of fish indicate that Hg concentrations were still very high in 1973, despite the imposition of and apparent compliance with Hg discharge regulations in 1971. These data made it necessary to make an immediate assessment of the Hg flux and the known and potential sources of Hg in the system. To calculate the flux, it was assumed that Hg is conservative in the water. For this reason, the Hg contained in the SPM was not included in the calculations, but assumed to be destined for sedimentation. It is also necessary to assume that waters of the fjord can be described as a simple box model in a quasi-state condition over a period of one to two years, in order to calculate the residence time of water in the fjord.

Table I shows the results of these calculations, which indicate that about 8.5 tonnes Hg arepresent in the water and 1.1 tonnes Hg is held in the SPM. The minimum flux is then calculated to be 7-6 tonnes Hg yr^{-1}.

Post 1971 - Mass Balance

To account for the Hg flux it is necessary to examine the known sources of Hg in the system (Table I). Examination of natural inputs from the Saguenay River, assuming a Hg concentration of 0.02 µg kg^{-1} in the water and 0.25 mg kg^{-1} in the SPM (conc 2.3 mg l^{-1}), shows that the river can be expected to deliver 1417 kg yr^{-1} Hg in the dissolved phase and 27 kg yr^{-1} in the SPM. This amounts to 19 percent of the calculated flux. Consideration of reported Hg concentrations in various products, allowable industrial discharges, chlorine production, and Hg consumed by local pulp and paper mill account for another 1369 kg Hg yr^{-1} to the system.

It is clear that natural and known industrial inputs cannot account for the Hg flux to the system, and other mechanisms or sources are required to explain a deficit of 4.8 tonnes Hg yr^{-1}. The following have been considered: (1) residual Hg in the water, (2) a release of methyl Hg, (3) transfer of contaminated sediments from the river, and (4) other potential industrial losses. Each will be discussed in turn.

(1)   Although it may be fortuitous, the deficit of 5.8 tonnes Hg yr^{-1} is almost identical to the estimated (4.7 tonnes Hg yr^{-1}) rate of Hg sedimentation in the 25 years. For this reason the possibility that dissolved mercury concentrations are biased by residuals of the pre-1971 conditions must be examined to estimate the degree to which conditions prior to 1971 are reflected in the conditions of 1973 when the measurements were made.   Previous calculations indicate that the industrial flux through the system is unlikely to be more than 250 tonnes in the 25 years prior to 1971 and was dominated by the Saguenay discharges.   On this basis the 1973 conditions would be biased in favor of the 1971 amounts in the water column by a maximum of 471 kg Hg.   This obviously is not enough to account for the deficit.

(2)   Since most of the Hg in the water column was found to be organic, it is possible that the Hg was released by methylation from the sediments.   Calculations indicate that the methylation rate would have to be approximately 17.9 kg Hg km^{-1} yr^{-1} to account for the deficit.   This is unlikely because such a rate would exceed the experimental rate of 0.7 kg Hg km^{-1} yr^{-1} found for the river's sediments by Beak (1970) and rates quoted by Krendel (1973).   Although Hg is methylated and released from the sediments, it is unlikely to exceed 2 kg km^{-1} yr^{-1} or 11 percent of the outstanding deficit.   Thus, methylation cannot account for the deficit.

(3)   The entrainment and transport of contaminated river sediments to the fjord to account for the excess Hg flux can also be estimated.   To account for an imput of 4-3 tonnes Hg yr^{-1} from this source (deficit less amount supplied by methylation), the Hg concentration of river derived SPM would have to be about 22 mg kg^{-1} Hg.   It would require an input of 2×10^5 tonnes yr^{-1} of SPM (mean concentration of 4 mg l^{-1}) in the water above the natural level of 2.3 mg l^{-1}. Although this mechanism cannot be entirely ruled out, it implies that the SPM would remain in suspension for a long time in the fjord and transfer all its Hg to the water.   This is unlikely because of the residence time of the particles in the fjord and the strong adherence of Hg to the SPM.   It is also not supported by the distribution pattern of Hg in the SPM in the fjord.

(4)   Finally, other potential but unrecorded industrial sources are examined.   Figure 5 shows average breakdown of Hg losses from Canadian chlor-alkali plants after the imposition of discharge regulations in 1971.   The most significant feature here is that 52 percent of total losses are untraceable and cannot be accounted for by the industry.   If the Hg loss budget for the Arvida plant were similar to that shown in Figure 5, an overall loss rate of 4673 kg Hg yr^{-1} could be expected, of which the expected losses of 3970 kg Hg yr^{-1}

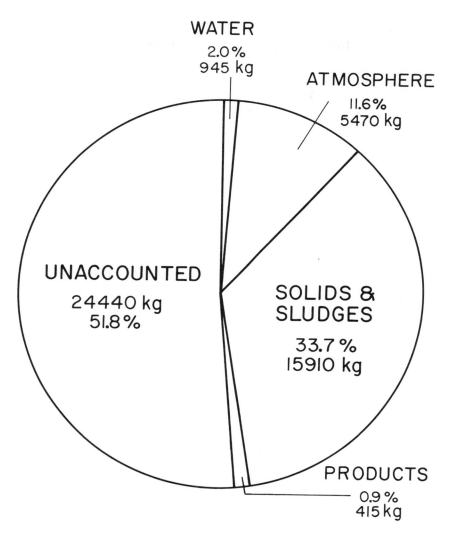

WATER
2.0%
945 kg

ATMOSPHERE
11.6%
5470 kg

UNACCOUNTED
24440 kg
51.8%

SOLIDS &
SLUDGES
33.7%
15910 kg

PRODUCTS
0.9%
415 kg

TOTAL Hg CONSUMED 47,180 kg
CHLORINE PRODUCED 431,800 tonnes
LOSS RATE = 0.11 kg Hg / tonne Cl_2

Figure 5.   Breakdown of Hg losses from chlor-alkali plants
in Canada after the imposition of effluent discharge controls.

from solid sludges and particularly the untraceable losses
represent 82 percent of the outstanding flux.

In view of the high loss of mercury from Canadian
chlor-alkali plants by routes that cannot be defined by
industry, it is instructive to examine the actual mercury
inventory of the chlor-alkali plant in Arvida for the post-
1971 period. Over a three-year period (1971-75) it is found
that the losses from this operation were not only higher by
a factor of two than the average Canadian chlor-alkali plant
but also a higher percentage (64 percent of the total losses)
could not be traced. This reveals that their unaccountable
and untraceable losses (6949 kg yr^{-1}) far exceed the amount
required to balance the mercury budget for the fjord. It is
suspected, therefore, that the chlor-alkali plant was the
primary source of the mercury passing through the fjord in
1973. The losses are hopefully being reduced as further
improvements in industrial housekeeping are made.

Small but significant quantities of biologically
available Pb and Zn also accompany the industrial discharges.
This may lead to an excessive accumulation in the sediments
and biota, as they have done for Hg. There is no evidence
to indicate, however, that these discharges have resulted
in an increase in the concentrations of Cu, Co, Ni, Cr and
V in the sediments above their natural levels or represent
a danger to the biota.

Calculations based on a natural level of 0.075 µg 1^{-1}
Hg in the fjord waters indicate that if industrial inputs
were curtailed, the mercury would return to natural levels in
about three or four years, and the recovery of the commercial
pelagic fishery might occur in two years. It should, however,
be noted that the high levels of mercury in the biota might
be maintained for some time despite the reductions in industrial inputs. The reason for this is the apparent decrease
in the supply of terrestrial organic matter, which acts as
the main scavenger of mercury in the system. The sediments,
on the other hand, are only expected to become decontaminated
by methylation and burial by recently deposited material, a
process that could take hundreds of years.

If, however, industrial discharges are maintained at
their 1973 level, not only will contamination of the fjord
continue, but there exists the danger that the productive
commercial fishery in the adjacent St. Lawrence estuary will
be affected. This seems, unfortunately, to be the present
case despite some evidence in 1975 that Hg levels in the
water were declining. A recent paper by Bourget and Cossa
(1976) indicates that mussels along the adjacent St. Lawrence
estuary have a decreasing gradient in mercury levels from
the mouth of the Saguenay fjord seaward that appear to be
directly related to Hg discharges from the Saguenay.

REFERENCES

Beak, T. W. Consultants Ltd. (Toronto). *Environmental Mercury Survey*, Unpublished report, (1970).

Blight, G. "Mercury and the Contamination of Freshwater Fish," *Fish. Res. Board Can. MS Rep.* 1088:1-27 (1970).

Bourget, F. and D. Cossa. "Mercury Content of Mussels from the St. Lawrence Estuary and Northwestern Gulf of St. Lawrence," *Mar. Poll. Bull.* 7:237-239 (1976).

Fimreite, N. "Mercury Uses in Canada and Their Possible Hazards as Sources of Mercury Contamination," *Environ. Pollut.* 1:119-131 (1970).

Hatch, W. R. and W. L. Ott. "Determination of Submicrogram Quantities of Mercury by Atomic Absorption Spectrophotometry," *Anal. Chem.* 40:2085-2087 (1968).

Loring, D. H. "Mercury in the Sediments of the Gulf of St. Lawrence," *Can. J. Earth Sci.* 12:1219-1237 (1975).

Loring, D. H. "Distribution and Partition of Zinc, Copper and Lead in the Sediments of the Saguenay Fjord," *Can. J. Earth Sci.* 13:860-971 (1976a).

Loring, D. H. "Distribution and Partition of Cobalt, Nickel, Chromium, and Vanadium in the Sediments of the Saguenay Fjord," *Can. J. Earth Sci.* 13:1706-1718 (1976b).

Loring, D. H. and J. M. Bewers. "Geochemical Mass Balances for Mercury in a Polluted Canadian Fjord," *25th Intern. Geol. Cong. Abs.* 2:352 (1976).

Loring, D. H. and D. J. G. Nota. "Morphology and Sediments of the Gulf of St. Lawrence," *Fish. Res. Board Can. Bull.* 182:1-147 (1973).

Marlowe, J. I. "Weddelite in Bottom Sediment from the St. Lawrence and Saguenay Rivers," *J. Sed. Petrol.* 40:499-506 (1970).

Pocklington, R. "Carbon, Hydrogen, Nitrogen and Lignin Determinations from theGulf of St. Lawrence and Adjacent Waters," *Bedford Inst. Oceanogr., Dartmouth, N.S. Rep. Ser.* BI-R-75-6:1-12 (1975).

Pocklington, R. and C. D. MacGregor. "The Determination of Lignin in Marine Sediments and Particulate Form in Sea Water," *Intern. J. Environ. Anal. Chem.* 3:881–893 (1973).

Rantala, R. T. and D. H. Loring. "Multielement Analysis of Silicate Rocks and Marine Sediments by Atomic Absorption Spectrophotometry," *Atom. Absorp. News* 14:117–120 (1975).

Reimers, R. S., P. A. Krenkel, M. Eagle and G. Tragitt. "Sorption Phenomenon in the Organics of Bottom Sediments," in *Heavy Metals in the Aquatic Environment*, P. A. Kendel, Ed. (New York: Pergamon Press, 1973) pp. 117–129.

Thomas, R. L. "The Distribution of Mercury in the Sediments of Lake Ontario," *Can. J. Earth. Sci.* 10:194–204 (1972).

Ui, J. "Discussion" (F. M. and P. A. D'Iri), in *Heavy Metals in the Aquatic Environment*, P. A. Krenkel, Ed. (New York: Pergamon Press, 1973).

Walkley, A. "A Critical Examination of a Rapid Method for Determining Organic Carbon in Soils," *Soil Sci.* 63:251–263 (1947).